TŌKYŌ

TŌKYŌ

JOHANN FLEURI | PIERRE JAVELLE

INTRODUCTION
P. 7

CHŪO
中央区

P. 12

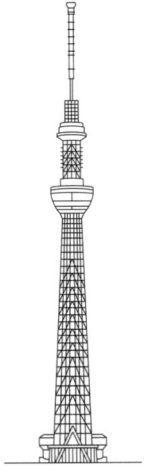

TAITŌ
台東区

P. 44

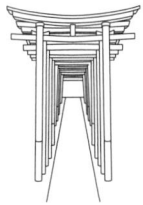

BUNKYŌ
文京区

P. 78

SHINJUKU
新宿区

P. 110

SETAGAYA
世田谷区

P. 142

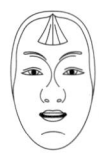

SHIBUYA
渋谷区

P. 168

MEGURO
目黒区

P. 196

CHIYODA
千代田区

P. 226

INTRODUCTION

Travelers setting foot in Tōkyō for the first time will immediately be struck by an intense sense of discovery, anticipating the fascinating experiences to come. Japan, much like its extraordinary capital, is a country like no other. Its globally unique identity and personality make it a place of fantasies and dreams, far removed from any normal point of reference. With its tangled web of transport networks, the proliferation of its suburbs, and the packed crowds teeming at the exit of every office, the capital makes a striking impression. The city sprawls out, invading space not just horizontally but also vertically, creating a unique urban landscape.

Tōkyō is vast. More than just a city—together with neighboring areas, the Metropolis of Tōkyō was established as a prefecture (a regional authority) in 1943 and has become one of the most densely populated conurbations on Earth, with nearly forty million inhabitants (around a third of the total national population) crammed into eight percent of Japan's sovereign territory. It is divided into twenty-three "special" wards and so has plenty of opportunity to showcase the various facets of its personality. Emperor Meiji formalized its status as the imperial capital in 1889, renaming Edo ("gate of the bay") as Tōkyō ("capital of the east"). This was actually no more than a formality, as Edo had been the seat of government of the Tokugawa shogunate since 1603 and was to remain so for Japan's two centuries of isolationism (*sakoku*, "closure of the country").

It is difficult to imagine that Tōkyō was originally no more than a small fishing village. The town was not fortified until the end of the fifteenth century, but in 1590 the shōgun Tokugawa Ieyasu (1543–1616) ordered a military base to be established here that was to lay the foundations of the future capital. Edo became the political and cultural center of the country, enjoying 265 years of peace, a time during which it prospered, despite, from 1639, gradually closing itself off to the outside world. This policy of withdrawal, which was to end with the Meiji Restoration of 1868, undoubtedly helped shape Tōkyō's mystery-shrouded identity. The Japanese capital sought to catch up during the Meiji era (1868–1912), constructing brick buildings, erecting telecommunication networks (1869), introducing steam trains (1872), and even building zoological gardens (1882).

In 1889, the government adopted the Constitution of the Empire of Japan while in the streets hairstyles were becoming more Westernized. During the Taishō era (1912–1926), Tōkyō gradually adopted a more consumerist approach, increased school attendance among girls, and established itself culturally, particularly in theater and opera. The first elections of representatives to the National Diet (the Japanese parliament) were held in 1928, Haneda airport was completed in 1931, and Tōkyō opened its port to international trade in 1941. This opening up took the brakes off the economy and spurred the growth of the population, which had exceeded six million inhabitants by the start of the Second World War, equaling New York or London at the time.

Tōkyō has risen from the ashes twice during the twentieth century—first, in the wake of the Great Kantō Earthquake of 1923, which claimed more than 140,000 victims and destroyed 500,000 homes, leaving nearly two million people without shelter, and then again after the Allied air raids of the Second World War. Tōkyō endured a total of 102 bombing missions that reduced the population of the Japanese capital to no more than 3.49 million inhabitants by October 1945, around half the pre-war total. Tōkyō bounced back in the 1960s, enjoying a period of meteoric growth as innovation and new technology entered Japanese homes. The oil crisis of 1973 put a stop to this, but growth restarted in the 1980s, ultimately raising Tōkyō to prominence as one of the most influential cities in the world. The bursting of the economic bubble in the 1990s put an end to the "Japanese miracle" and the metropolis found itself facing serious financial difficulty, however. Management of the crisis would entail two major fiscal reconstruction programs.

Tōkyō continued to be a major presence on the international stage, arousing admiration for its modernity, creativity, and unparalleled resilience. Dubbed "the safest city in the world" in 2019 by the authoritative British magazine *The Economist*, it is also one of the most attractive cities for students. It hosted the summer Olympics of 1964 and the postponed games of 2021. With more Michelin stars than any other capital in the world, Tōkyō is a city for gourmets. There seems to be a restaurant at every street corner luring passersby with enticing scents—there are approximately 160,000 restaurants in the Japanese megalopolis (by comparison, there are "only" 200,000 in all of France). And gastronomic Tōkyō's great secret? Its ability to dish up tasty food to suit every budget, from local eatery to bistro to Michelin-starred extravagance.

Tōkyō also has a distinctive topography. Due to its history, Edo was originally structured around its fortified castle according to a very strict hierarchy, with the city divided into two zones and two cultures. The families of the lords and other high-ranking individuals lived on the hill closest to the castle (the site of the current Imperial Palace) in an area known as Yamanote ("the mountain's hand"), while the rest of the population occupied the lower regions of the city, an area called Shitamachi ("lower town"). The upper classes living on the heights were sheltered from flooding but those closer to the rivers were more exposed, with some even living in marshy areas. Even today, the residents of Yamanote have a reputation for being cold and standoffish while those from Shitamachi are said to be more trustworthy. This may not be intended to be taken literally, but it is undeniable that each area has developed its own subculture over the centuries. Yamanote has also given its name to the loop railroad line linking the city's major stations since 1925. Much like its ambivalent topography, the two faces of modern Tōkyō are sources of constant surprise. Although packed with delights, the metropolis can also seem as cold and hard as its concrete and as merciless as the endless working days of its *salarymen*. It is worth breaking through this shell, however. Unlike timeless and imperial Kyōto, Tōkyō is not a city you merely visit so much as experience. The capital invites exploration on foot, with each neighborhood functioning like a microvillage in which locals rub shoulders with one another and every business has its regulars. The only way to discover Tōkyō is to venture out into its streets and alleys and get lost for hours. Stroll around, browse its stores, and sample its cafés—only then will Tōkyō begin to show its face and its true colors.

Tōkyō Tower, located in Minato special ward, is 1,091ft (332.6m) high. When it was built in 1957, its architect, Tachū Naitō, took inspiration from the Eiffel Tower but adapted the structure to resist the region's earthquakes and high winds.

THE HISTORIC HEART OF THE CITY

CHŪO

中央区

Beneath the modern and luxurious exterior of Chūō ward, there lurks both Tōkyō's feudal past and the city's historic central business district. Looking out over the Sumida River, it has retained an appealing, if slightly dilapidated charm.

P.12

A tea house in the historic Hamarikyū Garden, nestling between skyscrapers.

OPPOSITE

Having been spared the destruction visited upon Tōkyō, Ningyōchō district remains a glorious survivor from the Edo period.

While there is no real "city center" to speak of in Tōkyō, the capital's beating heart lies in Chūō ward, and there are several reasons for this. For a start, it was here that the "center" of Tōkyō was located when it was still called Edo (1457–1868) and historically, it was the city's main commercial area, even though it has now been largely overtaken by Shinjuku in the northwestern part of the capital since the economic bubble of the 1980s.

Until the Second World War, the streams and canals that wove their way through Chūō played a major role in the daily routines of its inhabitants, with goods and people mostly ferried about in in small boats. With transport methods having evolved, the area's links with the water are now less obvious at first glance, but Chūō is doing its best to preserve this heritage by still allowing those living by the waterways to use them to get about, especially on the water buses plying the Sumida River or serving the magnificent, stately Hamarikyū Garden, just beside Tōkyō Bay.

Chūō is divided into three separate areas: Nihonbashi, Kyobashi, and the island of Tsukishima. The two main points of interest are the district of Ginza, where the capital's biggest and most luxurious stores are located, and the old fish market in Tsukiji, which has retained its quirky charm and its many delicious sushi restaurants, despite the relocation of its wholesale section.

Despite the rather frosty impression presented by its offices and tower blocks, the district of Nihonbashi has always been one of Chūō's main attractions due to what it represents. Nihonbashi Bridge, with its retinue of bronze lions, has reigned over the city since the Edo era and marks the starting point of the magnificent Five Routes built in the seventeenth century, including the Tōkaidō and Nakasendō roads that both linked Edo with Kyōto. The bridge was also used as the reference point when calculating distances between Edo and other towns in Japan. Unfortunately, since an expressway was constructed directly overhead in the 1960s, the bridge has been poorly maintained, but despite this retains unique historical and symbolic value.

Chūō is now one of the city's smallest wards by area. Although it has no more than 142,000 residents if those who enter the ward just to work or shop are included, it has been estimated that more than 650,000 people pass through on a daily basis.

CHŪŌ
THE ESSENTIALS

01

TSUKIJI MARKET

The many sushi restaurants in the old fish market in Tsukiji still serve delicious lunches of fresh fish even though the wholesalers have relocated to Toyosu district.

02

KABUKI-ZA THEATER

This old theater holds daily performances in several languages.

03

NIHONBASHI BRIDGE

This bridge hidden away beneath an expressway was the starting point of the Five Routes of the Edo period (seventeenth century).

04

COREDO DEPARTMENT STORES

The Coredo Nihonbashi and Muromachi department stores are particularly elegantly designed, fusing tradition and modernity in perfect harmony.

05

NINGYŌCHŌ

Ningyōchō was the old entertainment district during the Edo era and was very popular for its kabuki performances. It was also well known for the local artisans who made dolls and marionettes.

06

GINZA DEPARTMENT STORES

The décor is so elegant in the luxury Ginza Six department store, which opened in 2017, that shopping is more like visiting a museum.

07

MITSUKOSHI STORES

The Mitsukoshi stores were founded in 1673 and are the oldest in Japan, selling a wide range of fashion goods and accessories.

ABOVE

Tachinomi *are bars that are often no more than counters at which you can stand to grab a drink in the street.*

OPPOSITE

Man-made Tsukishima ("Moon Island") is located in Tōkyō Bay and is renowned throughout the city for its famous street serving monjayaki.

P.22-23

The Hamarikyū Garden is a haven of tranquility among the skyscrapers of Chūō district.

EXCURSION
HAMA-RIKYŪ
STATELY GARDENS

Hamarikyū is a *daimyō-teien*, a garden belonging to a lord, and it was here that samurai would once gather to practice archery and horse riding before taking tea and enjoying the scenery.

"Gardens are at the heart of Japan. All our culture is represented there; our archipelago, with its mountainous relief surrounded by water; pure water, drawn from the mountains, which allows us to make tea, rice, and sake of great refinement. Gardens are both a representation of nature and a natural representation of the elements," explains Shinji Isoya, a researcher and a leading specialist in Japanese landscape architecture. Of the nine gardens in Tōkyō, Hamarikyū is his favorite, as it is one of the *daimyō-teien*, "disproportionately large gardens that only the lords of an era would have the power and the means to have built. They had many uses, being a privileged place to stroll and admire the seasons, but also an easily defendable site for samurai who also did military service."

With an area of 74 acres (30 hectares), Hamarikyū was first laid out in 1654 during the fourth Tokugawa shogunate. At the time, it was a place where archery and horse riding would be practiced. "They also developed systems to hunt birds and catch fish in the lake," the professor continues. The garden was gifted to the city of Tōkyō by the imperial family in 1945 but was not opened to the public until 1946, having been rebuilt in the wake of the great earthquake of 1923 and the bombing of the Second World War. It is now a serene and tranquil place for a stroll, seemingly far from the hustle and bustle of a city that looms on the horizon only a stone's throw away. A haven of peace in the heart of the capital, Hamarikyū is recognized as being an authentic traditional garden and a symbol of the esthetics of the Edo period. Some of its trees are centuries old. In Japanese tradition, tea houses are situated to provide the best panoramic view of a garden, and Hamarikyū has two, Hoba-tei and Nakajima-no-ochaya, which both offer the traditional tea ceremony.

SYMBOL OF NATURE

In Japan, a garden is a miniature representation of nature; its architecture may be highly sophisticated but it must never give that impression.

THE TEA CEREMONY

Tea houses *(chashitsu)* are designed to give the best view of a garden. Sweet food is eaten before taking tea, to soften the bitterness.

The residential area of Tsukishima has managed to hang on to some small stores such as this bookshop.

The street where monjayaki *is sold comes alive at the end of the day in particular, and especially at weekends, when Tokyoites like to take their time over this local specialty.*

ABOVE

During the Edo period, the waterways teemed with merchants and craftspeople, but today it is mostly tourists you will find there, although they also provide a means for transporting small goods.

OPPOSITE

Although now hidden away under an expressway, Nihonbashi Bridge is a major part of Tōkyō's history and cultural heritage.

FOOD & DRINK

TAKE A BREAK AU TSUKIJI MARKET

HERITAGE

Formerly the largest fish market in the world, Tsukiji still has its covered section offering a huge range of seafood that is extremely popular with local residents.

SEAFOOD SNACKS

The freshest of seafood is served here all day long.

PATIENCE REQUIRED

There can be a bit of a wait for the most popular eateries in Tsukiji.

FISH AND RICE

Another specialty is *kaisendon*, a bowl of rice topped with slices of raw fish.

SNACKS AND CRUSTACEANS

These small, sweet crabs are eaten whole.

SNACK ON THE GO

No time to sit down for a meal in a restaurant? Street vendors dish up food directly to enjoy on the go, such as these grilled scallops.

BAZAAR AND ACCESSORIES

Both snacks and dried fish to be cooked at home are on sale.

LUNCHTIME SERVICE

Employees and students flock to Tsukiji for lunch.

THE ALLEYWAYS OF THE COVERED MARKET

As with many covered markets, the way to discover the best spots is to get lost in its lanes and alleyways.

ABOVE

With its narrow counters and tables cobbled together from whatever is lying around, dining in Tsukiji is all about simplicity.

OPPOSITE

Although Tsukiji is primarily a fish and seafood market, there are also stores selling all kinds of kitchen gadgets.

GASTRONOMY

DINING ON MONJA
À TSUKISHIMA

Monjayaki, or *monja* to its devotees, is Tsukishima's specialty: a traditional dish cooked and eaten directly from a grill placed in the center of the table—the essence of sociable, convivial dining.

Tsukishima is undoubtedly a real foodie district, and though it may feature less frequently in travel guides, it is still worth a detour. There are no fussy table manners here, and the cooking is equally unpretentious, lively, and decidedly no-frills. Tsukishima is located on an island in Tōkyō Bay and extends along the shores of the Sumida River. This mainly residential area is a favorite with residents thanks to its local specialty, *monjayaki*. This very popular, savory Japanese "pancake" is eaten from a hot grill in the center of the table and shared with friends. Topped with meat, noodles, vegetables or seafood, depending on the diner's preference (and the options offered by the restaurant), it takes the form of a runny egg batter that the chef nimbly cooks before your eyes. It should be eaten as soon as it is ready, usually washed down with a beer.

A variation on *okonomiyaki* but with a firmer texture, *monjayaki* is a must-try in Tsukishima, which has a whole street dedicated to the dish. *Monjayaki* is also what is known as a "Kantō" dish, in other words, from a region located north of Honshū rather than from Kansai, farther south, where *okonomiyaki*, a Hiroshima specialty is preferred. Take exit 7 out of Tsukishima Station to enter the famous street of over seventy restaurants specializing in *monjayaki*. Despite the wide range of options on offer, patience may be required to get a table in the evening. If you are struggling to decide between the many options, try Iroha, which was established in 1955 and has two outlets in the street. A wide choice of toppings is available, with *mentaiko* (cod's roe) and cheese being a popular combination as they go together so well. To explore the flavors of other dishes cooked directly on the grill, look out for *okonomiyaki* and other fried noodles, which usually feature on the menu in such places.

LOCAL SPECIALTY

This kind of pancake topped with vegetables, fish, seafood, or meat is a
Kantō specialty and has made Tsukishima a very popular spot.

The majestic Kabuki-za theater at the eastern end of Ginza district stages daily performances of major works of kabuki theater.

切符預かり所
Will Call

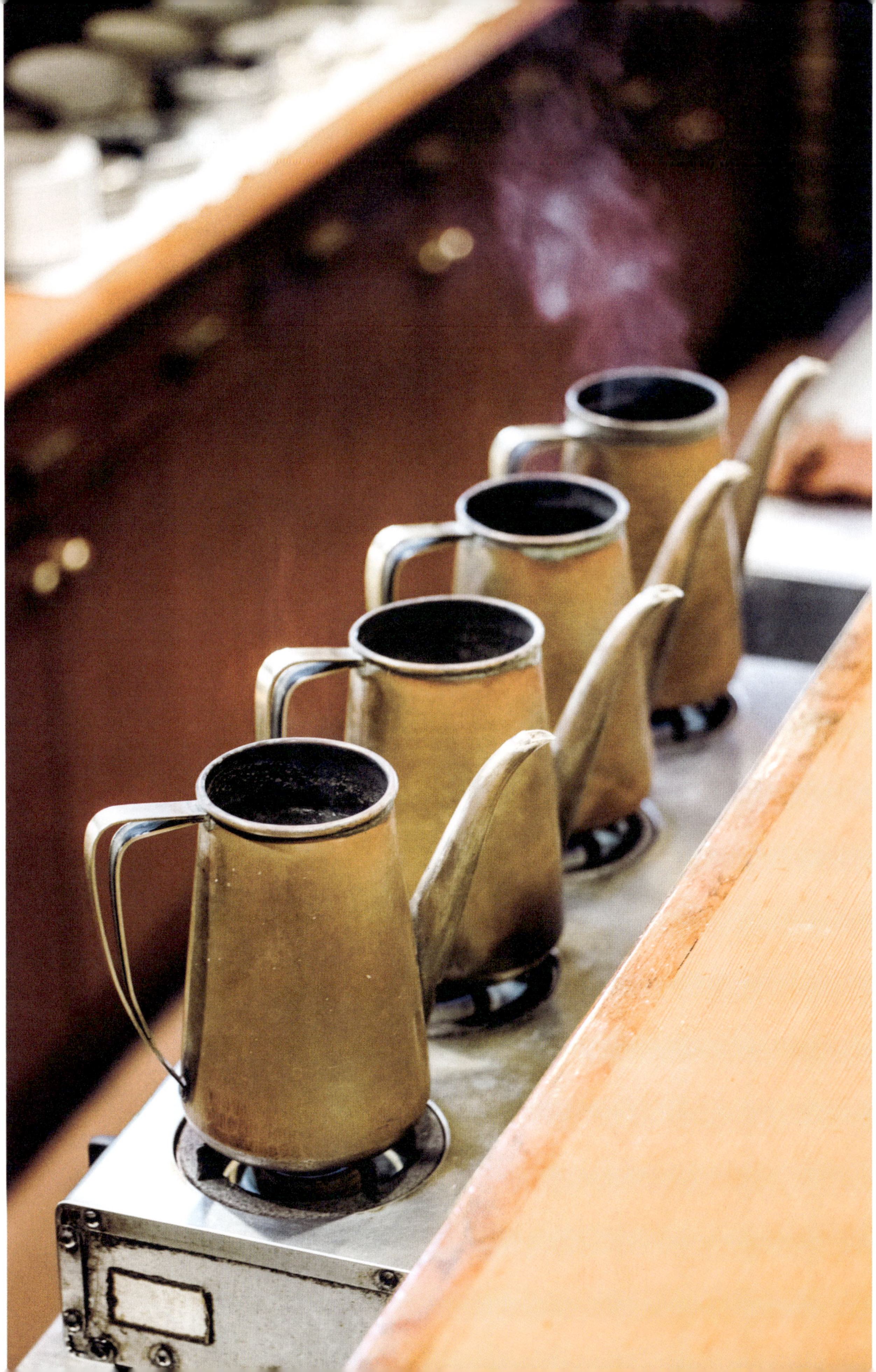

ABOVE

Café Béchet, located right in the heart of Ginza, maintains Tōkyō's old coffee-making traditions (kissaten).

OPPOSITE

The coffee is made using the "hand-drip" method, i.e. filtered entirely by hand.

UNDERSTANDING
TŌKAIDŌ
FROM TŌKYŌ TO KYŌTO

As the fastest route between Tōkyō (then Edo) and the imperial city of Kyōto, Tōkaidō was the most important road in Japan during the Edo era. The journey started at the Nihonbashi Bridge.

Nihonbashi Bridge is a place of major cultural and historical importance in Tōkyō's history. It was the entrance gate to the city and the departure point for the Tōkaidō road for many years. The two lions overlooking the bridge have been protecting Tōkyō from evil spirits since the seventeenth century. Construction was ordered by the shōgun Tokugawa Ieyasu, with the twin aims of creating a crossroads in the middle of Honshū and defining a base point from which to measure distances, with the bridge designated the national point zero.

The Tōkaidō was by far the most important of the Five Routes that crossed this part of Japan, providing travelers with the quickest way from Edo, the center of power, to Kyōto, the imperial city of the time. This arterial road was used by merchants, feudal lords, noble families, and the military, with the 319-mile (514-kilometer) route along Honshū's east coast mainly being covered on foot.

Fifty-three relay stations along the way allowed travelers to take a break but were also used by the government to demand taxes and check identities. The Tōkaidō crossed several provinces and travelers had to be in possession of a passport and valid papers to be permitted to pass the various stations, under penalty of imprisonment or even—in extreme cases—the death sentence. Regulations were very strict as Edo was entirely cut off from the rest of the world during the "closed country" period (1639–1853). Any attempt to cross a "checkpoint" illegally would therefore risk capital punishment.

Some of these relay stations and stretches of the Tōkaidō have been perfectly preserved as historical monuments and can be visited, such as at Hakone, west of Tōkyō. There are tea houses still operating along the road that have been in situ since it was built.

The Tōkaidō is far more than a mere road and has inspired great works of art and literature—many artists from the nineteenth century onward have represented it in sculptures, paintings, short stories, and poems. It has been immortalized in prints by Hiroshige, for example, who painted every one of its fifty-three stations, and in the *haiku* of Matsuo Bashō, and has also served as a setting for many novels.

TRAVELING DURING THE EDO PERIOD

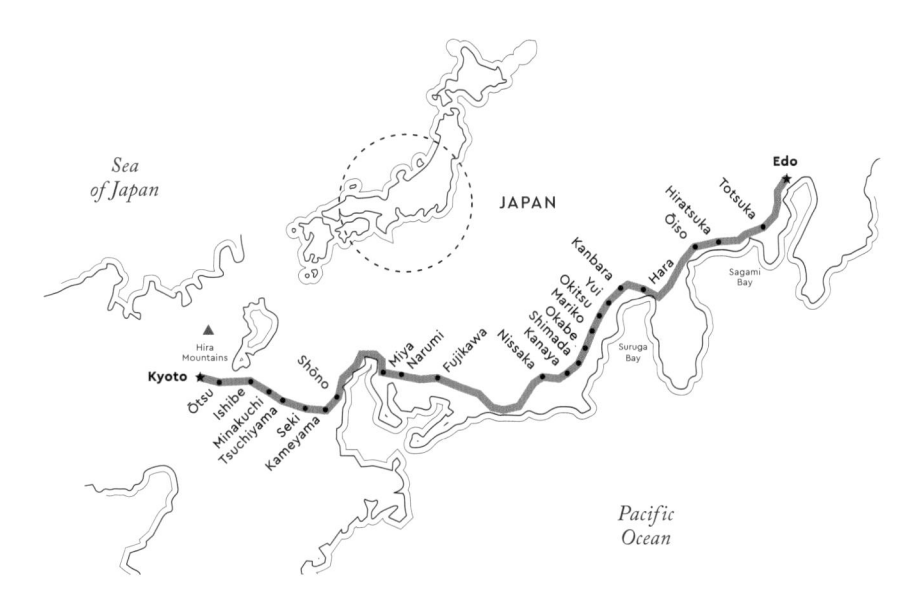

1 / TŌKAIDŌ

The Tōkaidō road was 319 miles (514 kilometers) long, with fifty-three relay stations at intervals. These were used as rest stops and checkpoints to establish a traveler's identity and travel authorization during the era of *sakoku* ("closure of the country").

2 / NIHONBASHI BRIDGE

Nihonbashi Bridge was the departure point for the Five Routes built in the seventeenth and eighteenth centuries (including the Tōkaidō) and also served as point zero for calculating distances between Tōkyō and other cities in Japan. It has been overshadowed by an elevated expressway since the 1960s.

ABOVE

Tōkyō is so well served by public transport that few residents have a car or even a driver's license. Owning a car is more to do with luxury or having a passion for automobiles.

OPPOSITE

The swastika is a key religious symbol used in Japan to designate Buddhist temples, especially on maps.

花見せんべい
板倉屋
魚久
佐々木酒店
鳥近
第三番
百度石
条例により
客引き・客待ちを許さない！
久松警察署
久松防犯協会

42 Tōkyō | CHŪŌ

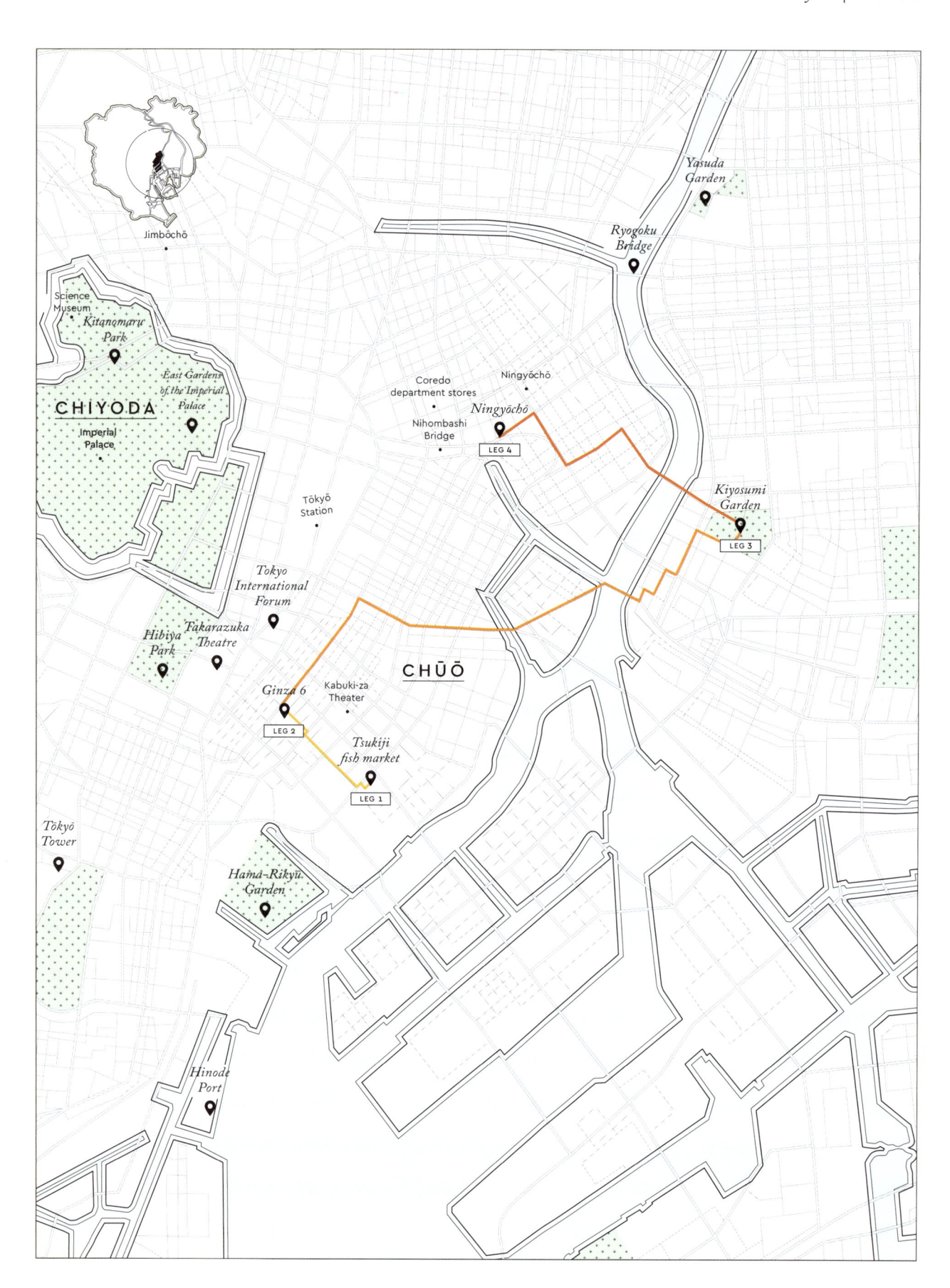

WALKING TOUR

THE HEART OF TŌKYŌ

Chūō ("center," in Japanese) ward is still the heart of the capital for the people of Tōkyō, with its nucleus in Shitamachi, the cradle of the city's commerce.

LEG 1: TSUKIJI MARKET

Tōkyō's fish market was moved in 2018 for health reasons and to modernize its infrastructure. Located in Tsukiji since 1935, it had expanded over the years to become the largest fish market in the world. The decision to relocate came as a disappointment to local residents, but the covered market is still active and lively even though the wholesalers have indeed upped sticks for Toyosu district. You can still come here to stroll round, sample its unique atmosphere, and enjoy a lunch of excellent sushi. The restaurant owners have stayed put and adopted a new system so they can continue to serve fresh fish around the clock, although it is best to visit during the morning. It's good to know that the traditional early morning public tuna auction that used to be held at Tsukiji is still open to the curious, although it is now held at Toyosu and advance booking is required.

LEG 2: SHOPPING FEVER IN GINZA

Ginza is still the go-to district for locals who love fashion, fine dining, luxury products, and upscale brands. Its stores really grab the attention and tourists come from all over the world to shop here. It is also a mecca for the city's gastronomic stars. Make a detour to the Ginza Six department store designed by architect Yoshio Taniguchi, which opened in 2017; the building is worth a visit in itself. With a roster of 241 boutiques and a 43,000-square-foot (4,000-m²) garden on the roof, this shopping heaven also includes a contemporary art gallery and a Noh theater.

LEG 3: KIYOSUMI GARDEN GETAWAY

Kiyosumi Garden was laid out during the Meiji era as the very model of a traditional Japanese garden. It was originally part of the residence of Kinokuniya Bunzaemon, a prominent Edo-era merchant, and became a precious refuge for citizens during the great earthquake of 1923. The landscaping of the garden, which includes a pond with three small islands and a bridge from which you can observe the carp and turtles, together with the many birds that also gather here, creates a truly beautiful and harmonious scene. The gates close at 5 P.M.

LEG 4: DINING IN NINGYŌCHŌ

Ningyōchō has been nicknamed "Doll Town" for a number of reasons, not least because it was home to Japan's first kabuki theater in 1624. There is a long history of marionette theater performances (*bunraku*) in this entertainment district, and all kinds of craftsmen and puppet makers have naturally settled in this part of the city. Ningyōchō was also a major trading hub, but people now come here to rediscover its delightfully old-fashioned atmosphere, to dine in one of its restaurants, see the puppet clock, try a traditional pastry, or even drink some *amazake*, a kind of sugary, rice-based, non-alcoholic drink.

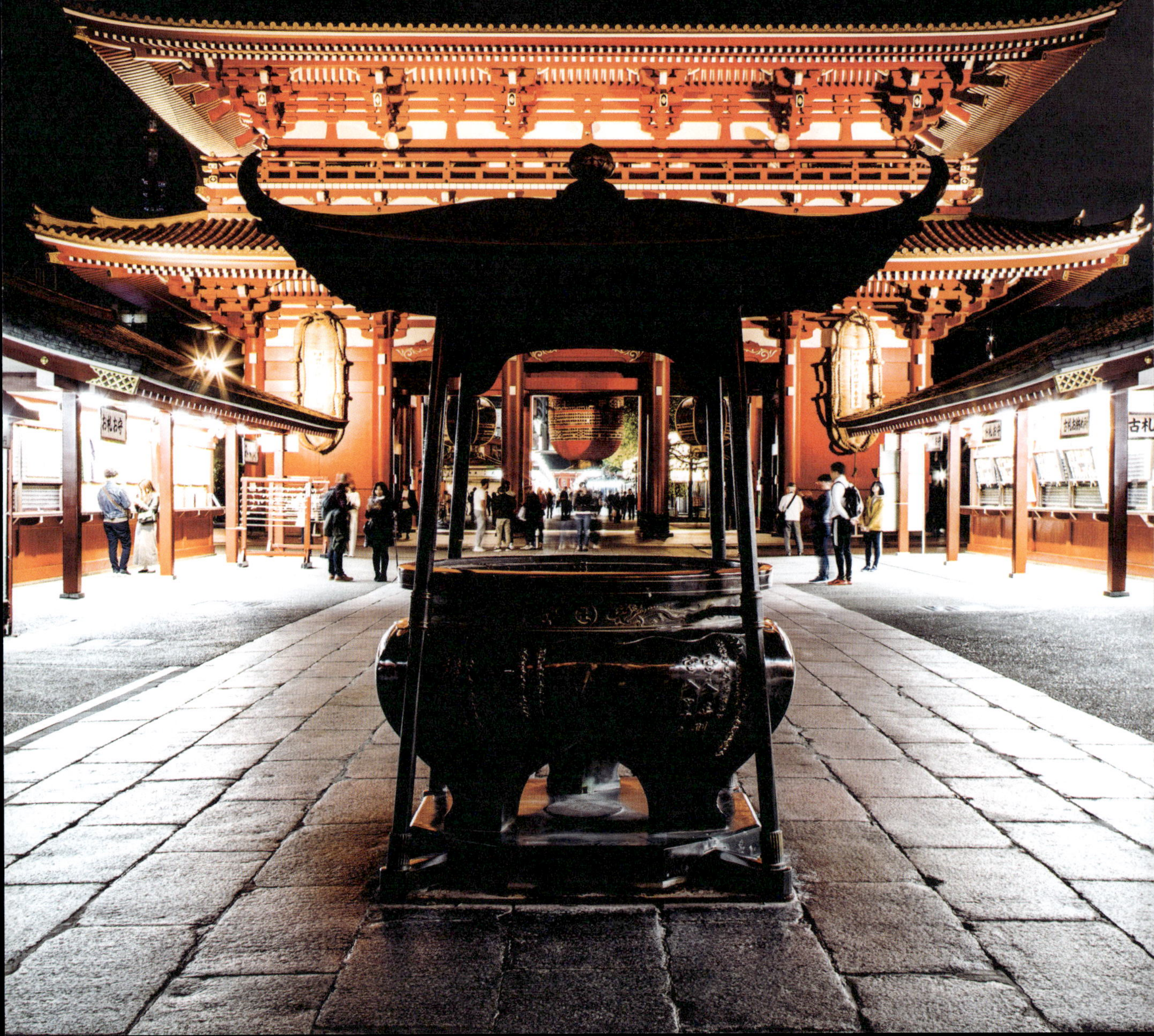
古札

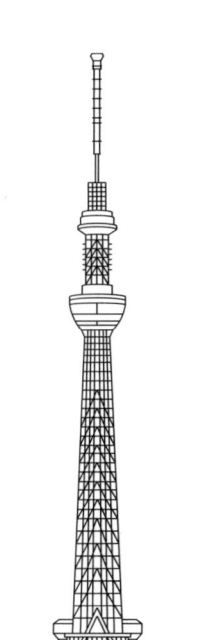

LIFE LIVED TO THE RHYTHM OF THE SUMIDA RIVER

TAITŌ
台東区

Taitō is Tōkyō's smallest ward and home to the Sensō-ji Buddhist temple and the districts of Ueno and Asakusa. Its rich local life and enthusiasm for popular culture mean that it is one of the most popular areas with tourists.

P. 4 4

The imposing incense burner at Sensō-ji temple is used for a purification ritual that involves enveloping the body in smoke.

OPPOSITE

Kafū Nagai was a popular author with a rebellious spirit; his novels, essays, and plays are a wonderful depiction of twentieth-century Tōkyō.

Taitō is located north of Chūō in the east of the metropolis and is not to be missed on a first visit to the Japanese capital. For centuries, life in Taitō revolved around the Sumida River, which has long been the principal thoroughfare for locals, used by merchants and craftsmen in particular.

A hint of these times still hangs in the air in Taitō in the tradition of outspokenness inherited from the Shitamachi and dating back to the Edo period. It's easy to find traditional Japanese culture here, as the district has developed less frantically than the rest of the capital and many of its charming spots have been preserved. Beneath this seductive veneer lie many delights of a rich past for travelers. Every alleyway, slightly dilapidated building, old store, and the whole atmosphere here gives Taitō a completely different feel from what might be experienced in the bustling Ginza district, for example.

Food and gastronomy are another great tradition and Taitō is a paradise for gourmets, with many restaurants offering traditional Japanese cuisine that goes back more than a hundred years. Ameya-Yokochō market, near Okachimachi Station, is a riot of small stands and outlets where you can grab a bite on the go, perhaps at one of the famous *nomitachi*, bars where customers stand to order a drink and nibble on some snacks—there is no seating. In Asakusa, close your eyes and try *unaju*, an eel dish served on rice, or cakes shaped liked dolls that are stuffed with red bean paste.

On the cultural front, there are many temples to explore and museums of art, history, natural history, and science to browse, along with many local craft stores. Tōkyō's largest and most popular summer festivals are also held here. If you fancy a journey back in time, treat yourself to a trip on the historic Toden Arakawa line, which was rebranded as the Tokyo Sakura Tram (Tokyo Sakura Toramu) in 2017. This charming tramway crossing the city from east to west between Minowabashi and Waseda was built more than a hundred years ago and makes it easy to explore Taitō at a leisurely pace that allows you to contemplate the scenery.

永井荷風

六区通り

中華料理 康楽

TAITŌ
THE ESSENTIALS

KAPPABASHI

Kappabashi street is where catering professionals come to stock up on crockery, knives, and kitchen utensils, although that shouldn't prevent the general public from doing the same, if they so wish.

09

TŌKYŌ NATIONAL MUSEUM

This is one of the largest art museums in the world, with more than 110,000 exhibits from all over Asia, including eighty-nine national treasures.

10

UENO PARK

This city park is particularly popular with residents at weekends and when the cherry trees are in blossom, and many families and groups of friends will congregate here at that time of the year.

11

UENO ZOO

Ueno Zoo is the oldest in Japan, opened on March 20, 1882. There are more than 3,000 animals from 400 different species, including the zoo's mascots, two giant pandas.

12

NATIONAL MUSEUM OF NATURE AND SCIENCE

This museum is a treasure trove of facts and figures about everything from dinosaurs to the latest technology, taking in space exploration and the study of ecosystems.

13

NATIONAL MUSEUM OF WESTERN ART

The museum houses the collection amassed by the industrialist Matsukata Kōjirō and specializes in Western art from the Renaissance to the turn of the twentieth century, with works by everyone from Hans Holbein to Picasso, taking in Delacroix and Monet.

14

SHITAMACHI MUSEUM

The Shitamachi Museum conjures up local life in the district during the Edo and Meiji periods, aimed at educating the young Japanese.

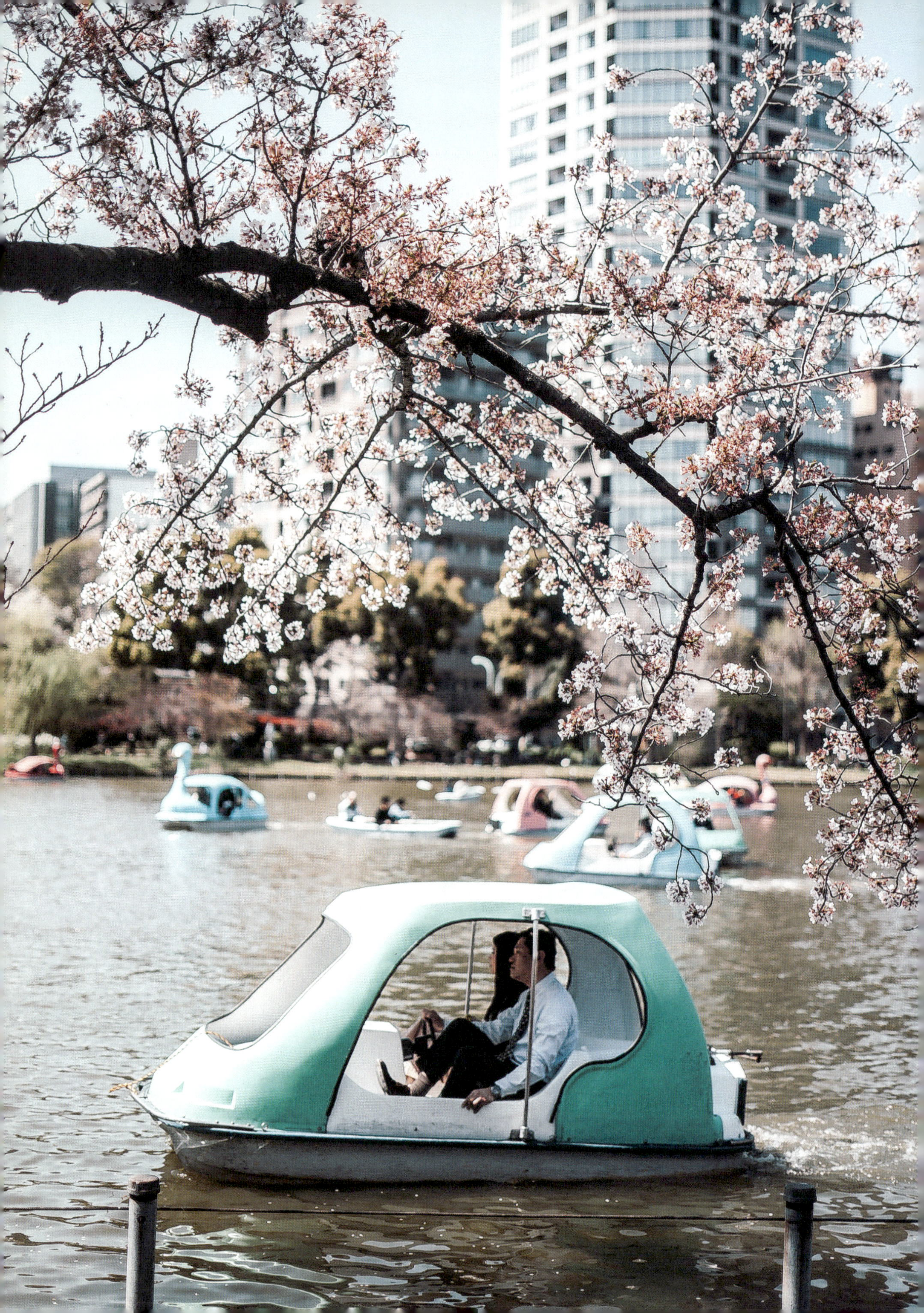

ABOVE

Ema, *small wooden tablets on which a petition or a prayer can be written, can be bought at temples and shrines. They are hung in places of worship.*

OPPOSITE

During cherry blossom season, which in Tōkyō peaks at the end of March, paddleboats can be hired to enjoy the view from the water in Ueno Park.

When hanami, *the time for contemplation of flowers, is in full swing, picnics are organized in Ueno Park as an opportunity to catch up with friends and family.*

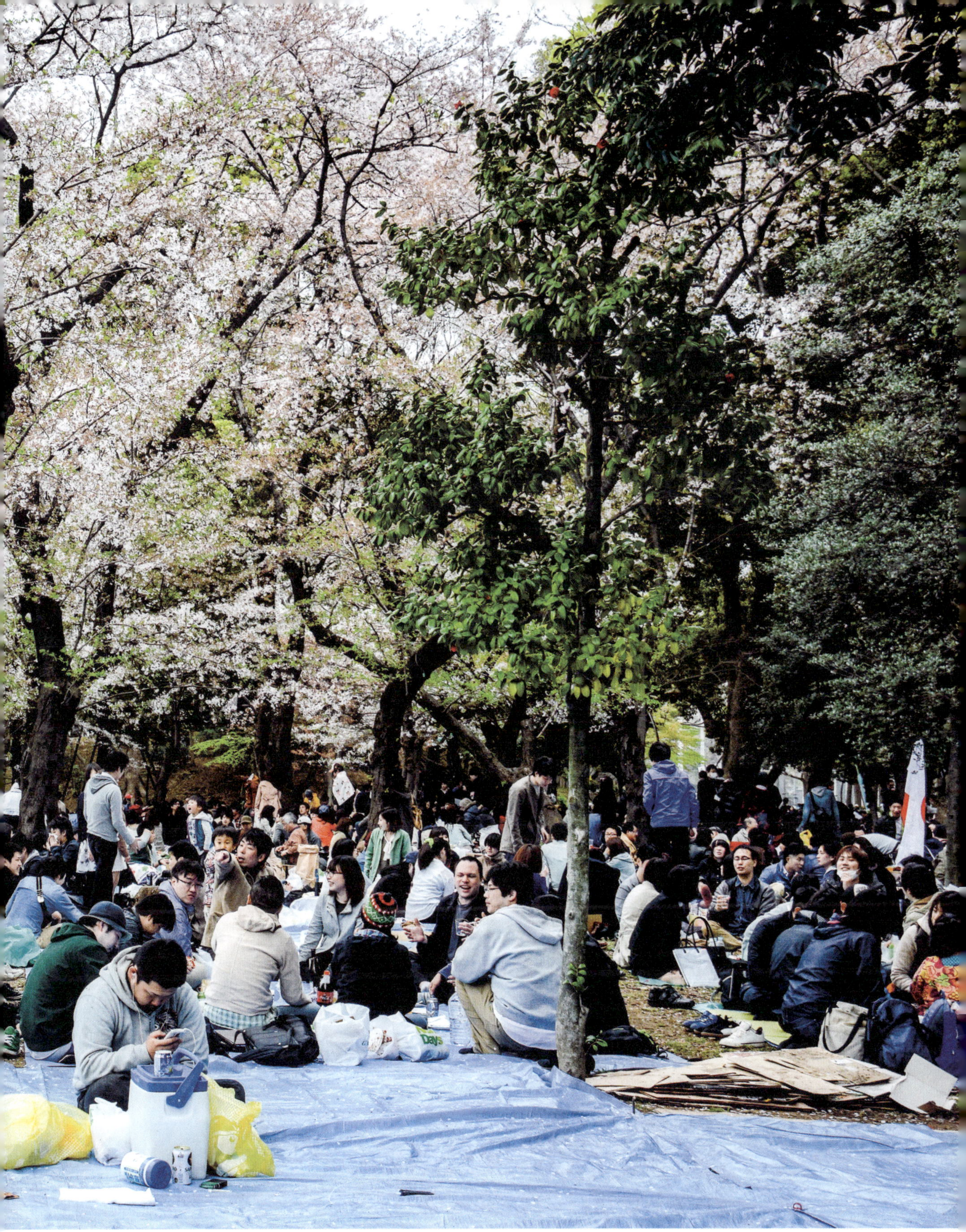

ABOVE

The Fuglen café (originally a Norwegian brand) is a lovely spot for coffee or tea during the day and beer or cocktails in the evening.

OPPOSITE

The Tokyo Skytree is the symbol of the city, with two observatory decks from which you can admire the Japanese capital from heights of 1,150 ft (350 m) and 1,475 ft (450 m).

UNDERSTANDING
SENSŌ-JI
BUDDHIST TEMPLE

In Tōkyō, and in Japan in general, religious buildings are either Buddhist temples or Shinto shrines. Sensō-ji, the symbol of Asakusa, is a perfect example of a Japanese Buddhist temple.

Shinto is the oldest known religion in Japan. Literally "the Way of the Gods," it combines both polytheist and animist elements and is based on the worship of nature and *kami*, divine spirits that embody a place or natural elements such as the winds, rivers, and mountains—in Shinto everything has a soul, including rocks. Buddhism was imported from China and Korea in the sixth century. Founded by the Buddha, it is based on the hope of enlightenment and breaking the cycle of reincarnation, and has a body of scriptures (sacred texts). In Japan, its history extends over three eras: the Nara (710–794), Heian (794–1185), and post-Heian periods (after 1185). Each of these saw the introduction of new doctrine and the development of existing schools of thought with the result that there are now no less than thirteen main schools. Many Japanese have links with both religions.

The structures of Buddhist temples and Shinto shrines share a common basic esthetic but they differ in architectural details that only an expert could identify. In a Shinto shrine, the *torii* (gate) that divides the sacred space from the secular world is larger, with greater use of vermillion red, and there are no representations of divinities.

In Buddhist temples, meanwhile, particular emphasis is placed on their numerous statues and on the *kouro*, the elaborate vessel used to burn sticks of incense and perform purification rituals.

The architecture of Buddhist temples underwent major changes in the wake of the Meiji era, with the new government imposing *Shinbutsu bunri* in 1868, effectively banning the mixture of Buddhas and *kami* (Shinto) in places of worship, in order to create a clear distinction between the two religions and calm a nationalist, "anti-Buddhist" rebellion. Perceived as a religious movement with foreign roots, Buddhism was rejected as contradictory to Shinto, the authentic and historic Japanese religion. Nearly 30,000 Buddhist temples were destroyed in an attempt to weaken its presence in the Japanese archipelago.

Constructed in the seventh century, Sensō-ji is the oldest Buddhist temple in Tōkyō and has become the symbol of both the Asakusa district and of the Japanese capital itself, with millions flocking to visit it every year. The majestic temple is dedicated to Kannon, the goddess of mercy.

THE ARCHITECTURE OF A BUDDHIST TEMPLE

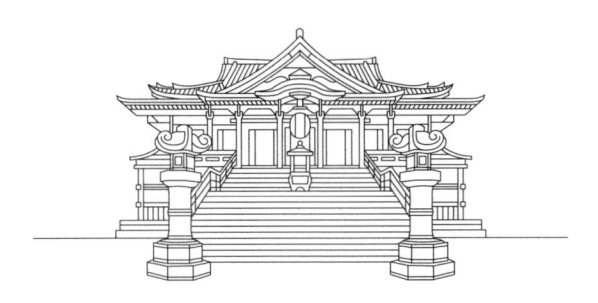

1 / MAIN HALL

The main hall at Sensō-ji houses a statue of the goddess Kannon that is said to have been discovered in the Sumida River by fishermen nearly 1,400 years ago.

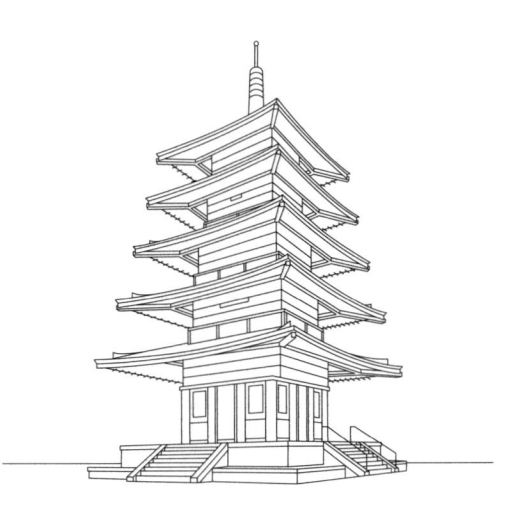

2 / PAGODA

The 180-ft (55-m) steel-framed, five-story pagoda beside the main hall was renovated in the 1990s.

3 / THUNDER GATE

Immediately recognizable by its enormous red lantern, the *Kaminarimon* ("thunder gate") was erected in 941. It was largely destroyed by fire in 1865 and rebuilt in the 1960s.

Nakamise-dori is a large street opposite Senso-ji temple that draws thousands of tourists every year; its stalls overflow with souvenirs, snacks, and all kinds of gadgets.

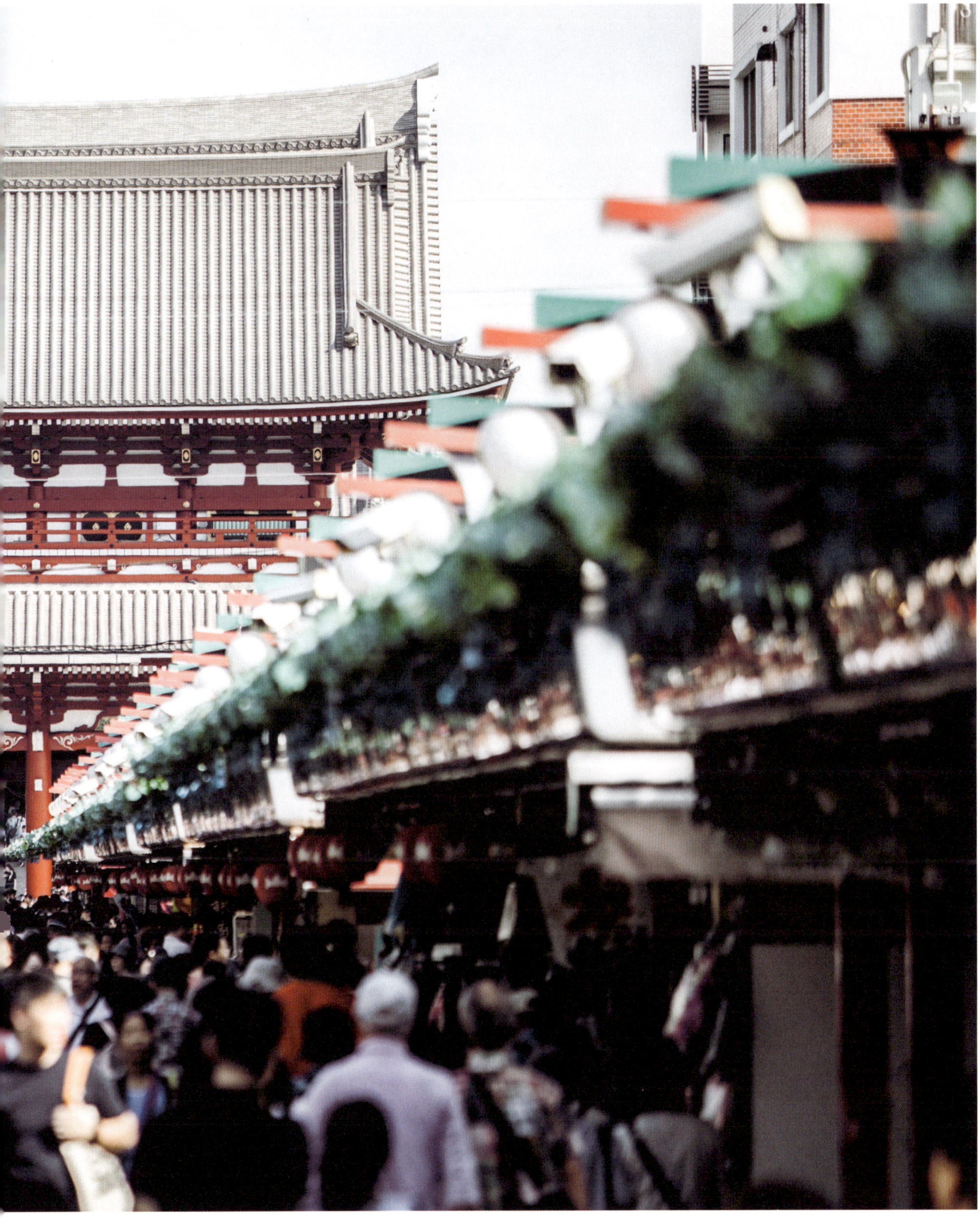

ABOVE

Omikuji *("sacred lots")* are fortunes written on small scraps of paper that are drawn at random in shrines and temples.

OPPOSITE

The current pagoda at Sensō-ji was built in 1973 to replace the one destroyed by bombing in the Second World War, the location of which is marked by a pillar on the eastern side of the site.

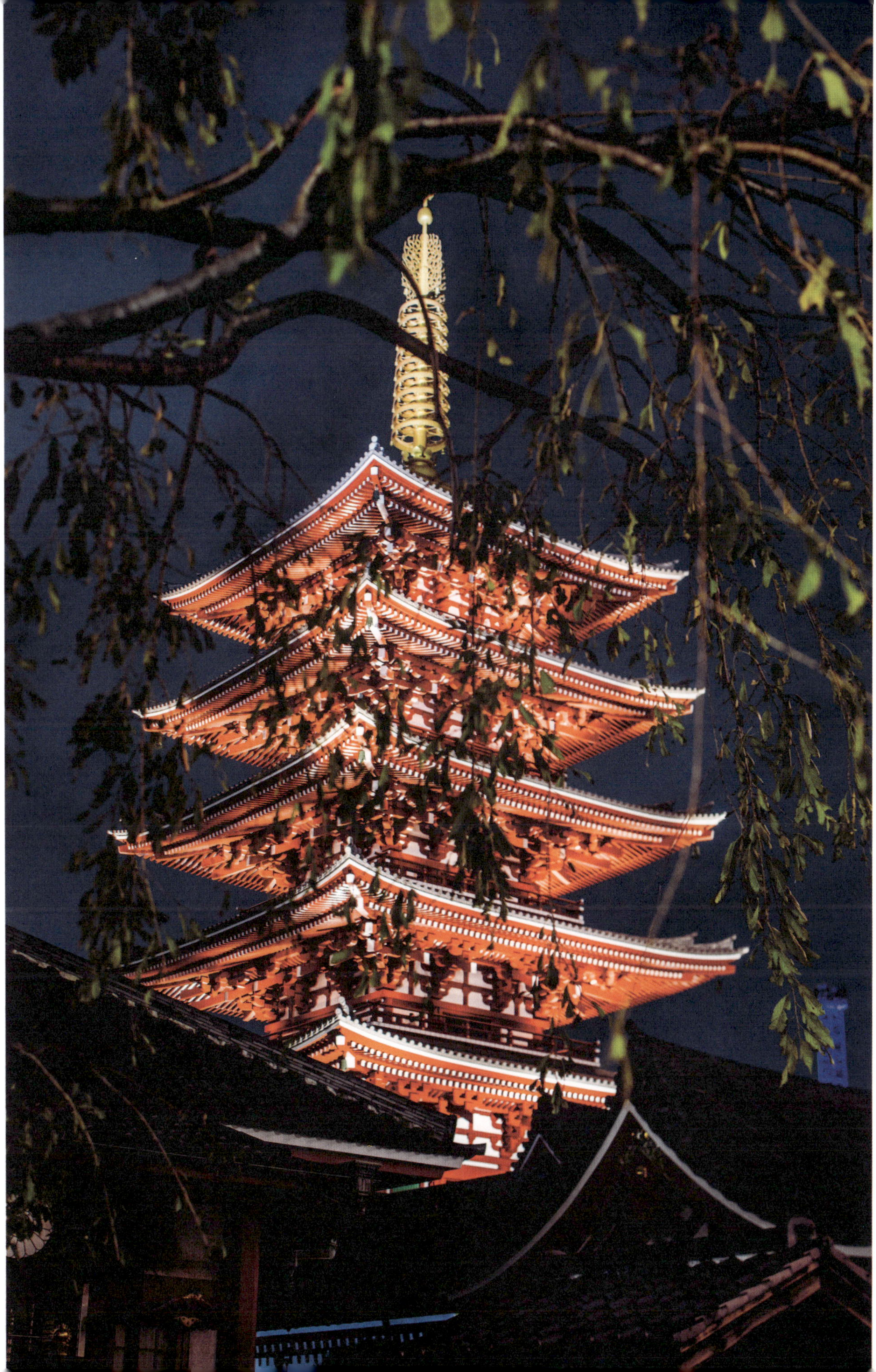

LIFESTYLE

ASAKUSA

A LOCAL DISTRICT FOR LOCAL PEOPLE

With its thousand-year-old temple and whole areas that seem frozen in the past, Asakusa has a feel that is quite unlike anywhere else in Tōkyō.

Asakusa is the center of what is known as "Tōkyō Shitamachi." The Japanese capital was once roughly divided into two areas: the steep streets of the upmarket districts of the city to the west of the Imperial Palace (Yamanote); and to the east, the workers' districts of the "lower town" (Shitamachi), in particular those located close to the Sumida River. Although these traditional terms are no longer used officially today, the characteristic features of the Shitamachi area are still very much alive in Tōkyō culture, referring to a particular atmosphere and style of cuisine, as well as a certain glibness, a kind of eloquence all its own.

It is said, somewhat stereotypically, that the residents of this district are by definition rougher but also more honest, direct, and open, and more reliable that the people of Yamanote. People born and raised in the Shitamachi district are considered true *Edokko*, or "children of Edo," definitively establishing them as heirs to Edo culture.

You need only visit some of the museums dedicated to Shitamachi culture in Ueno, and especially Asakusa, to understand this deep attachment to the history and values of the past. The gleaming Sensō-ji temple, built in the seventh century, is the district's star attraction and more than 30 million visitors pass through this Buddhist place of worship, the oldest in the capital, every year. It is reached via Nakamise-dori, a shopping street overflowing with traditional stores selling souvenirs and traditional pastries. This colorful road has entered folklore and is very popular with visitors, but resist the temptation to linger too long. In Asakusa, it's far more pleasant to simply stroll and lose yourself in its many adjacent side streets, browsing the wares of the last craftsmen left in Shitamachi, grabbing a drink at a locals' bar, or even watching a kabuki performance. Asakusa is renowned for its *okonomiyaki*, a sort of thin pancake topped with various ingredients (vegetables, meat, or seafood) that is a heartier cousin of *monja* and made on a hot grill, from which it can be eaten directly.

Just around the corner from Sensō-ji is the tiny Hanayashiki amusement park, which is definitely worth a visit. It was built in the mid-nineteenth century and seems frozen in time, with the rollercoasters, maze, and haunted house that children still enjoy to this day.

KAMINARIMON

Kaminarimon, the "thunder gate," the symbol of Asakusa district,
marks the entrance to Sensō-ji temple.

不動産
永谷
(株) 永谷上野営業所
3836-1234
上野松坂屋向い
永谷の演芸場
お江戸
上野広小路亭
やきとん
大王
上野アメ横店
大王
上野アメ横店
永谷
2F
40席
あり

ABOVE

Asakusa has many restaurants selling soba, *the famous buckwheat noodles.*

OPPOSITE

The izakaya *in the alleys and lanes of this historic district serve simple and unpretentious food.*

Tōkyō | TAITŌ

FOOD & DRINK

STREET FOOD AND TACHINOMI

AMEYOKO

Ameyoko market (a contraction of Ameya-Yokochō, "sweetshop alley") runs parallel to the railroad line between Ueno and Okachimachi stations.

RED BEANS

Japanese desserts are often based on red bean paste, such as these stuffed pancakes known as *dorayaki*.

YAKITORI

Yakitori are small morsels of grilled meat (usually chicken) served on skewers.

GOURMETS

Tōkyō is a gourmet paradise, with 160,000 restaurants.

GETTING TO KNOW YOU

The district's restaurants are frequently very cramped and people eat elbow to elbow. Solo diners will have the chance to meet their neighbors.

ON THE HOOF

The locals will sometimes enjoy a bite to eat at a *tachinomi*, a bar with just a counter at which customers stand.

BARS

Ueno and Okachimachi are popular districts with many small *tachinomi*.

MARKET

Ameyoko market has almost 200 stalls selling all kinds of foodstuffs.

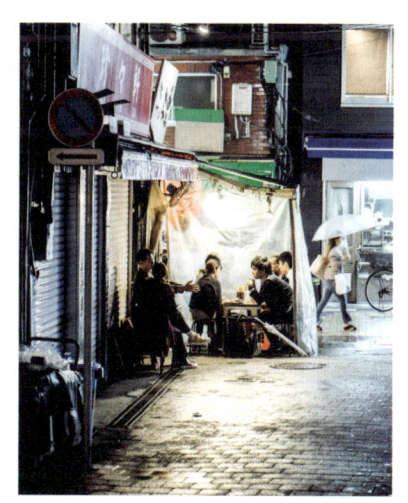

CONVIVIALITY

People often meet up after work for a meal with friends or colleagues at an *izakaya*.

The giant Ameya-Yokochō market has 161,459 sq ft (15,000 m²) of bars, local restaurants, and food stores. You will also find all kinds of fashion accessories on sale.

うえちゃん
上中
都まんじゅう
WINDY CITY
ゲーム
エアトリ
CURRENCY EXCHANGE
LAW
IN
都まんじゅう
商店 TEL03-3833-6668
出会い
外貨両替

PORTRAIT

HANAYASHIKI

AMUSEMENT PARK

Hanayashiki is a unique spot that is very popular with families.
Japan's oldest amusement park has a nostalgic charm
enjoyed by people of all ages.

This tiny amusement park opened its doors in 1947 and has changed little since then, remaining very popular with Japanese families over the decades. The park is located behind Sensō-ji temple in the heart of Asakusa and its retro appeal will round off a visit there with a spot of fun and relaxation.

Hanayashiki ("Flowery Mansion" in Japanese) takes its name from the site on which it was built, an old botanical garden laid out in 1853. It gradually metamorphosed into a pleasure garden and then a zoo. After suffering damage in the Great Kantō Earthquake (1923), it was destroyed completely during the Second World War before being rebuilt in its current form in 1947.

Hanayashiki boasts around twenty rides arranged across a very compact site, but even the youngest visitors can enjoy classics like a merry-go-round, a Ferris wheel and a rollercoaster; the "Yomiuri rocket coaster" opened in 1953 and was the first of its kind in Japan.

If thrill-seeking is not your thing, you can also enjoy gentle rides on swans and pandas or in a helicopter, and there's even a coconut shy stand in the park. The Pyong Pyong is a ride on which children over the age of two can jump like small frogs. If you are feeling brave, the "Edo no Kimodameshi" haunted house will test your nerve.

The "Bee Tower" was demolished in 2016 to make way for the Asakusa HanaGekijyou, a small theatre that opened its doors in 2019. The stage is also used for putting on shows, and the park's website advertises various concerts, martial arts displays and more.

If you are feeling peckish, restaurants in the park sell everything from ice creams and burgers to crêpes and *takoyakis* (octopus dumplings that are an Osaka speciality). As a final bonus, this unique park guarantees a good view of both the temple and the Tokyo Skytree.

FESTIVE OASIS

Hanayashiki is a very compact park where all the attractions are contained in an area of just over 20,000 sq ft (1,860 m²).

VIEW FROM A HEIGHT

This park has the oldest rollercoaster in Japan, built in 1953. It offers views of Sensō-ji and the Tokyo Skytree.

Shinobazu Pond in the heart of Ueno Park luxuriates in a carpet of lotus plants, whose leaves can cover the entire surface of the water during summer.

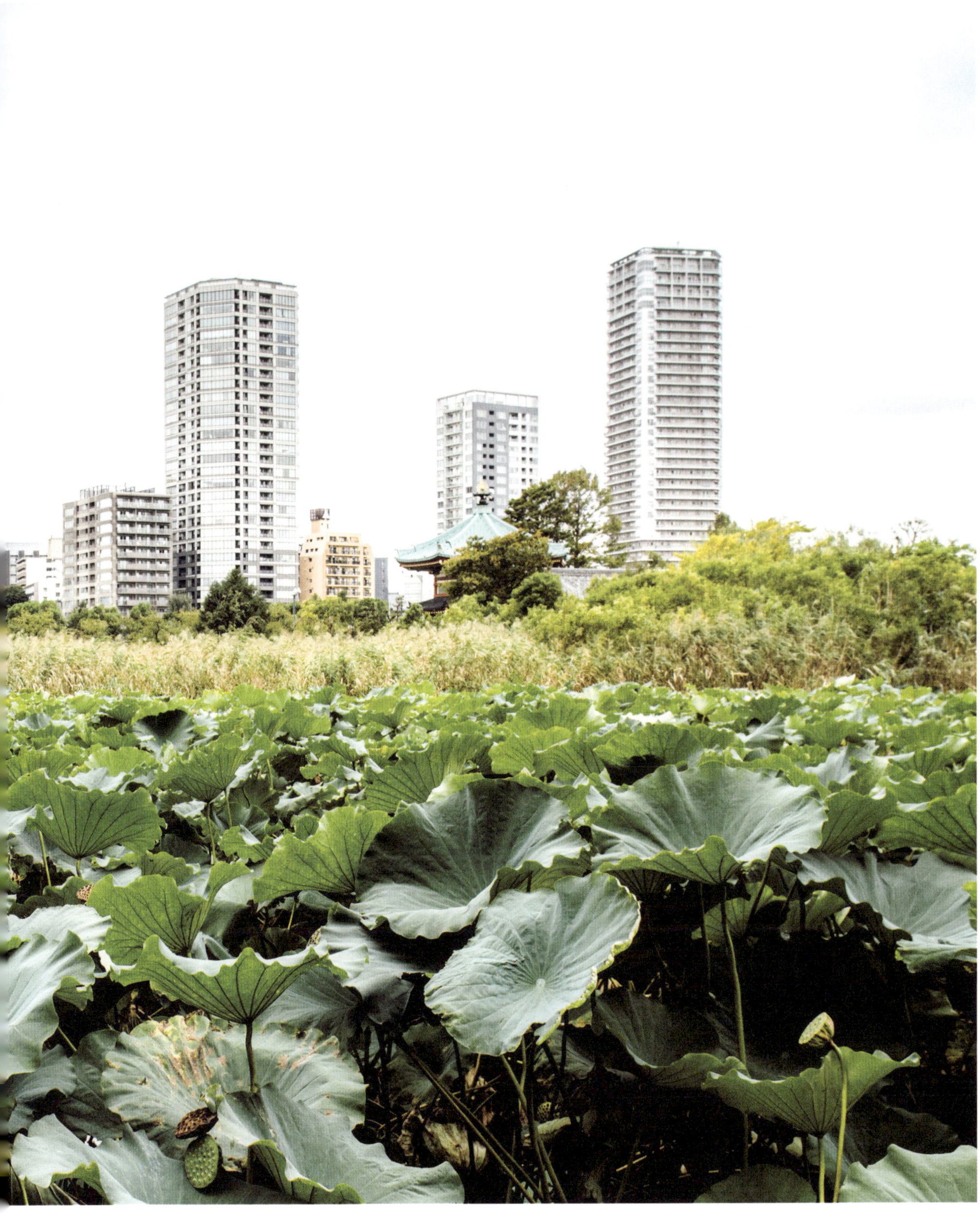

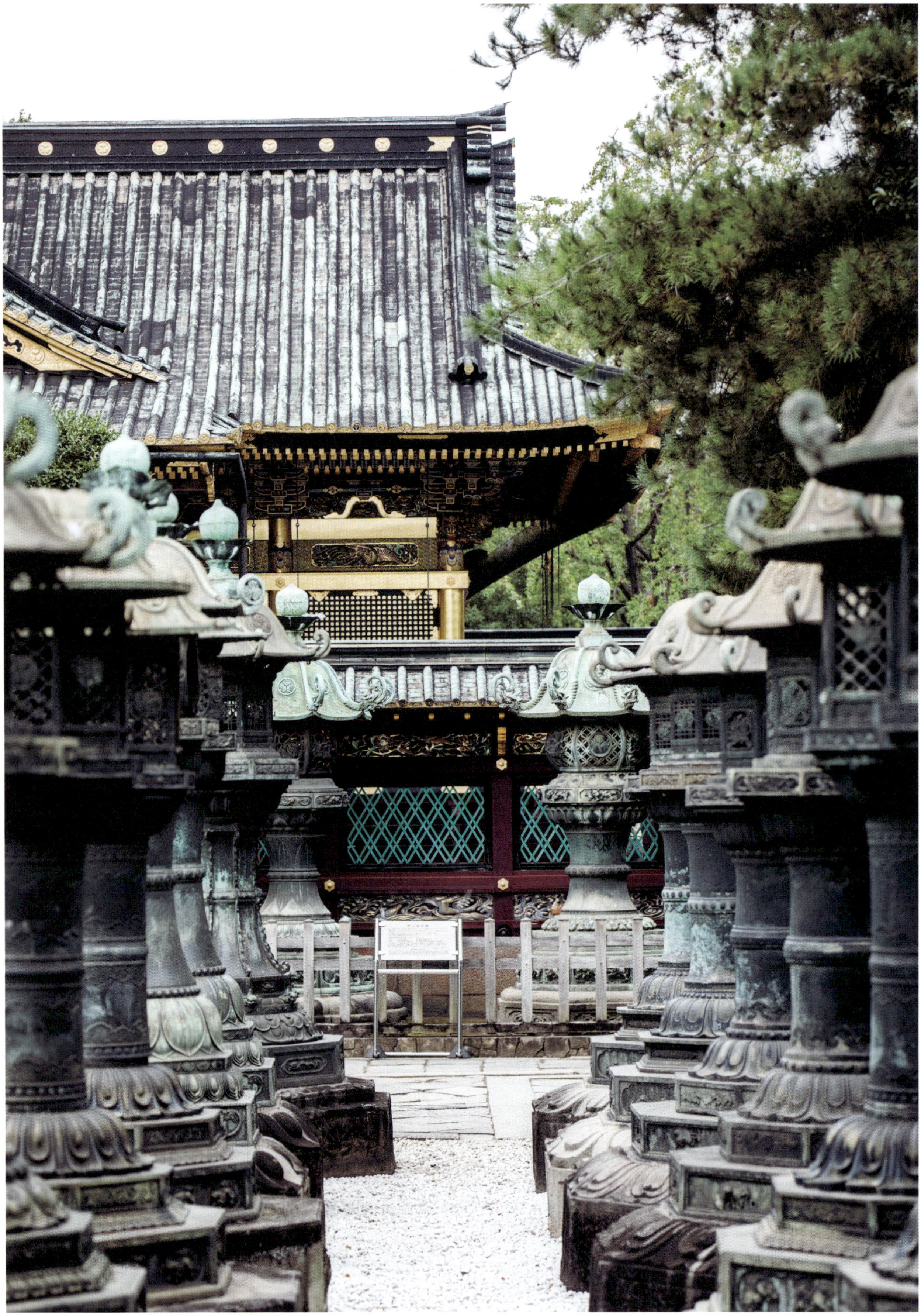

ABOVE

The National Museum of Western Art is the premier public art gallery in Tōkyō and welcomes more than a million visitors every year.

OPPOSITE

The Ueno Toshogu Shrine is dedicated to the spirit of the shōgun Tokugawa Ieyasu (1543–1616). Its forty-eight bronze statues were donated by nobles from all over the Japanese archipelago and have been recognized as examples of "world heritage".

76   *Tōkyō* | **TAITŌ**

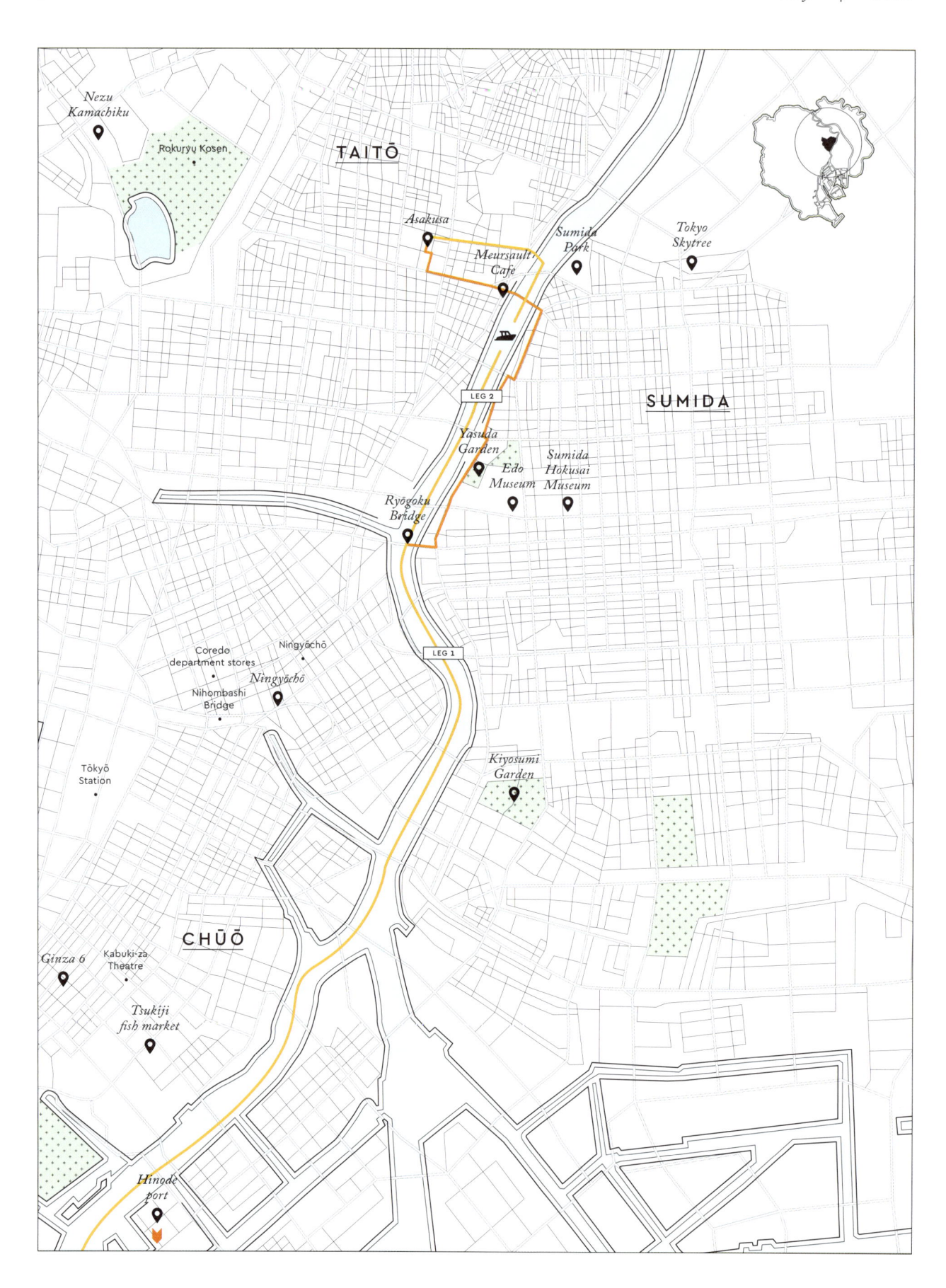

TAITŌ

- Nezu Kamachiku
- Rokuryu Kosen
- Asakusa
- Meursault Cafe
- Sumida Park
- Tokyo Skytree

SUMIDA

- LEG 2
- Yasuda Garden
- Edo Museum
- Sumida Hokusai Museum
- Ryōgoku Bridge
- Coredo department stores
- Ningyōchō
- Ningyōchō
- Nihombashi Bridge
- LEG 1
- Tōkyō Station
- Kiyosumi Garden

CHŪŌ

- Ginza 6
- Kabuki-za Theatre
- Tsukiji fish market
- Hinode port

WALKING TOUR

ALONG THE SUMIDA RIVER

The Sumida River is the focal point of the eastern part of Tōkyō and has shaped the cultural and artistic life of the Japanese capital since the Edo era. It is also a showcase for the peaceful nature of the local life that goes on along its banks and is the site of one of the country's biggest summer festivals.

LEG 1: FROM RYŌGOKU TO ASAKUSA

The Sumida River flows through the Japanese capital for seventeen miles, crossing seven wards. As a tributary of the Arakawa River, it passes through several of the city's northern districts, reaching Asakusa, where it plays a major role, before flowing into Tōkyō Bay. It passes beneath no fewer than twenty-six bridges, including the Ryōgoku-bashi immortalized by Hiroshige and Hokusai, and is the gateway to numerous picturesque canals. Starting a riverside stroll at Ryōgoku provides the opportunity to visit the Edo and Hokusai Museums, or to attend a sumo tournament beside the Sumida at Ryōgoku Kokugikan. The walk along the riverbank to Asakusa is very pleasant, taking in several parks (including Sumida and Hamachō) and passing the former Yasuda Garden, which was first laid out between 1688 and 1703.

LEG 2: A CRUISE ON THE WATER

At Asakusa, it's easy to hop onto one of the numerous cruise shuttles that take less than an hour to reach Tōkyō Bay. The trip provides the opportunity to see Asakusa from a different angle, as well as to spot several of the city's other iconic structures, such as the Tokyo Skytree tower and the Rainbow Bridge. There will also be time to admire the Hamarikyū Garden from the water and take in the districts of Tsukishima and Odaiba before reaching the port of Hinode at the southern end of the city. Another option is to take a water bus from Asakusa, allowing you to cross the river quickly.

ALTERNATIVELY: TALES OF THE RIVERBANK

If you prefer to keep your feet on *terra firma*, exploring on foot is just as pleasant. Take a stroll along the riverbank while taking the pulse of local life beside the Sumida. Just a stone's throw from Asakusa Station is the charming Cafe Meursault, which is open all day and where you can enjoy brunch, a coffee, or an aperitif while enjoying the stunning view of the river from the café terrace. There are plenty of places (Sumida Park, for example) where you can enjoy a picnic and inspect the soaring outline of the Tokyo Skytree, officially recognized as the "tallest telecommunications tower in the world" since 2011. Thousands of locals flock to the annual Sumidagawa Hanabi Taikai, Sumida's great firework display, a tradition that dates back to the Edo era. Always held on the last Saturday in July, it is one of the oldest and most famous summer festivals in Japan and offers the chance to enjoy the cool of the evening during the merciless heat of the Japanese summer.

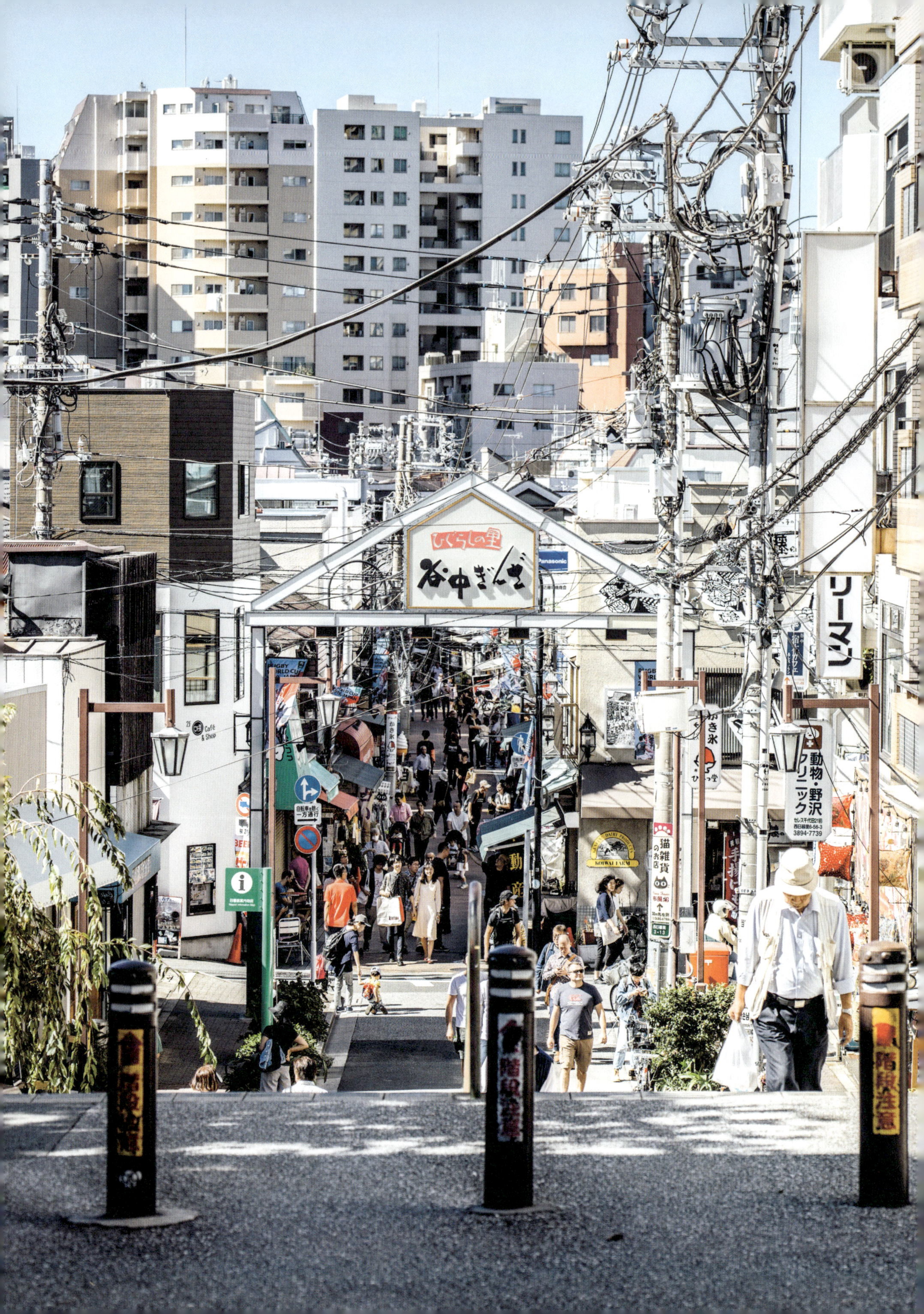

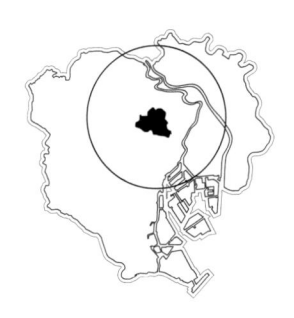

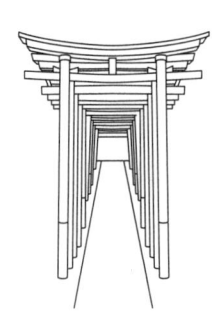

ROMANTIC

BUNKYŌ
文京区

For many of the capital's inhabitants, Bunkyō is its most romantic district with several attractions for the traveler: a centuries-old shrine, the Kōrakuen Garden, described as one of the most beautiful landscapes in the country, and the delightful "Yanesen triangle", which takes you on a gentle trip back through time.

P. 70

Many Tokyoites would say that the best view of Yanaka is from this flight of steps, the Yūyake Dandan. A place to visit at sunset on a romantic evening out.

OPPOSITE

Koishikawa Korakuen is one of the capital's oldest and most beautiful gardens.

In a survey conducted in 2015, the people of Tōkyō voted Bunkyō their favorite place for a first date, giving a range of reasons, from the impulse to fall in love inspired by the area and the pleasure of taking a stroll along its streets as a couple, to the strong sense of community that it has retained—everything in Bunkyō conspires to create the perfect romantic atmosphere.

Bunkyō is also where the Tokyo Dome is situated, the famous baseball stadium that hosts home matches for the Yomiuru Giants, not to mention concerts by many of today's most well-known music artists. Just north of the stadium is the small Nezu Shrine, built in the eighteenth century. Although it is one of Japan's oldest and a fine example of the capital's unique heritage, visitors still often pass it by. The magnificent Kōrakuen Garden next to the Tokyo Dome, one of the three most beautiful gardens in Japan, is also well worth a visit, and a little farther on is the no less remarkable Koishikawa Botanical Garden.

The jewel in Bunkyō's crown remains the Ya-ne-sen triangle, however, an acronym of three districts: Yanaka, Nezu, and Sendagi. Yanesen residents are fiercely attached to their neighborhood and have preserved its old-fashioned charm over the years, highlighting its best aspects and nurturing the atmosphere of the past that pervades its walls.

Just around the corner from Nezu Shrine is Yanaka, one of the few areas to have survived at least in part the earthquake of 1923 and the bombing of the Second World War (hence its nickname, "Old Tōkyō"). Accessible from Nippori Station, the district is characterized by its disarming simplicity and its cheerful residents. Yanaka banishes all thoughts of the ultra-modern shopping centers in Shinjuku, Shibuya, or Akihabara—its small retro stores with their traditional Japanese pastries and tea are charming and its traditional and authentic ambience makes for a welcome change of pace and a trip back in time.

Yanaka Cemetery, barely a minute's walk from Nippori Station, is also worth visiting. This calm, green oasis covering more than 25 acres (10 hectares) was built in 1874, and locals flock here every spring to enjoy the stunning sight of the plum trees in bloom (*ume*). More temples are scattered throughout the district and it's easy to extend your walk by adding one or two to your itinerary. As you may have gathered, Bunkyō is particularly suitable for exploring on foot at a leisurely pace. This is by far the best way to truly get to know the area.

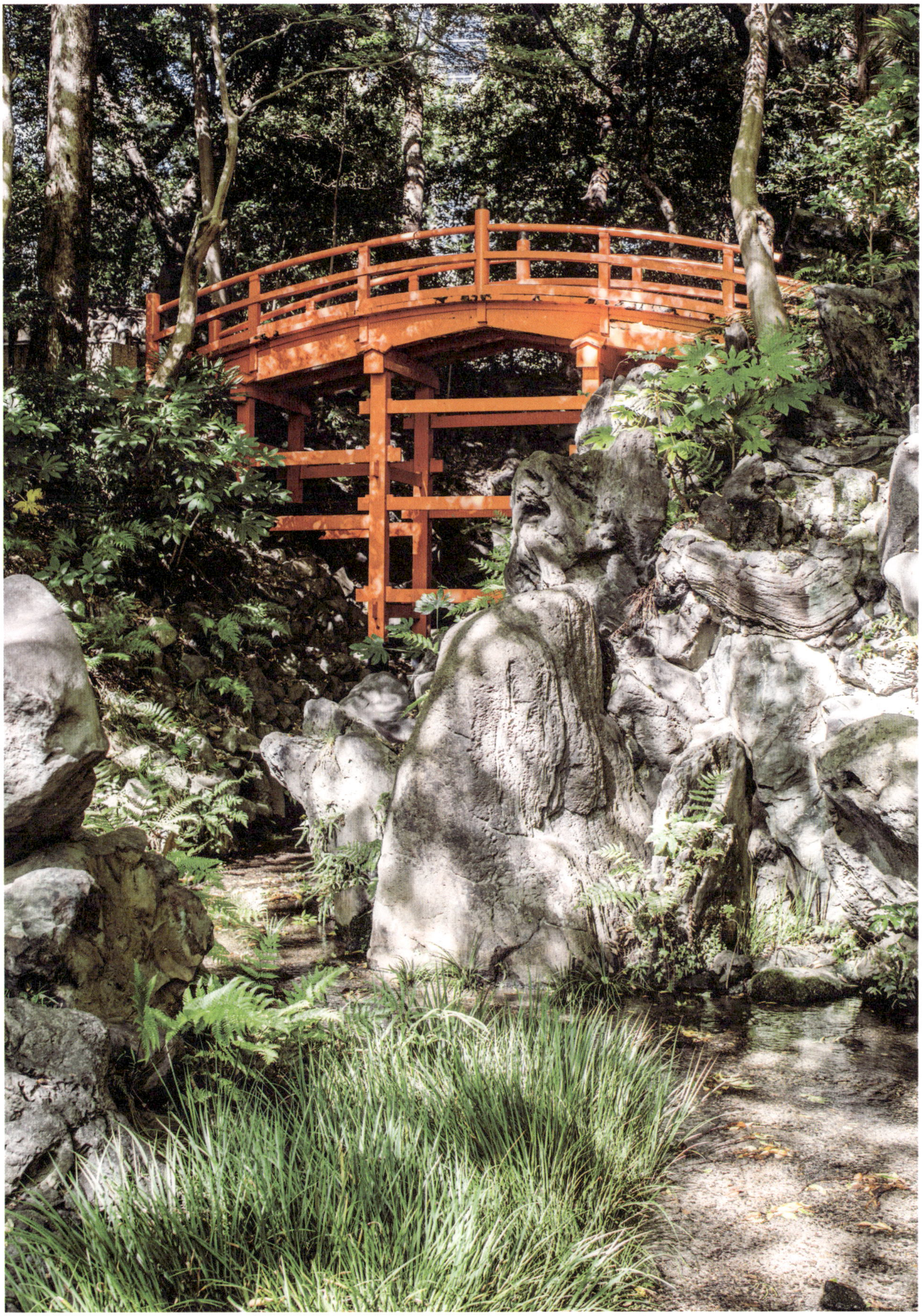

BUNKYŌ
THE ESSENTIALS

15

TEMPLE TENNŌ-JI

Look out for the bronze Buddhas, several centuries old, in this temple founded beside Yanaka Cemetery in 1274. The site is dedicated to Bishamonten (Vaiśravana), the god of riches and courage.

16

GOKOKU-JI TEMPLE

A Buddhist temple whose main hall houses one of the capital's most beautiful collections of art from the Genroku period.

17

NAKIRYU *RĀMEN*

Nakiryu was opened by Kazumasa Saito in 2012 and is one of only two rāmen restaurants in Tōkyō to have won a Michelin star.

18

YAYOI KUSAMA MUSEUM

A museum exhibiting manga, popular magazines, and advertizing posters from the Meiji (1868–1912), Taisho (1912–1926), and Shōwa (1926–1989) periods.

19

TOKYO DOME

The complex includes several spaces for entertainment in the broadest sense, from a spa to an amusement park and a children's playground.

20

YANAKA CEMETERY (YANAKA REIEN)

More than 7,000 tombs are here, including that of Tokugawa Yoshinobu, the last shōgun of the Edo period (1603–1868).

21

KŌRAKUEN GARDEN

One of the three most beautiful traditional gardens in Japan, with a lake, small hills, winding paths, plum trees, pines, rice paddies, and tea plantations.

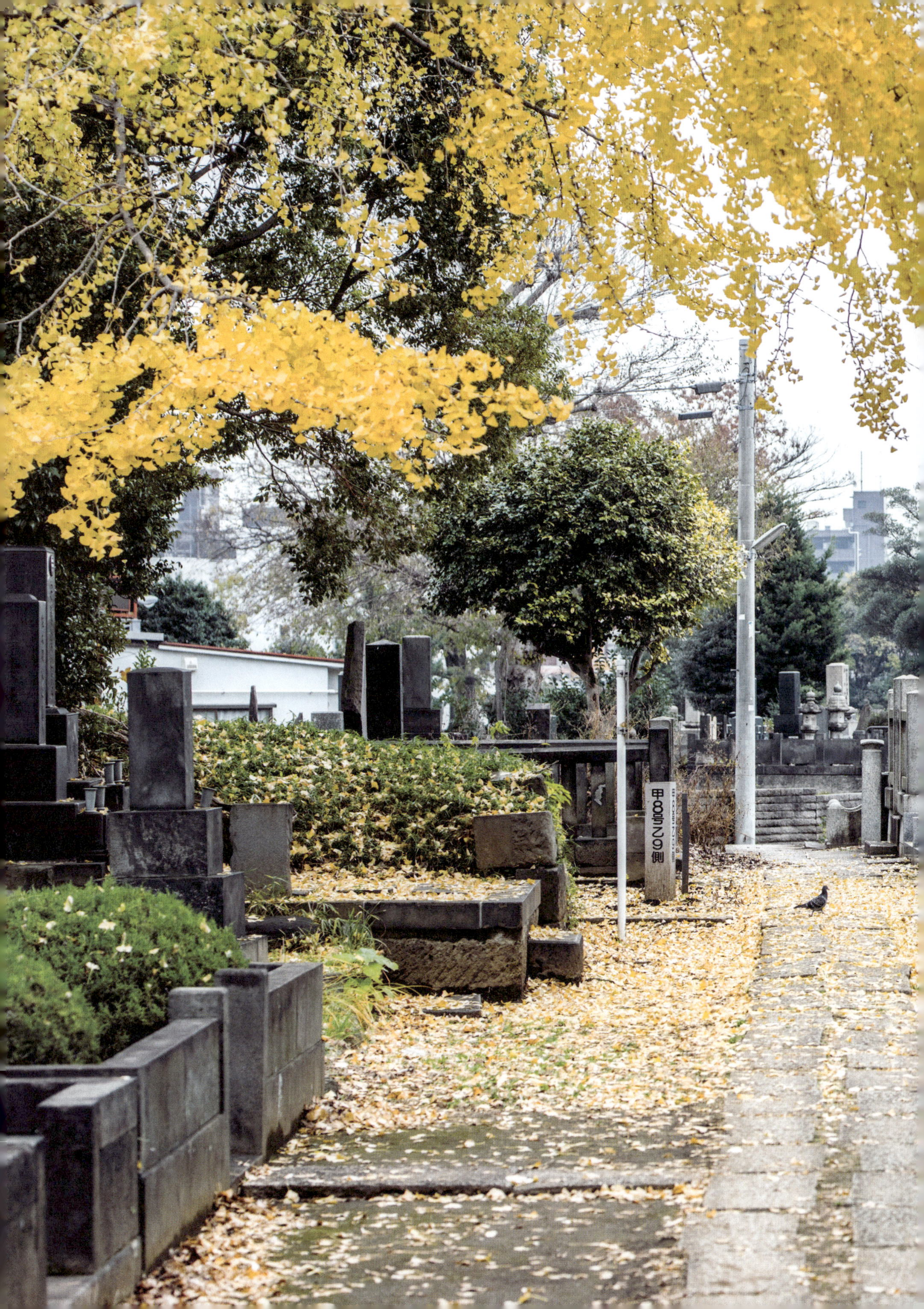
甲8号乙9側

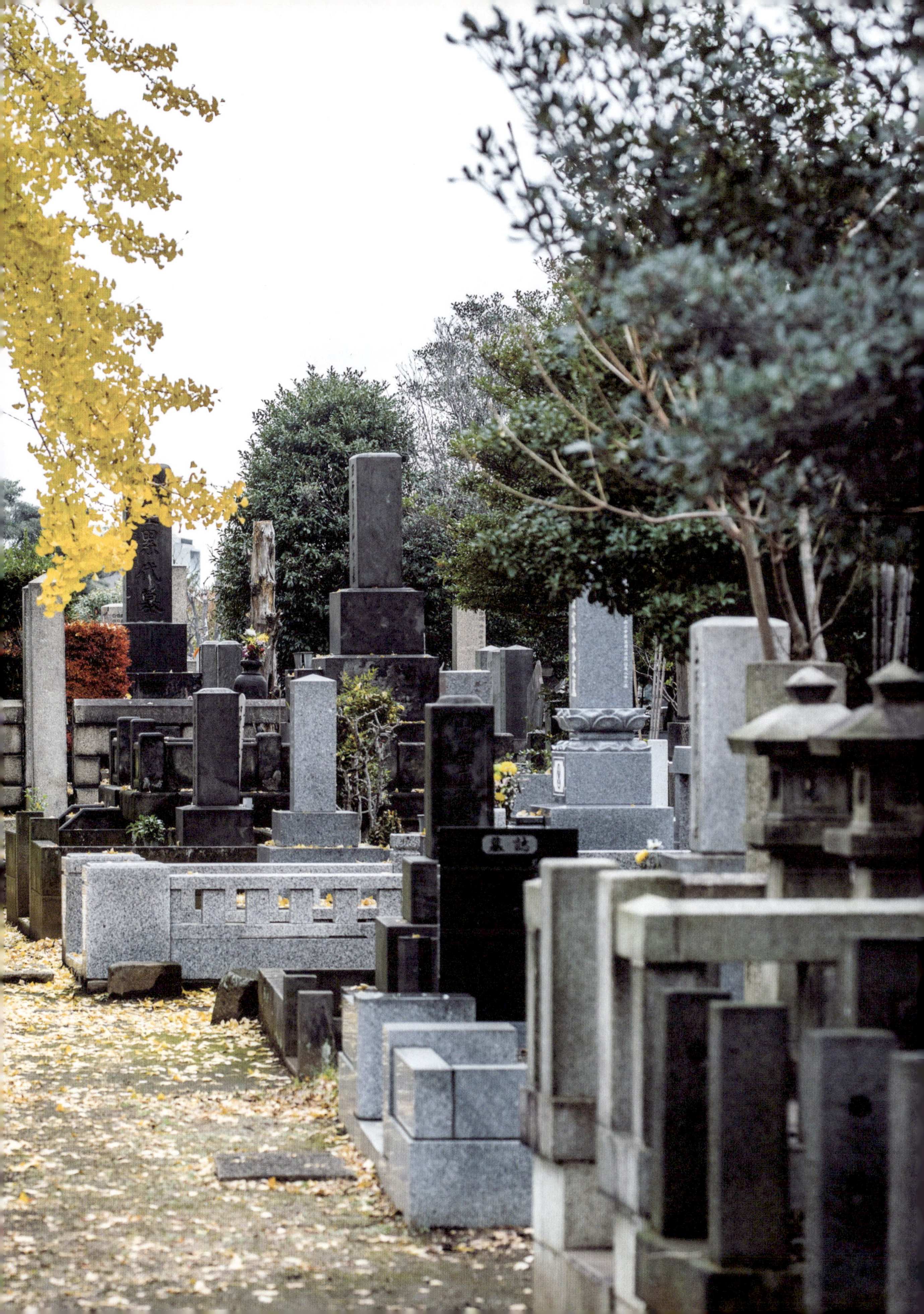

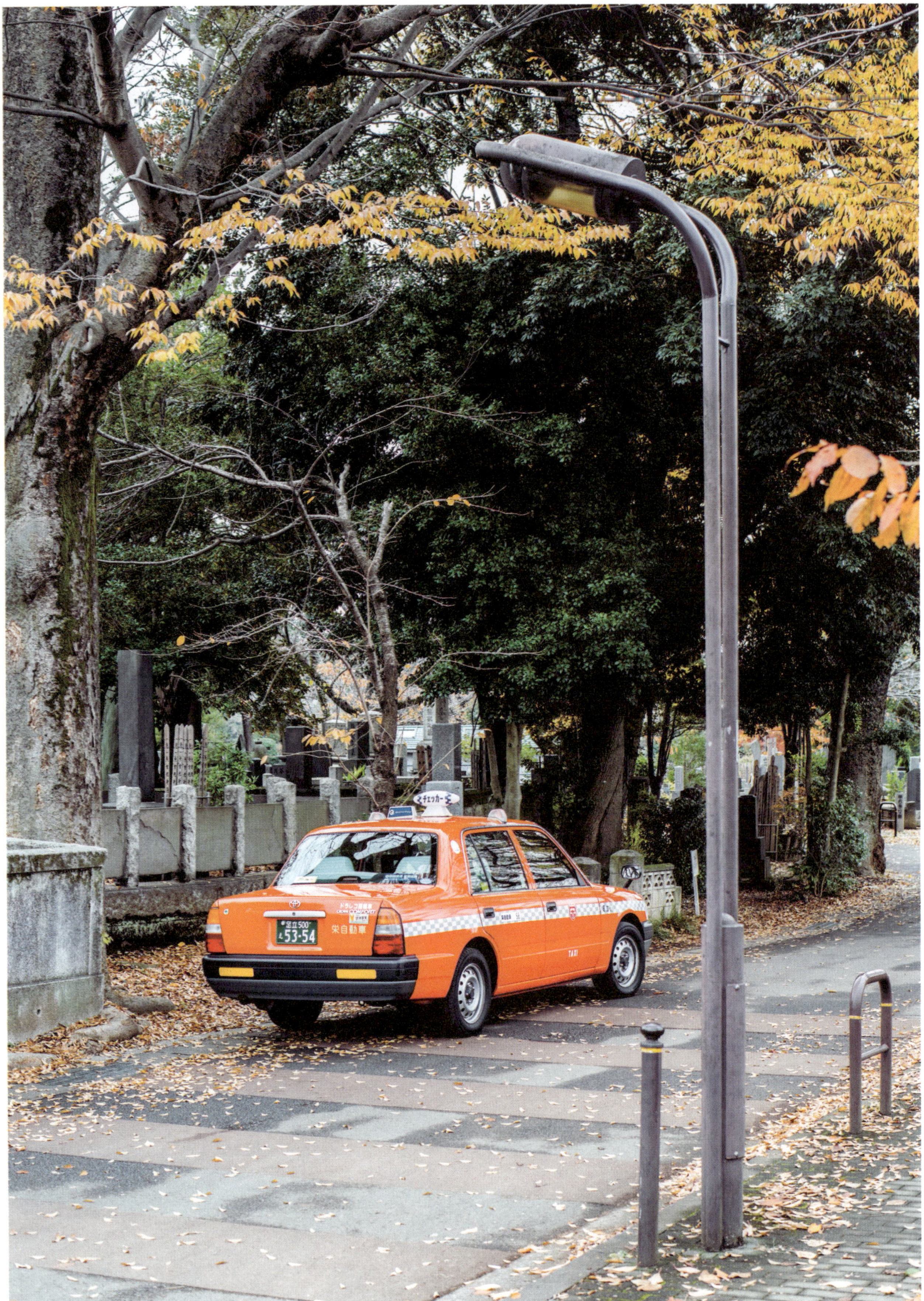

チェッカー
足立500
え53-54
栄自動車
TAXI

ABOVE

It is traditional to clean gravestones and tombs at the time of the spring and fall equinoxes.

OPPOSITE

The small road crossing Yanaka Cemetery has been dubbed "Sakura-dori" as it is lined with cherry trees that make a dazzling spectacle when in blossom.

P. 84-85

Yanaka cemetery (Reien Yanaka) was founded in 1874 and is one of the city's most famous burial grounds.

LIFESTYLE

THE STORES OF YANAKA GINZA

CAT STREET

Yanaka Ginza is known in the city as Cat Town and you can't miss the numerous stores and boutiques selling candies covered with pictures of cats.

ARCHITECTURE

The interior partition walls, doors, and windows of these old houses are made of *shōji*, screens made of rice paper.

CIBI

Cibi is a cozy concept store with a wide selection of muffins.

HITAMACHI AMBIENCE

The street and its businesses have not really changed much since the last century.

TOKYO BIKE SHOP AND RENTAL

Before heading off on your rental bike, why not enjoy a delicious coffee in this bike shop located in an old brewery?

PROMENADE

Yanaka Ginza attracts people out for a stroll who come to enjoy the calm atmosphere of this local district.

DELICIOUS DISHES

Don't miss the Soboro chicken with ginger at Cibi.

ARTISAN

The pedestrian street has a number of traditional stalls.

SNACKS

Visit with an empty stomach to enjoy the irresistible snacks.

ABOVE

A cluster of houses with modernist architecture stands near the exit at Yanaka Cemetery.

OPPOSITE

A school bus parked in front of Kaneiji kindergarten, which is located next door to Kanei-ji Buddhist temple.

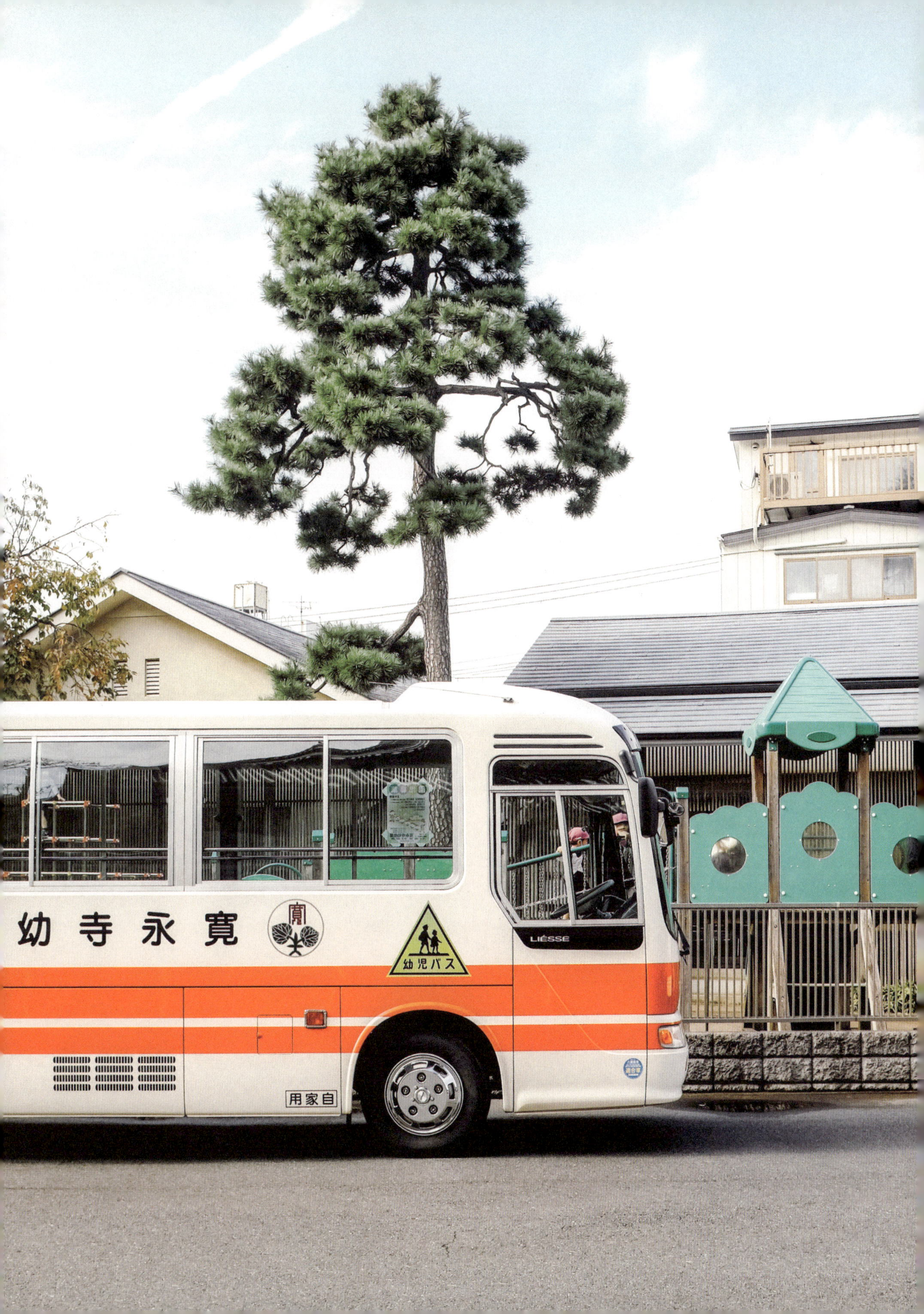
寛永寺幼
幼児バス
LIESSE
自家用

Nezu was built in the same style as the famous Nikkō Toshogu Shrine and is surrounded by golden sculptures that contrast with its bright red pillars.

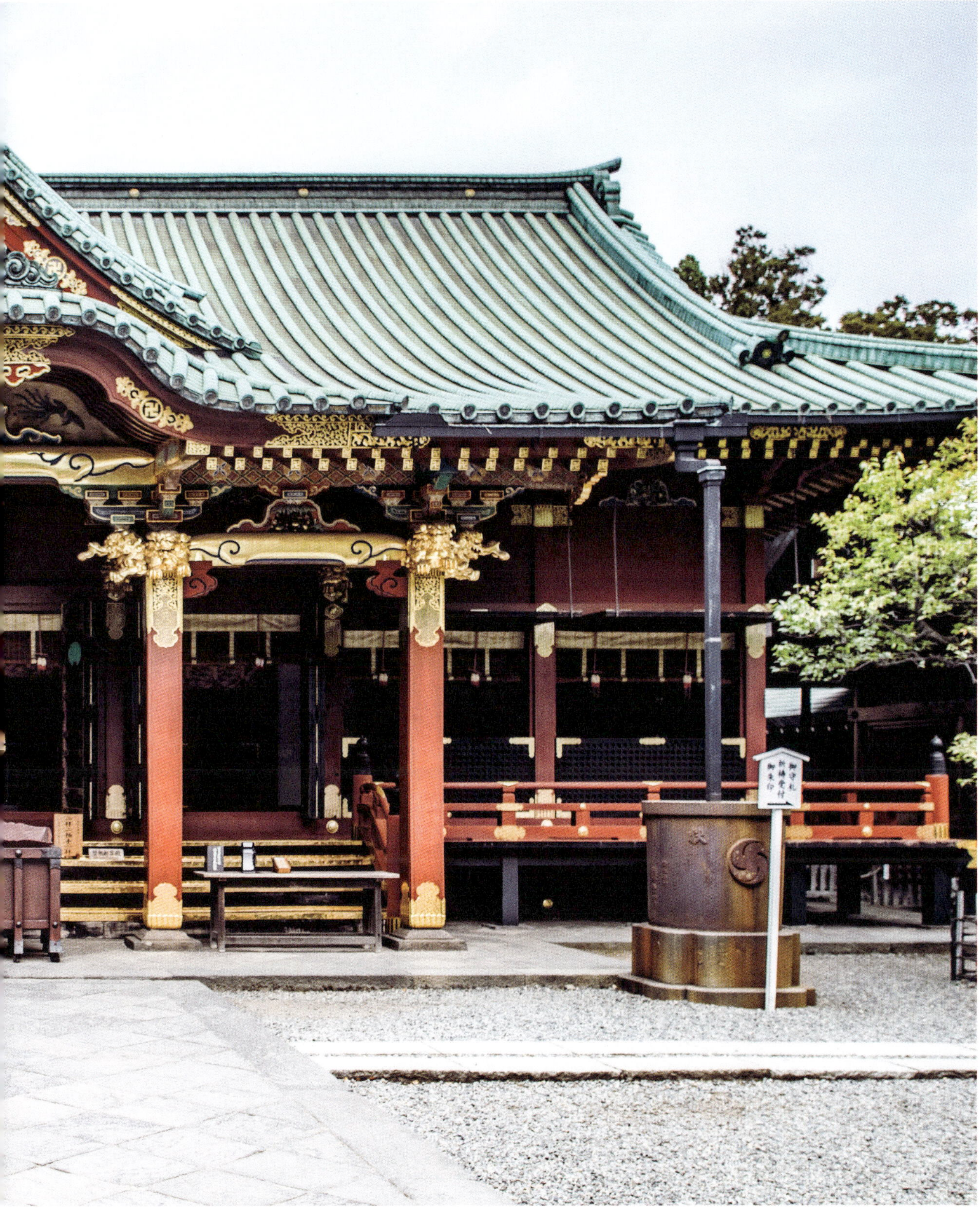

EXCURSION

NEZU-JINJA

A CENTURIES-OLD TEMPLE

Nezu Shrine was founded in the eighteenth century and, as one of the *Tōkyō-jissha* ("the ten shrines of Tōkyō"), is also one of the Japanese capital's oldest religious buildings.

This Shinto shrine built in 1705 miraculously escaped damage during the many air raids of the Second World War and several of the buildings in the shrine's complex have been designated as nationally "Important Cultural Property". It is much loved by the local population and is also known for having been frequented by Natsume Sōseki, the famous Japanese novelist. The prevailing atmosphere of centuries of history and spirituality lends it a special charm.

The shrine follows the colorful esthetic of *Ishi-no-ma-zukuri*, a style typical of Shinto architecture and notably also found two hours from the capital at Nikkō Tōshō-gū. Visitors can stroll through the series of small red gates that surround the complex, seemingly protecting it from the outside world and the bustle of the city. The entrance is marked by two great red doors (Karamon and Rōmon) before which visitors must bow before going inside. Shinto ritual now requires you to purify yourself by rinsing your hands in the washbasin (*chōzuya* or *temizuya*) before entering the hall of worship. Take hold of the handle of a ladle (*hishaku*) with your right hand, scoop up some water, and then rinse your left hand, followed by your right. Now pour a little water into the hollow of your left hand and rinse your mouth with it. Wash your left hand again and let the rest of the water run away down the handle. On no account pour the water you have scooped up back into the basin, but instead pour it away at the base.

Visitors to Japan are allowed to take pictures within the precincts of temples and shrines but may not photograph the interiors of the buildings. Offerings are placed in a box provided for this purpose; there's no set amount, but people generally slip in a five-yen coin as it is considered a bringer of good fortune.

In spring (between April and May), the shrine is transformed by the flowering of azaleas of a dozen different colors. Those lucky enough to visit Nezu at this time will have a spectacular show to admire, created by the hundreds of varieties grown here in the garden. Tsutsuji Matsuri, a large local festival celebrating the azalea, is held at this time of the year, so visitors can sit and take in this whole magnificent scene while sampling some of the local food.

HIDDEN TREASURE

This succession of red *torii* (gates) leads to the adjacent Otome Inari Shrine, which is dedicated to the prayers of young women.

BELIEFS

According to popular belief, the red coloring often found on statues in places of worship helps to keep evil spirits and sickness at bay.

ABOVE

In the Buddhist religion, water symbolizes life and is the purest form of nourishment. It is also synonymous with purity and clarity.

OPPOSITE

The Buddhist temple at Gokoku-ji, to the east of Ikebukuro, is a remarkable wooden structure. It was built in 1681 by the fifth shōgun Tokugawa Tsunayoshi to honor his mother.

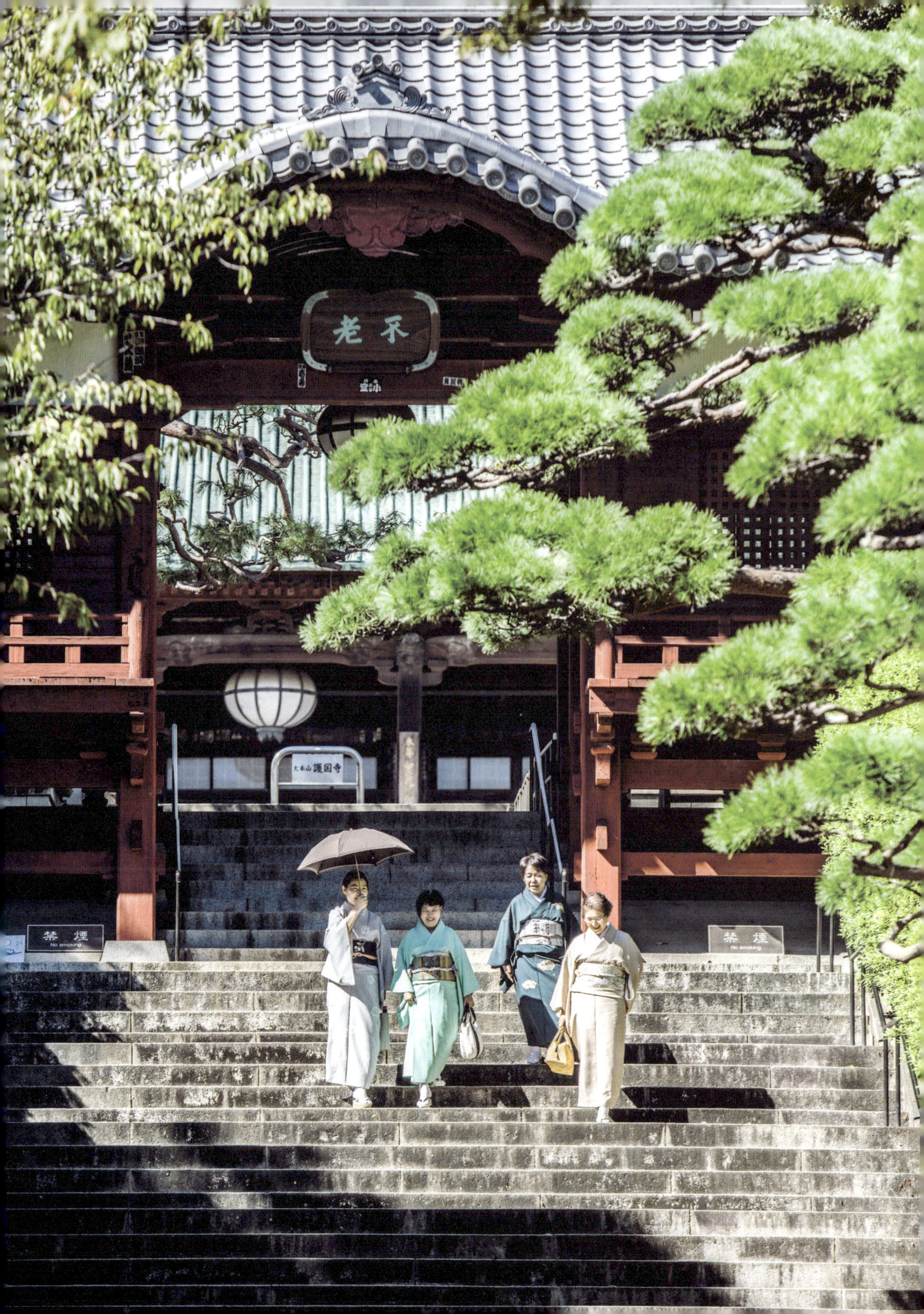

不老
大本山 護国寺
禁煙
No smoking
禁煙
No smoking

質 買取
さのや
0120-783-783
商店街
大塚
メディカル
クリニック
内科・皮膚科・肛門科
Tokyo Sakura Tram
7705

ABOVE

Yaki-imo *are delicious grilled yams that can be bought from street food traders or in supermarkets.*

OPPOSITE

A train on the old Toden Arakawa Line, now known as the Tokyo Sakura Tram; together with the Setagaya Line these are the only tramways in Tōkyō.

PORTRAIT

RYOZO NAGANUMA

BATHING AT KOTOBUKI-YU

Here at Kotobuki-yu, Ryozo Naganuma has been preserving the traditional public bathing culture of *sentō*, which has proved a big hit with local residents. It is a passion that has been with him since childhood.

Tōkyō now has around 600 *sentō* bathhouses, although there were once 2,500 during the Edo period. The number has been in constant decline since the second half of the twentieth century, with one of the capital's public baths closing its doors for the final time every week.

The principal cause for the reduction in numbers is that since the 1980s Japanese homes have been routinely fitted with Western-style bathrooms, but the problems of managing a *sentō* run this a close second. "Running a *sentō* is a pretty tricky job and it's often difficult to find someone to take over the business," explains Ryozo Naganuma, the forty-year-old owner and manager at Kotobuki-yu. He goes on to explain that maintaining and cleaning the premises is hard work.

Twenty-three people work at Kotobuki-yu, which opens every day at 11 A.M. and closes at 1.30 A.M. It is so popular that local residents stand in line at weekends patiently waiting for the chance to enjoy a nice hot bath, meet up with neighbors and friends, and to catch up on the local news. This makes it much more than a place where you come to wash and care for your body—it is first and foremost a place of social mixing, where the hierarchical barriers melt away. In Japan, they often say that when both are naked, there is no difference between a boss and a worker.

Ryozo Naganuma recalls his first *sentō* memories when just a small child, with emotion. "I would go to the baths regularly with my parents and siblings; it was a real pleasure as a family. My uncle was the owner of a *sentō* and I started working with him when I was twenty-two years old; I had my own business by the age of thirty-seven."

On entering a traditional *sentō*, the first thing you notice are the wooden changing rooms (*datsuiba*) and the adjacent bathroom section (*yokushitsu*), as it is customary to wash before entering the various hot baths. Kotobuki-yu has several outdoor baths (*rotemburo*) and a sauna in both its male and female sections. Once inside, don't be surprised to see a colorful picture decorating the walls, in this case a picture of two boxers in a landscape depicting Mount Fuji (each *sentō* has a different image). "I was a professional boxer," smiles Ryozo Naganuma. "I got my passion for boxing from my older brother and I still box even now, although only as an amateur."

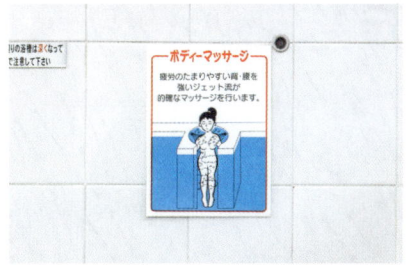

1 / FRESCO

The wall painting (*penki*) in a *sentō* defines its identity.

2 / RECEPTION

The admission fee is paid at reception, where you can also rent towels and buy soap.

3 / PASSION

Ryozo Naganuma, a former boxer, is the manager of the Kotobuki-yū *sentō*.

4 / MASSAGE

Bubble baths offer the chance for a very relaxing massage.

5 / OUTDOOR BATHS

Some *sentō* also have *rotemburo* (outdoor baths), which may be fed by a natural hot spring (*onsen*).

UNDERSTANDING
SENTŌ
THE GENTLE ART OF BATHING

Tōkyō still has several hundred public baths across its various districts. Visitors who are new to bathing in Japan are strongly recommended to visit a *sentō* accompanied by someone with previous experience.

To the Japanese, the *sentō* (the local name for the neighborhood public bathhouse) is rather old-fashioned. The building itself, with its elaborate roof, is always immediately identifiable by the *noren*, a sort of curtain placed across the entrance and decorated with the *kanji* (ideogram) for hot water.

The layout and procedure inside are pretty much the same in all such bathhouses: shoes are first placed in a locker before the entrance fee is paid at the reception. The baths are not mixed so bathers proceed to the male or female changing room. In the first room (*datsuiba*), they undress completely and put their things in the locker provided; this is where they will return when it is time to dry off and get dressed. Mirrors are available, and there may be hairdryers, lotions, and massage chairs that can be used for a few yen.

Once naked, bathers enter the bathing area (*yokutshitsu*) but must wash (there are stools and basins in front of the faucets) before they can enter the hot bath. In Japan, you never wash in the bath, either at home or at the *sentō*; everyone washes beforehand. Once clean, bathers can enter the hot water to relax and unwind. People with long hair are required to tie it up so that it doesn't touch the bathwater.

Sentō, or local public baths, don't have quite the cachet of the *onsen* (thermal spas and natural hot springs found throughout Japan) that people visit to relax during the vacations. Yet they are charming, with murals and decoration that differ from one bathhouse to the next. They range from classic bathhouses to "super *sentō*", which are larger, better equipped and more modern, with higher admission prices (the admission price for a classic *sentō* is fixed). Unlike *onsen*, people with tattoos are permitted to bathe in a *sentō*, but the super *sentō* may sometimes refuse entry as tattoos are associated with the *yakuza* (Japanese mafia).

THE LAYOUT OF A SENTŌ

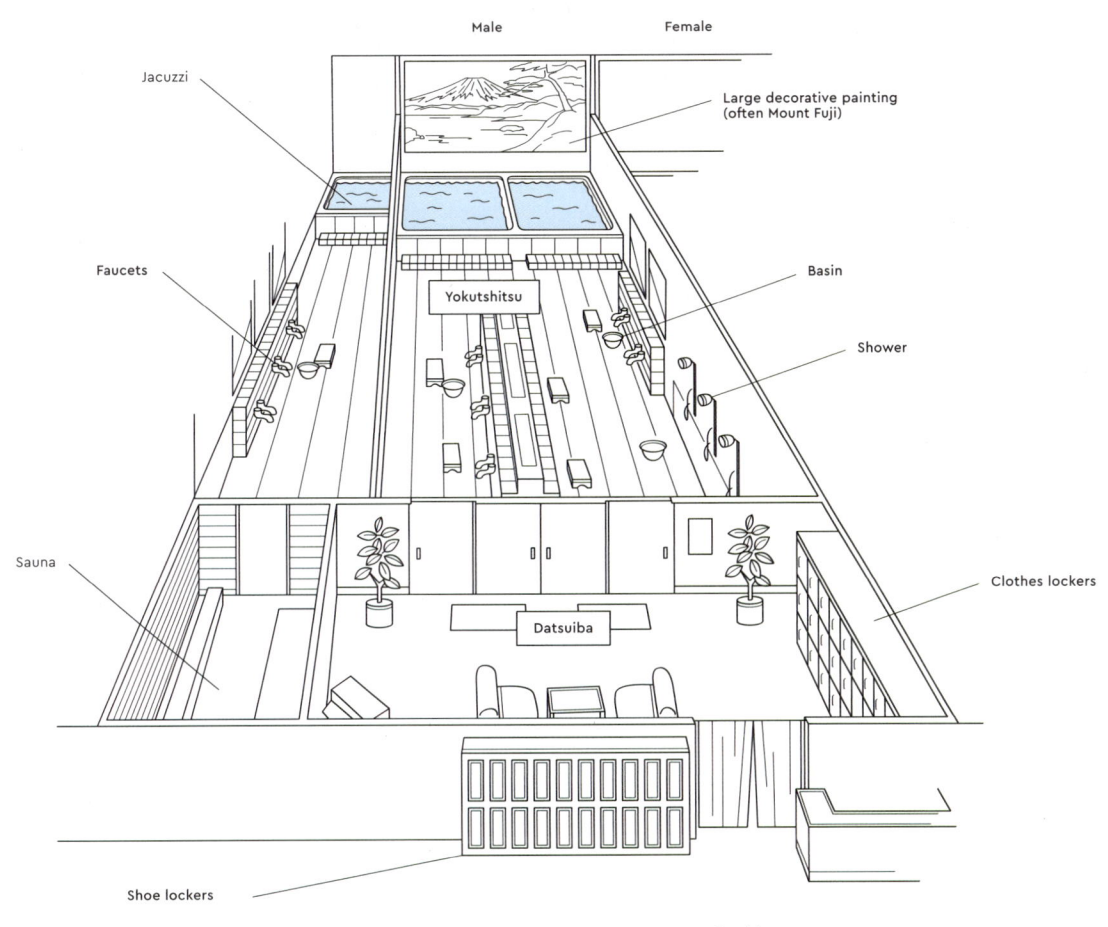

Male · Female
Jacuzzi
Large decorative painting (often Mount Fuji)
Faucets
Yokutshitsu
Basin
Shower
Sauna
Datsuiba
Clothes lockers
Shoe lockers

Bandai
(reception desk, where an admission fee is paid)

Soap and towels are not provided but can be hired or purchased.

BLUEPRINT FOR A SENTŌ

Sentō are often laid out in the same way and with a procedure to follow before sinking into the water in the hot baths. The water is heated using wood, gas or electricity, depending on the *sentō*, and can often be very hot (106–107 degrees Fahrenheit/41–42 degrees Celsius).

The Former Yasuda Residence is one of Tōkyō's last traditional homes and was renovated at the turn of the twentieth century. It is accessible from Sendagi Station.

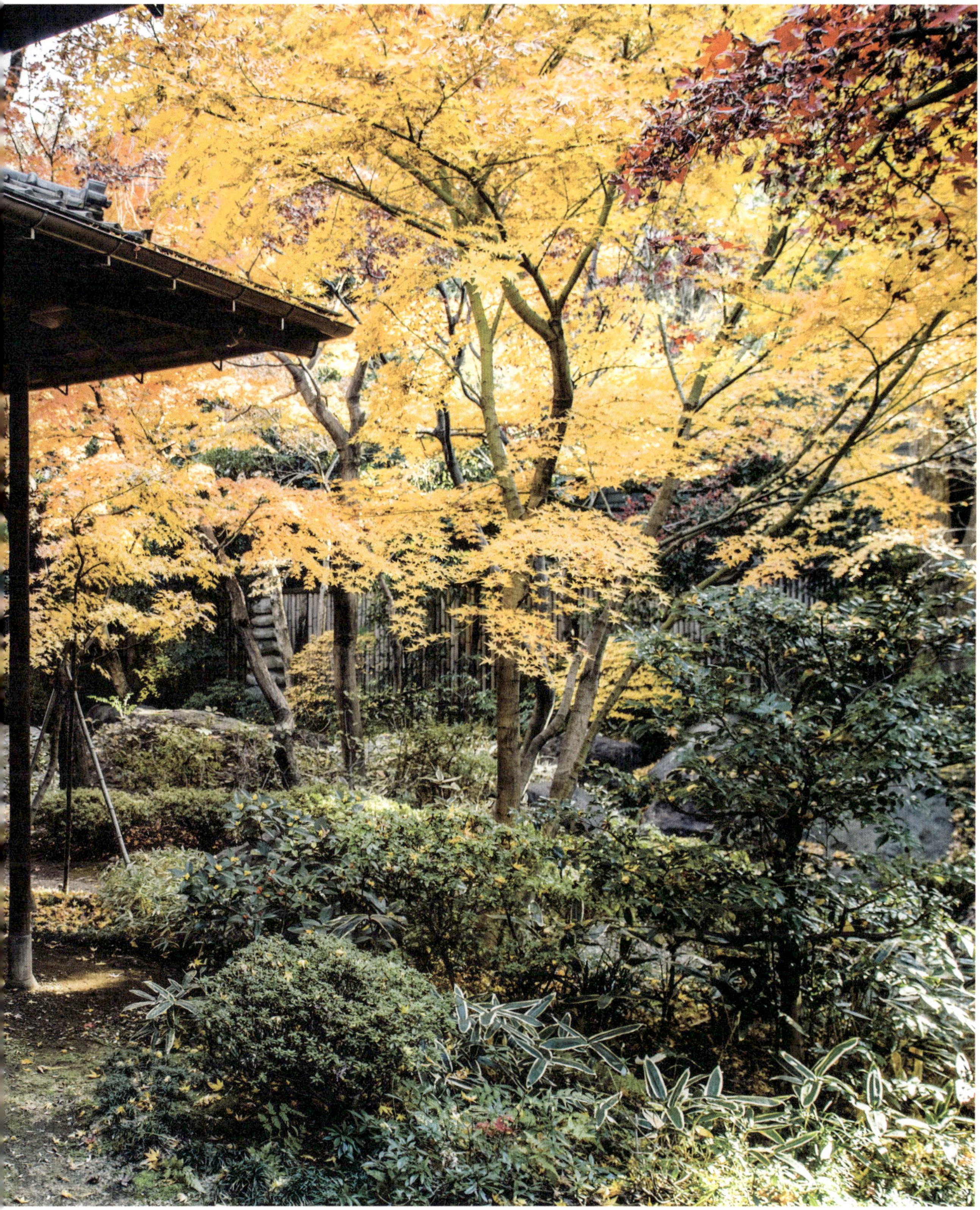

ABOVE

A beautiful Japanese garden surrounds the Former Yasuda Residence, lending it an aura of timelessness and of being shut away from the world.

OPPOSITE

Catch a glimpse of the maple trees in the garden through the sliding shōji *panels (which are made of rice paper).*

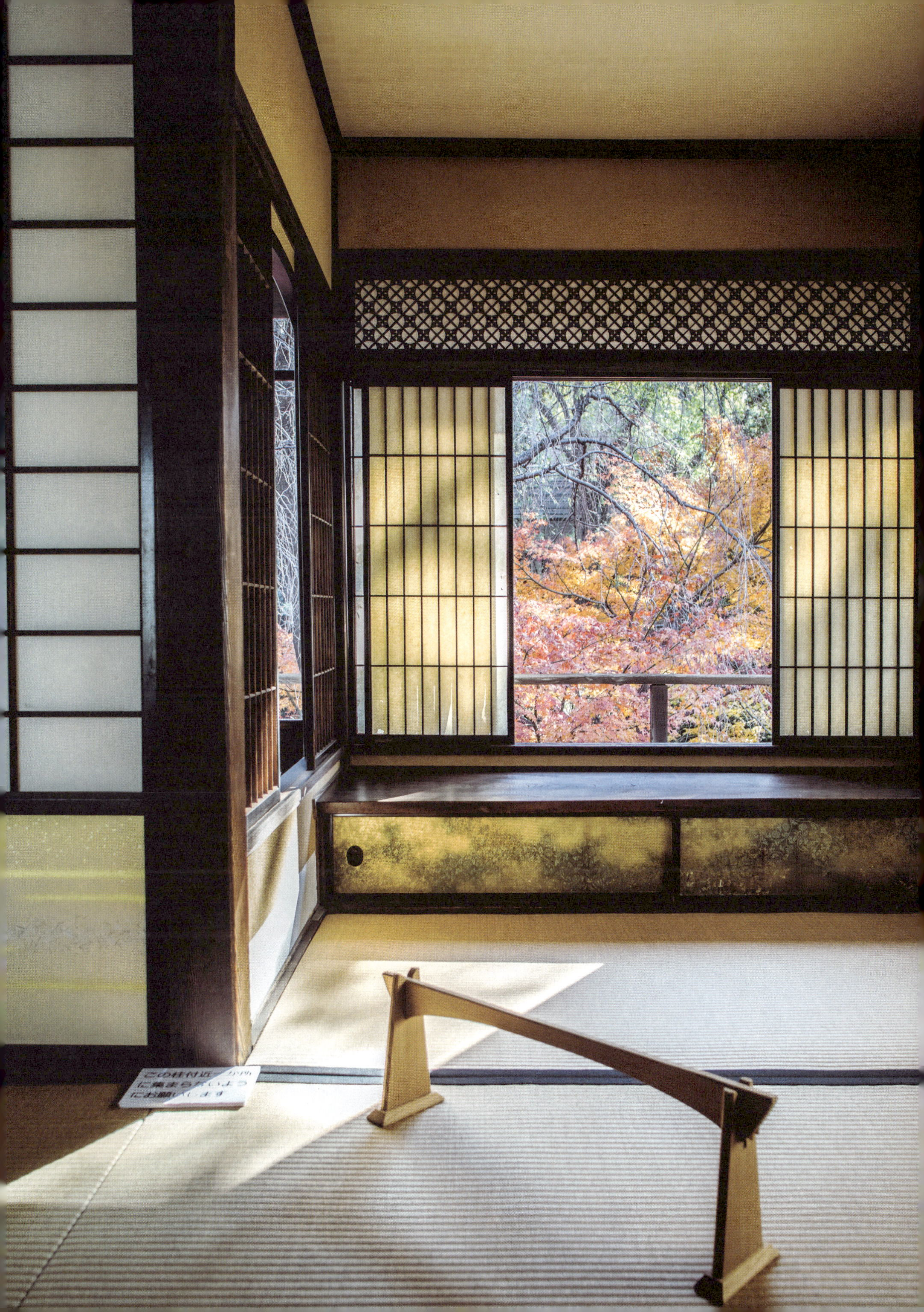
この柱付近
に集まらないよう
にお願いします

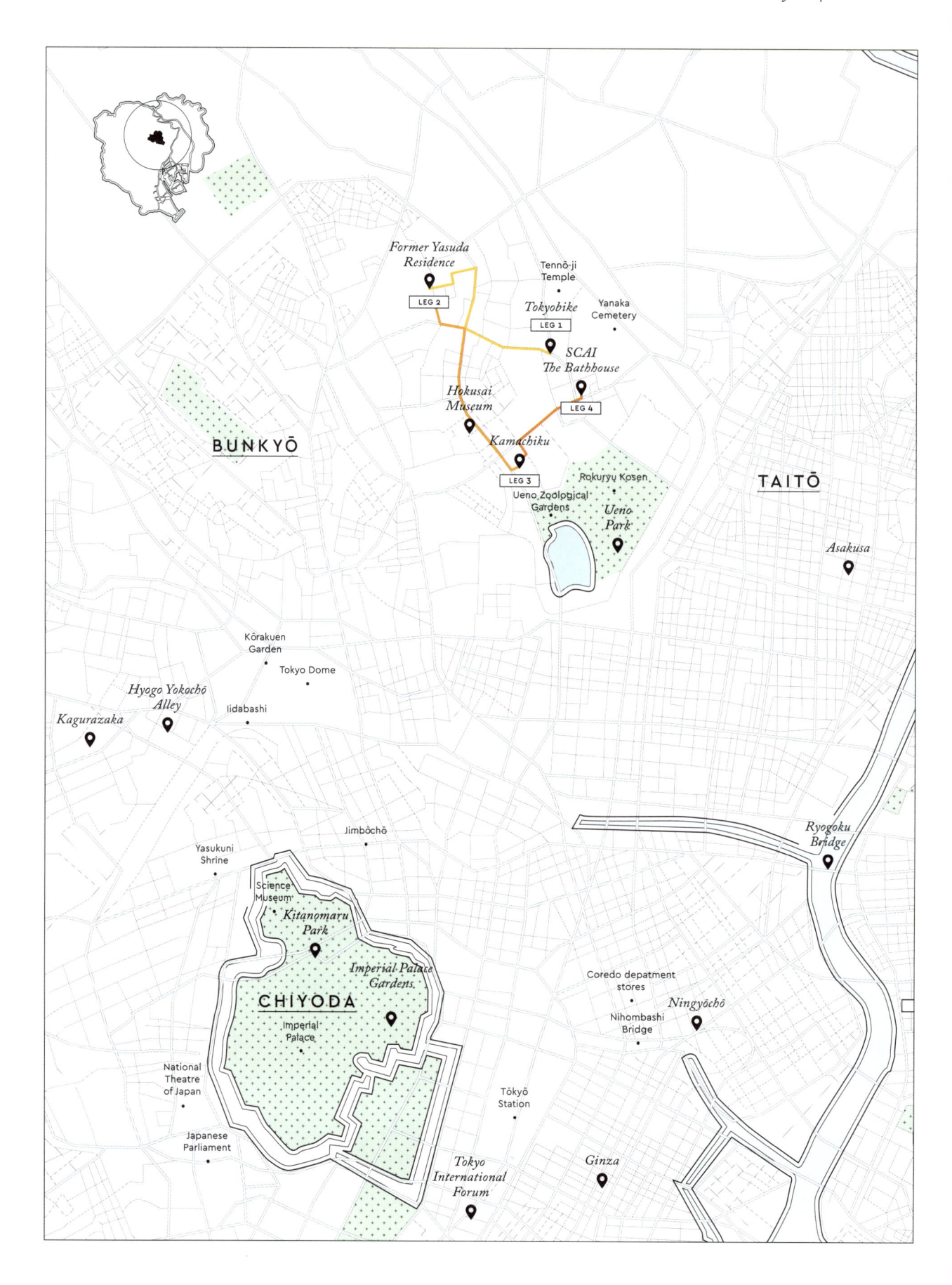

Tōkyō | BUNKYŌ

WALKING TOUR

YANESEN BY BIKE

Yanesen includes the districts of Yanaka, Nezu, and Sendagi and is one of the city's shitamachi or working-class areas. Whether passing through on foot or by bike, every detail is a reminder of its very particular esthetic.

LEG 1: HIRE A BIKE IN YANAKA

Yanesen is served by three train stations: Nippori, Sendagi, and Nezu. It is perfectly possible to explore the area on foot, but making use of the city's rental services and hiring a bike probably has the edge in terms of enjoyment. Tokyobike Rentals in Yanaka district hire out bikes from a shop housed in a 300-year-old sake brewery, where you can enjoy a delicious coffee before hitting the road. Cycling through Yanesen, look out for traces of the old Edo culture that can still be found in the architecture, stores, and cafés. Top tip: Tōkyō Station, the Tokyo Skytree tower, and Ginza district are less than twenty minutes' cycle ride from Yanaka.

LEG 2: VISIT THE FORMER YASUDA RESIDENCE IN SENDAGI

This house was built in 1919 by Yoshisaburo Fujita, who also created the Toshimaen amusement park. The last resident was Kusuo Yasuda, who made it his home until his death in 1995. The Former Yasuda Residence is significant for its architectural style, and it is rare to see such a well-preserved traditional house in Tōkyō. In the purest Japanese tradition, the house has two stories and makes the best use of the length and width of the rooms. It is encircled by a fine example of a dry landscape garden symbolizing the four elements that can be viewed from the solarium and main room. The residence is open to the public on Wednesdays and Saturdays, with volunteers providing commentary in English.

LEG 3: LUNCH AT NEZU KAMACHIKU

Take a lunchbreak at Nezu Kamachiku, an *udon* restaurant that has been serving thick wheat noodles for decades. The building housing the dining room is exceptional in itself, with a red brick roof and a small garden that the restaurant shares with the neighboring retirement home; it was renovated by the celebrated architect Kengo Kuma in 2005. While it is easy to find restaurants serving excellent homemade *soba* (buckwheat noodles) in Tōkyō, it is rare to come across *udon* of this quality. Kamachiku has been awarded a Bib Gourmand by the Michelin guide.

LEG 4: TAKE AN ART BREAK AT SCAI THE BATHHOUSE IN YANAKA

Once a 200-year-old public bath, SCAI The Bathhouse has undergone a particularly successful conversion to become a gallery of contemporary art in the heart of Yanaka district. It was opened in 1993 and has hosted numerous exhibitions, including by Lee Ufan, Toshikatsu Endo, and Mariko Mori, as well as the sculptors Kohei Nawa and Nobuko Tsuchiya. The venue also promotes meetings between avant-garde artists from Japan and further afield. Over time, SCAI The Bathhouse has built up a solid reputation in the art world and has also opened its doors to emerging talents by creating a space for experimentation.

海の家
鳥貴族
TORIKIZOKU
山内農場
5F
焼肉屋さかい
4F
カラオケ歌広場
カラオケ&パーティー館
薬
マツモトキヨシ
Tax Free Shop
HOTEL GRACERY
TOHO CINEMAS
IMAX
ジェミニマン
10.25
美女と野獣のディズニーが贈る、『眠れる森の美女』の新たなる伝説。
Disney
マレフィセント2
10.18 fri.
MARUHAN
2F店舗出入口はビル左側
KABUKI町
GODZILLA ROAD
お好み焼
大阪家
CENTRAL ROAD
新宿で会お
ゴジラロード
747
カラオケランド
Booth
ネットカフェ&カプセル
8F~5F
東京ビル
甘太郎
4F
3F
ACORN

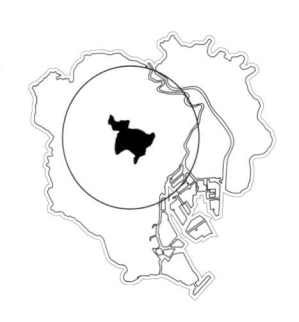

TRAIN - WORK - KARAOKE!

SHINJUKU
新宿区

Truly a city within a city, Shinjuku ward, with its population of more than 340,000, is often best known for its station, the busiest in the world. The district is a Mecca for shopping and entertainment but also shows its more provocative side in the adult-oriented district of Kabukichō.

P. 110

On entering Kabukichō district to the east of Shinjuku, look out for the iconic Toho Cinema and the huge head and formidable claws of the Godzilla statue outside.

OPPOSITE

Tōkyō's most iconic sights, including the Tokyo Skytree, can be seen from the Metropolitan Government Building's observation decks.

To the people of Tōkyō, Shinjuku generally means the area immediately adjacent to its impressive station, which is used by close to three million passengers every day, making it the busiest in the world. The station and its surroundings are like a giant, teeming anthill from which spill an incredible range of services connected with leisure and entertainment—the mind-boggling selection of karaoke bars, restaurants, cafés, and drinking holes is enough to make your head spin. Although Tōkyō has a choice of more than 160,000 places to find a bite to eat, the greatest concentration is to be found in Shinjuku.

While the area west of Shinjuku Station is dominated by offices, government departments, skyscrapers, and the imposing Metropolitan Government Building (the famous Mount Fuji is visible on a clear day from its observation deck), the eastern end is definitely party central. Under the watchful eye of an enormous animated statue of Godzilla, which has loomed large over the Toho cinema since 2015, eastern Kabukichō is the place to go for those in search of adult entertainment, with no shortage of love hotels, host and hostess bars, and other offerings of sexual services. Despite its rather disreputable reputation, there is no real danger here, provided you keep your eyes open and are careful as to which bars you choose to enter— some can charge tens of thousands of yen for one drink. In general, steer clear of bars with touts in the streets.

On the other hand, do take a walk along the lanes and alleys of Golden Gai, in the heart of Kabukichō, which is a magical place, with some 200 snack bars (*sunakku bā*) dating back to the 1960s crammed into a compact space. Some are so tiny they can accommodate no more than ten customers. Snack bars in Japan are unlike other bars—they are first and foremost places to relax, where people go to chat to their neighbors, who are often regulars, or with the barman. This is where a good command of the local language comes in!

Snack bar culture is still alive and kicking in Japan even if it is gradually being neglected by young people, who prefer more modern eateries. In some rural regions, snack bars are the only places for socializing for miles around. Launched during the first Tōkyō Olympic Games in 1964, they are now in decline in the face of the capital's constantly changing entertainment offering and the runaway success of the "karaoke box" in the 1980s. Before the arrival of the latter, a snack bar was in fact the only place where you could sing.

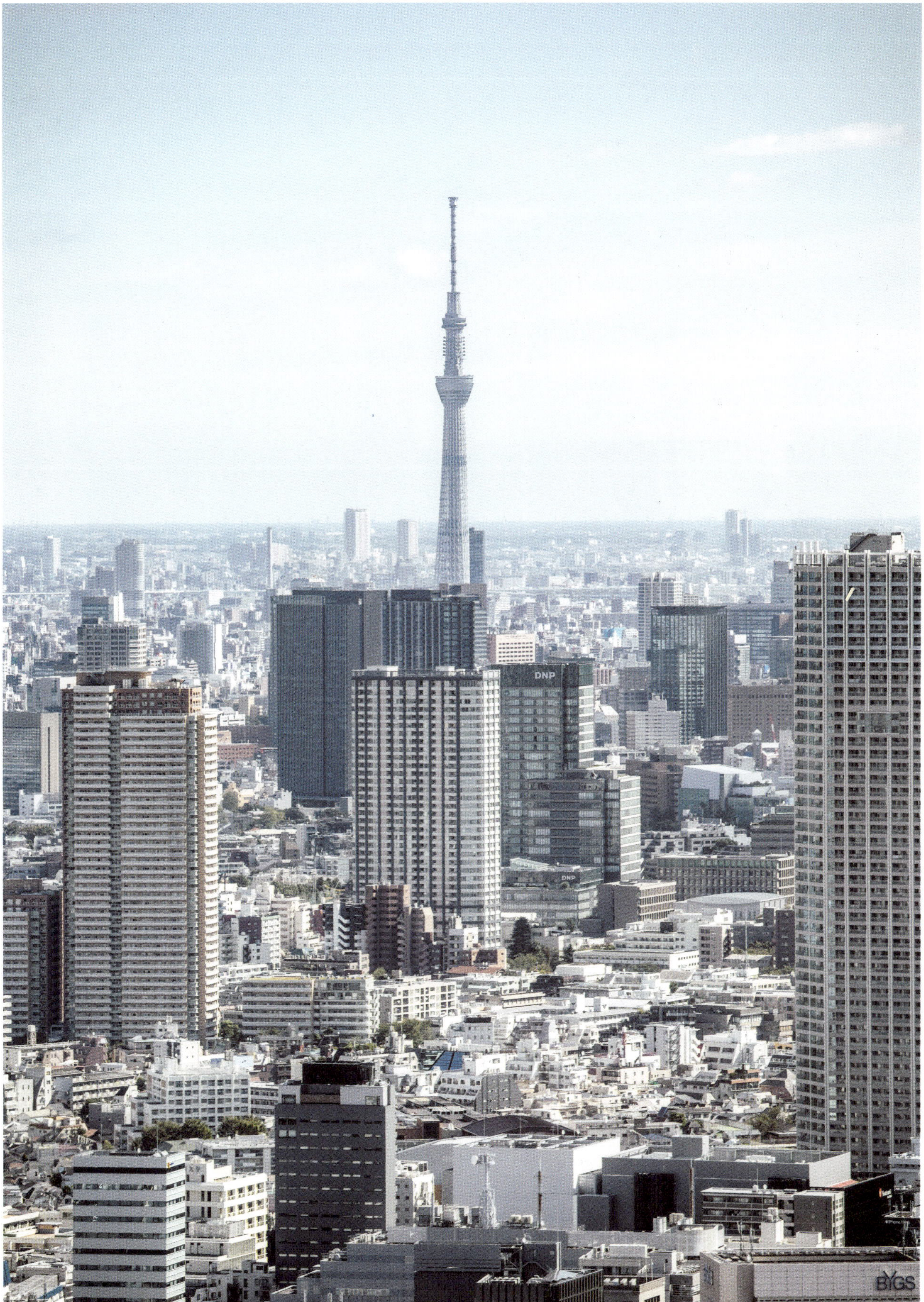
DNP
DNP
BYGS

SHINJUKU

THE ESSENTIALS

OMOIDE-YOKOCHŌ

Take a seat at the counter of one of the eateries selling *yakitori* and beer west of Shinjuku Station.

23

THE VIEW FROM THE METROPOLITAN GOVERNMENT BUILDING

The Metropolitan Government Building has installed a panoramic observation deck on the 44th story of its north tower. Admission is free and the deck is open from 9.30 A.M. to 10.30 P.M. On a clear day, you can see Mount Fuji.

24

KABUKICHŌ

The Japanese think of Kabukichō as the city's red-light district.

25

SHINJUKU-GYOEN

This stately garden is the jewel in Shinjuku's crown. Tokyoites flock here for lunch when the weather is good and the crowds in spring to admire the cherry blossom are particularly dense.

26

IIDABASHI

Iidabashi is a foodie area where French and traditional Japanese restaurants rub shoulders in perfect harmony. This is one of the most pleasant places to take lunch by the water.

27

TAKADANOBABA

Located north of Shinjuku, Takadanobaba is a district where you are likely to come across students, the Tezuka animation studios, and *rāmen* restaurants (such as Tsurugi with its grilled *rāmen*, or Ippudō, which sells the classics).

28

GOLDEN GAI

Golden Gai is a collection of 200 snack bars that have been open since the 1960s. The bars are little more than a counter with room for around a dozen customers and are good places for a chat, but you really do need to learn Japanese!

Kabukichō, with its streets lined with bars and sex shops, has a reputation as the city's red-light district.

驚安の殿堂
ドン.キホーテ
Tax Free Shop 免税店
Don Quijote
新宿
アイドル
ステージ
IDOL STAGE
販売
ブランド
BRAND
時計
WATCH
don.quijote
HOTEL GRACER
TOHO CINEMAS
IMAX
CENTRAL ROAD
ゴジラロード
マレフィセント2
MARUHAN
カラオケ
安全安心ステーション

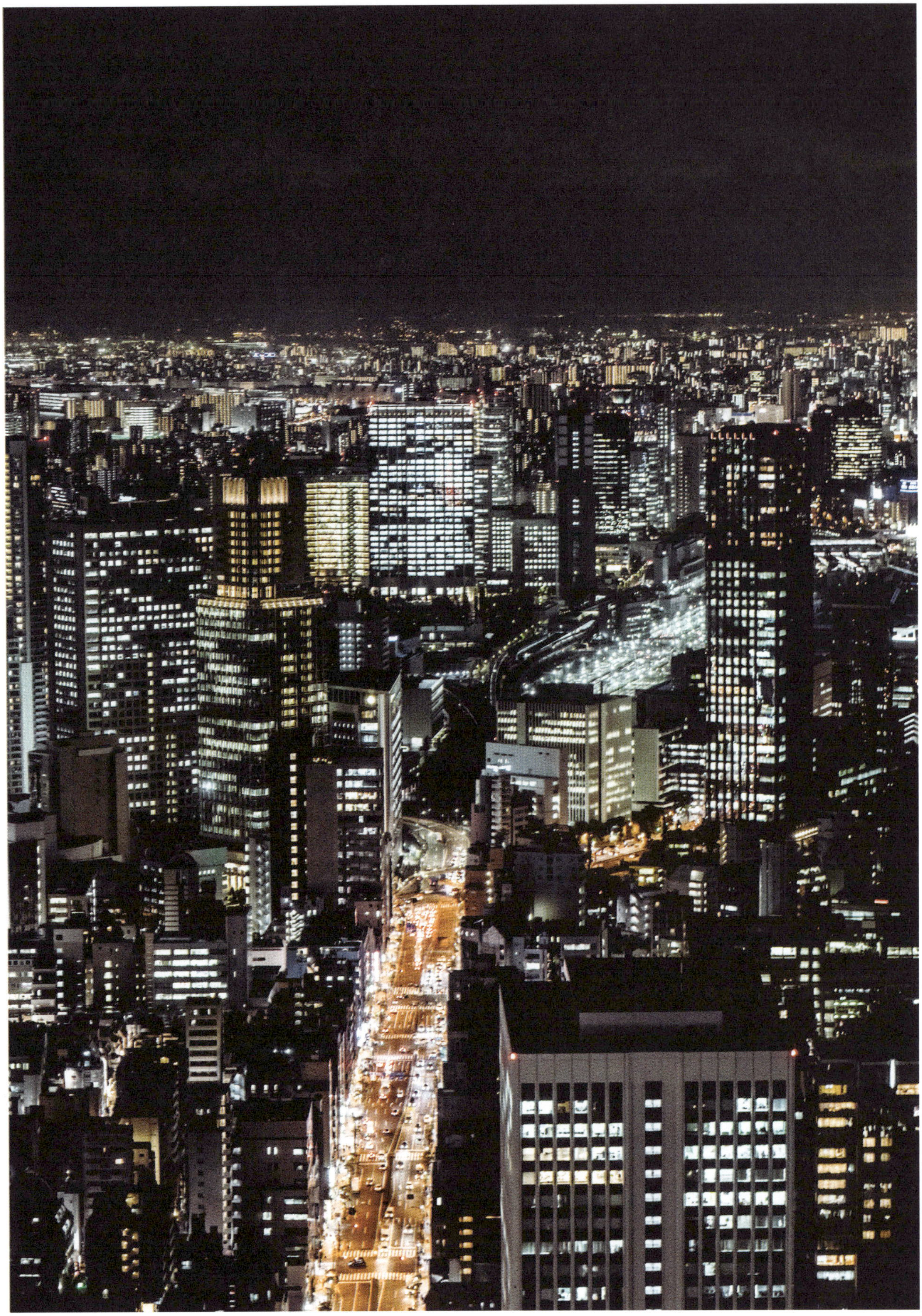

ABOVE

Although console video games are widely played at home, the Japanese also play with fellow gamers in arcades.

OPPOSITE

At night, the city comes alive with a million lights that can be seen from Tōkyō's various observation decks.

UNDERSTANDING
GASTRONOMY
WHAT'S ON THE MENU IN TOKYO?

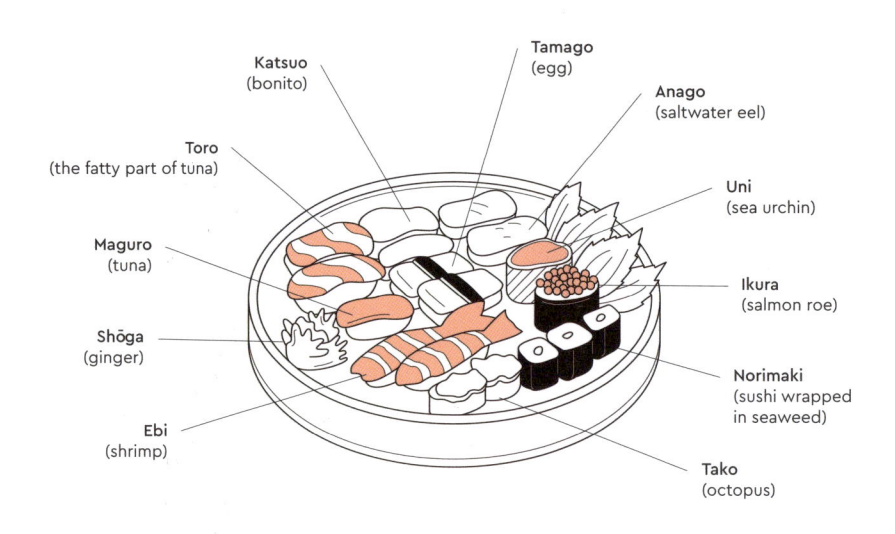

- Katsuo (bonito)
- Tamago (egg)
- Anago (saltwater eel)
- Toro (the fatty part of tuna)
- Uni (sea urchin)
- Maguro (tuna)
- Ikura (salmon roe)
- Shōga (ginger)
- Norimaki (sushi wrapped in seaweed)
- Ebi (shrimp)
- Tako (octopus)

SUSHI

Sushi may have earned international acclaim but it is still an essential part of Japanese cuisine. It is best enjoyed when prepared by an expert, as mastering sushi dishes takes years of experience. In Tōkyō, the ideal place is Tsukiji, with its many *sushi-ya*.

In Japan, restaurants often make one dish their specialty, which also features in the restaurant's name, for example *rāmen*, sushi or *tonkatsu*—a *rāmen-ya* is a *rāmen* restaurant, a *sushi-ya* sells sushi, and so on. In this way, Tokyoites always know what kind of dishes to expect before they have even crossed the threshold; people have no qualms about waiting half an hour or an hour (or indeed, longer) for a chance to sample the best dishes.

Tōkyō has no fewer than 160,000 restaurants that are open around the clock, with something to suit every budget, from gourmet restaurants (the city has more Michelin-starred restaurants than any other in the world, with 226 featuring in the Michelin Guide) to the small food stalls at the stations. Among the various types of restaurants are *izakaya*, very popular Japanese bars where employees like to meet up after work. Dishes are placed in the center of the table for sharing, and people can enjoy the likes of *edamame* (soya beans), *karaage* (battered, fried chicken pieces), *gyoza* (Chinese pork dumplings), *yakitori* (chicken skewers), *cha-han* (fried rice), potato salad, sashimi, and grilled fish (often *aji*, mackerel).

Food is washed down with beer, sake (known as *nihonshu* in Japanese), or cocktails made with *shōchū* (alcohol distilled from rice, buckwheat, or potatoes).

A QUICK TOUR OF SOME ICONIC DISHES

SOBA AND UDON

Soba and *udon* are varieties of noodles, with the former being made with buckwheat flour and the latter from wheat flour (they are a bit like *rāmen*, only thicker in diameter). Both types of noodles are served in a light broth and can be accompany tempura. *Soba* are eaten cold in summer.

SHABU-SHABU AND SUKIYAKI

These vegetable and noodle-based hotpot-style dishes tend to be eaten in winter. *Shabu-shabu* is a broth in which thin strips of meat or fish are briefly plunged before being eaten immediately. *Sukiyaki* has thicker and sweeter sauce and the meat is left to simmer for longer.

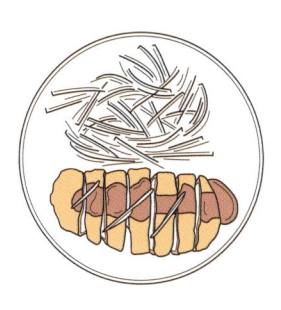

TONKATSU

Tonkatsu refers to a piece of breaded pork served with rice, shredded cabbage, and miso soup. Tonki, near Meguro Station, serves this dish and is a Tōkyō institution; their specialty is *hire-katsu*, a kind of mille-feuille of finely sliced pork.

RĀMEN AND VARIATIONS ON A THEME

A bowl of *rāmen* (wheat noodles) is a typical dish, whose broth (often pork-based) and ingredients (eggs, pork, *menma*, and so on) vary according to the region in which it is being served.

Tōkyō | SHINJUKU

Access to government offices, which are housed in a complex of tower blocks in Tōkyō's downtown area, is a real maze.

The Mode Gakuen Cocoon tower, see here in the distance, is a symbol of the western part of Shinjuku and the tallest tower to be used as an educational facility in the world.

EXCURSION

YAYOI KUSAMA MUSEUM

A HYMN TO CREATIVITY

This museum in Waseda district (Shinjuku ward) dedicated to the famous Japanese visual artist Yayoi Kusama celebrates her extraordinary and very varied work.

The avant-garde artist Yayoi Kusama now has her own museum in the Japanese capital, located in Waseda district in Shinjuku ward. The museum opened its doors in 2017 and is managed by the Yayoi Kusama Foundation to promote and explain the prolific output of this internationally renowned artist.

Operating solely on the basis of temporary exhibitions, with no permanent collection, the museum showcases the artist's major works, from her early years of creative production to the present day. The exhibitions are interspersed with activities and events such as conferences that highlight the artist's multi-disciplinary approach.

Yayoi Kusama was born in Matsumoto in Nagano prefecture in 1929. Experiencing auditory and visual hallucinations from a young age, she first began to represent these in images and perceptions in childhood. Her trademark recurring motif of polka dots first appeared in her work around 1939. From 1948, she studied traditional Japanese painting at a school of art in Kyōto. Admiring the work of the American artist Georgia O'Keefe (1887–1986), she decided to leave for the United States in 1957 and in 1958 settled in New York. Returning to Japan in 1973, she threw herself into writing novels and short story anthologies in parallel with her paintings.

Kusama's work has been exhibited all over the world, from London to New York, in museums, and at biennial and triennial festivals. A museum of her own is a first for her, and the design, dreamt up by the artist herself, offers a unique insight into the thinking of a contemporary artist who has had a profound impact on the world of art.

The museum is located at 107 Bentencho Shinjuku-ku, 162-0851 Tōkyō. Tickets must be booked in advance via the museum website (https://yayoikusamamuseum.jp/). No tickets are sold on site. Visits are limited to ninety minutes in a time slot selected when making the booking.

1 / DIVERSITY

This museum showcases the diversity of the media used by the artist in her creative process.

2 / NARCISSUS GARDEN, 1966/2020

This installation was created in 1966, with various versions exhibited at venues such as Australia's Queensland Art Gallery, the Whitney Biennal in New York, and the Paris International Contemporary Art Fair. It was presented in Tōkyō in 2020 as part of a temporary exhibition.

3 / POLKA DOTS EVERYWHERE

Kusama's trademark polka dots are already in evidence at the museum entrance.

4 / STARRY PUMPKIN, 2015

This giant pumpkin was installed as part of a temporary exhibition and is the ultimate achievement of Kusama's artistic approach. Simultaneously monolithic and yet delicate, the sculpture scintillates with the light from the thousands of tiles that cover its surface.

5 / ARCHITECTURE

This ultra-modern museum building designed by the Japanese architect Kume Sekkei allows visitors to explore the works of Yayoi Kusama over five floors.

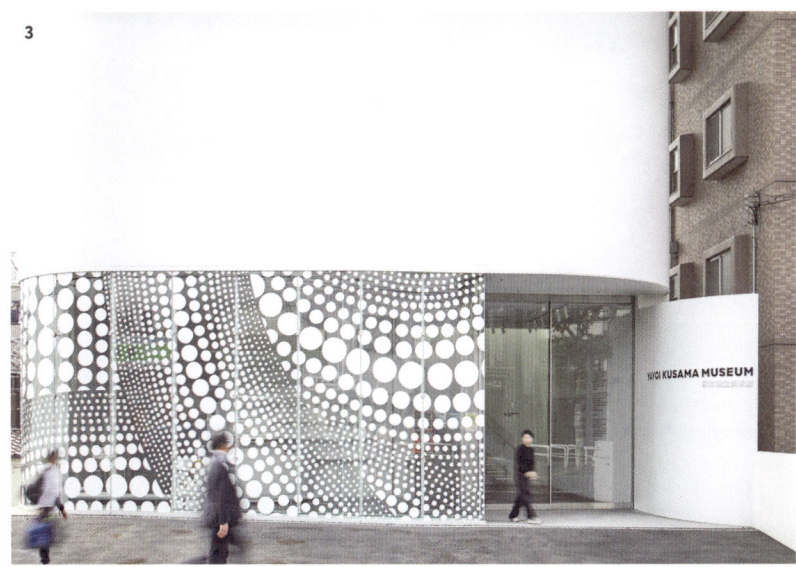

Designed by architect Kenzo Tange, the Shinjuku Park Tower (on the left) has an unusual roof and is the second highest tower in Shinjuku district.

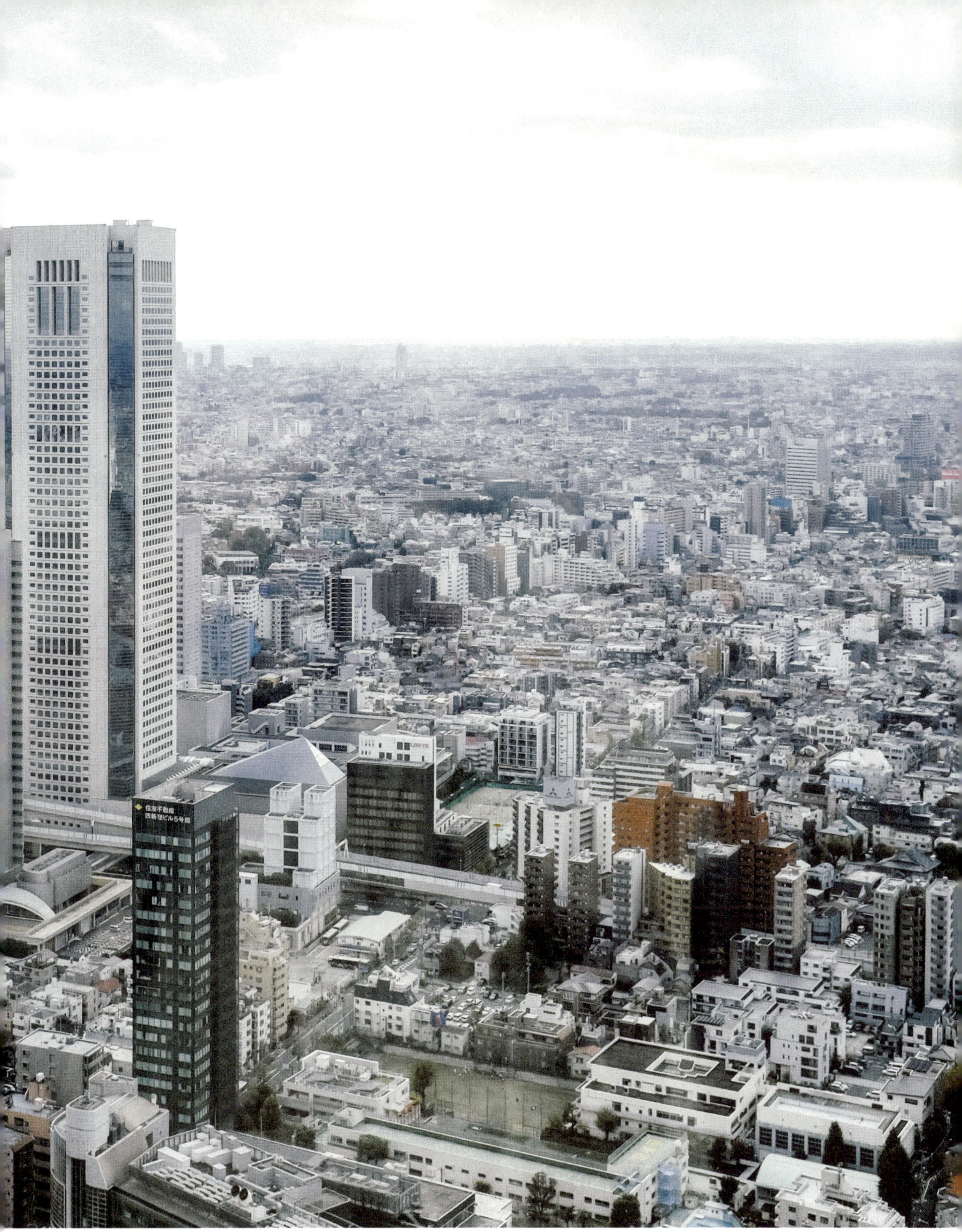
住友不動産
西新宿ビル5号館

*Shinjuku-sanchōme is the most commercial area in the district
and is also home to many restaurants.*

*Visit one of several breweries to try the finest vintage sake (*nihonshu *in Japanese; sake means alcohol in general), which is stored in barrels known as* komodaru *or* sakadaru.

Tōkyō | SHINJUKU

LIFESTYLE

GOING OUT IN SHINJUKU

ATMOSPHERE

The alleyways of Omoide Yokochō on the western side of the station are a popular destination for people looking for a warm and friendly place to eat.

TABLE FOR ONE

Solo dining in a restaurant is known as *ohitori-sama* ("just for one") in Japan and is a very common practice in Tōkyō.

SAMURAI

Kabukichō is home to a small samurai museum, so there is plenty of related merchandise in the stores.

CHEERS!

Beer remains the preferred alcoholic drink of Tokyoites.

TAIYAKI

Taiyaki are fish-shaped pastries stuffed with red bean paste or yams.

KARAOKE

A favorite pastime for young Japanese, and very common in Shinjuku!

DRINKING AND SINGING

Some karaoke bars have set menus with bottomless alcoholic drinks.

COUNTER

Some places have only a single counter, making chatting to your neighbors easy.

CONVERSATION

Kabukichō also has a few bars with hosts and hostesses who are paid to chat with customers.

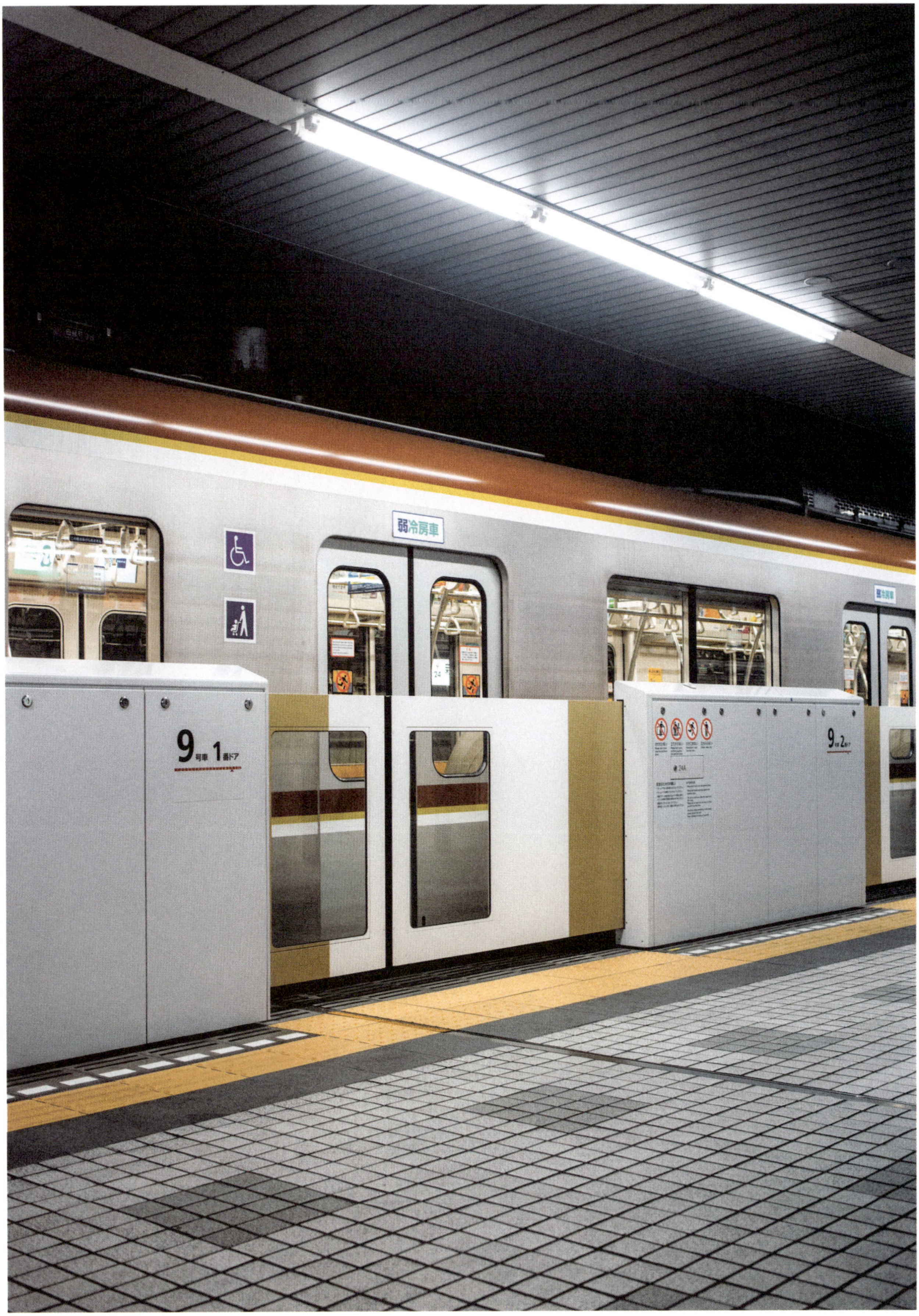
弱冷房車
9号車 1番ドア

ABOVE

Shinjuku Station is the busiest in the world, with almost 3.6 million passengers passing through every day.

OPPOSITE

The most difficult part of negotiating your way around the station is not getting lost in the immense labyrinth of its exits (200) and platforms (10).

PORTRAIT

THE LITTLE HOUSE OWNED BY
KOHEI FUKAZAWA

The house owned by Kohei Fukuzawa's grandmother was built in the heart of Akasaka-Mitsuke. Kohei Fukuzawa, a Tōkyō history enthusiast, is preserving his grandmother's house, built in 1948, as a precious reminder of life in the past.

Kohei Fukazawa's small house is quite unlike any other. A little out of the way in the charming Akasaka-Mitsuke district, this tiny and fragile structure is tucked in between soaring tower blocks, restaurants, bars, and hip stores, seemingly resistant to the ravages of time and the urbanization that saw this district develop so rapidly during the economic bubble of the 1980s. "It was built in 1948," he explains. "My grandmother lived here and my mother grew up here. I also spent several years here; it has immense sentimental value."

No longer the family home, it has been transformed into a café, exhibition space, and charming B&B, and Kohei Fukazawa edits guides to Tōkyō, focusing on both the history and the topography of the city. He dislikes the way that Tōkyō changes so much and demonstrates such little interest "in preserving the evidence of the past, preferring to make way for new things. Real estate prices exploded during the economic bubble and everything was built very quickly. There are no more public baths in the area around Akasaka-Mitsuke Station, for example, and everything has been demolished to make way for offices and entertainment venues."

Dubbed the *Tokyo Little House* as an homage to the book by Virginia Lee Burton, the house owned by his grandmother Tsuma was built just after the bombing during the Second World War in a district that at the time was no more than a bombsite. Within the living area upstairs is a bookable guest space, and it is here that Kohei Fukazawa has preserved the old-fashioned charm of yesteryear, with such features as a *washitsu* (Japanese sitting room with a *tatami* floor). The kitchen appliances have the kind of trailing electrical leads that are no longer manufactured and his grandmother's sewing machine has been left near the window. "Like many women of the time, she had a habit of using the walls as a notepad when she was on the phone, so don't be surprised to see addresses and numbers scribbled on the wall," he smiles. The double-glazed windows are the only concession to modernity.

His wife Kimiko has taken care of the design and decoration without disturbing the house's timeless charm. This is a rare opportunity to see such an architectural document of times gone by in Tōkyō.

FAMILY HERITAGE

The Fukazawas have meticulously preserved this unique house in memory of Kohei's grandmother and as a document of the past it represents.

TRADITIONAL ARCHITECTURE

The house consists of a living area and a café on the ground floor that is also used as an exhibition space. Visitors can stay in the bedroom upstairs.

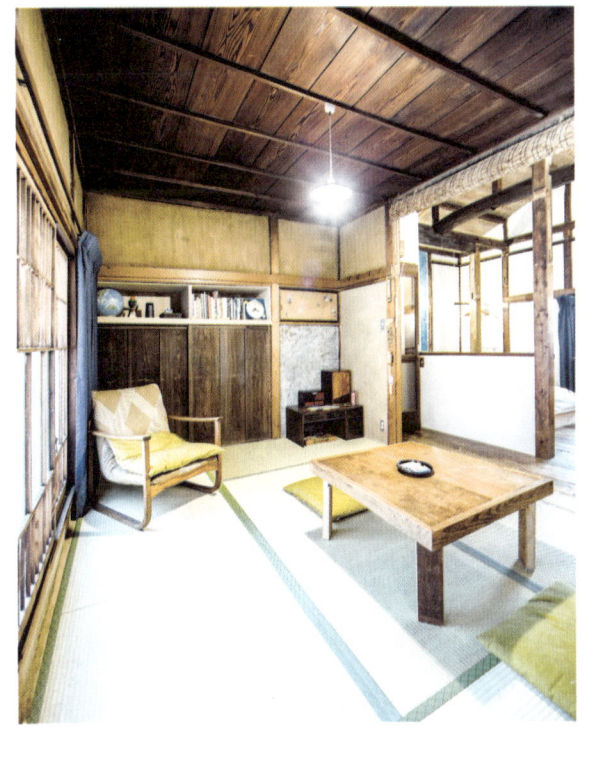

Shinjuku-Gyoen was landscaped in 1906 but was not opened to the public until after the Second World War. It is considered one of the most beautiful gardens in the city.

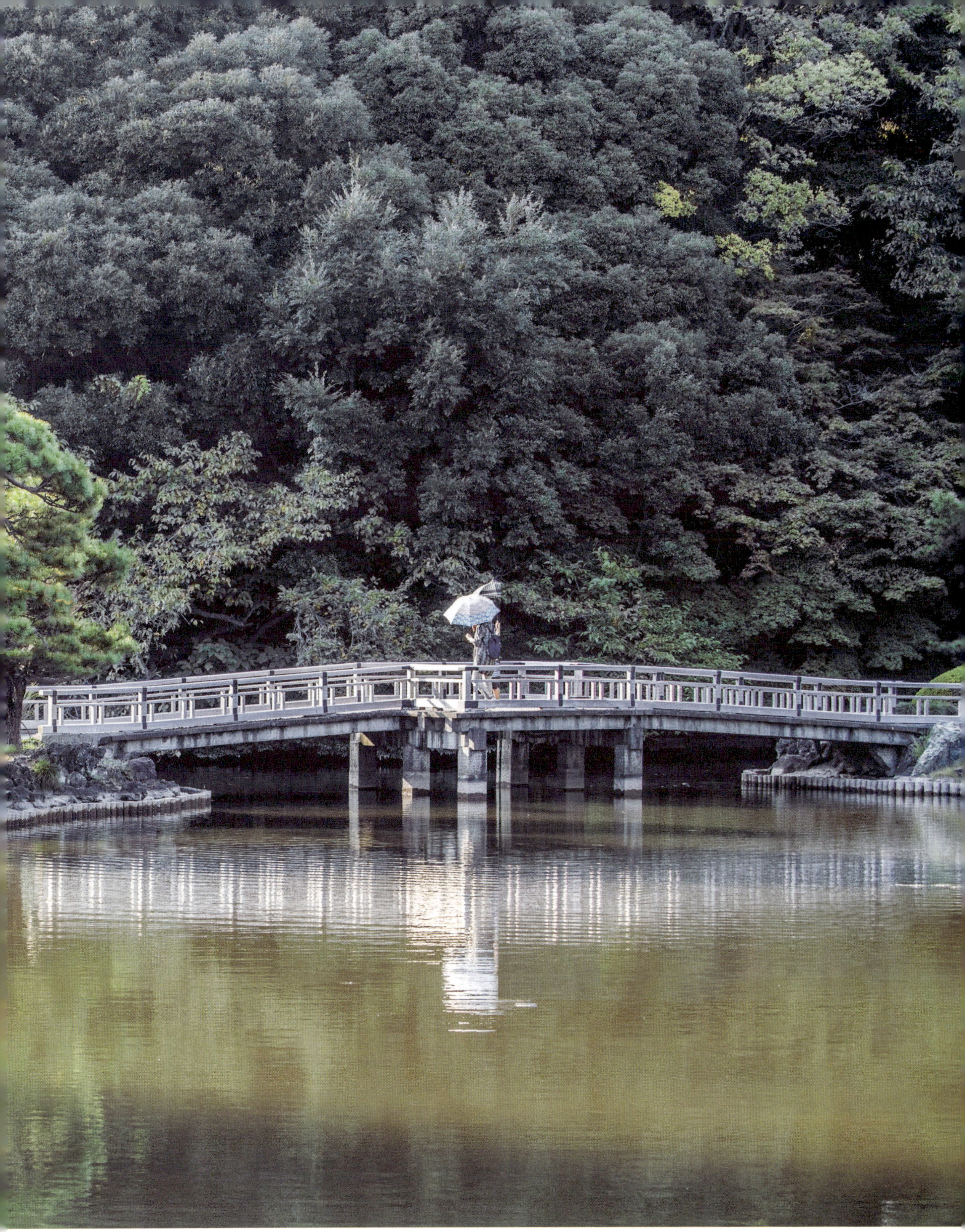

ABOVE

*In Japan, cranes symbolize longevity and good luck.
They often appear as a motif on kimonos and in art in general.*

OPPOSITE

*The Shinjuku-Gyoen Garden was built on the estate of a lord;
designated an "imperial garden," it was closed to the public.*

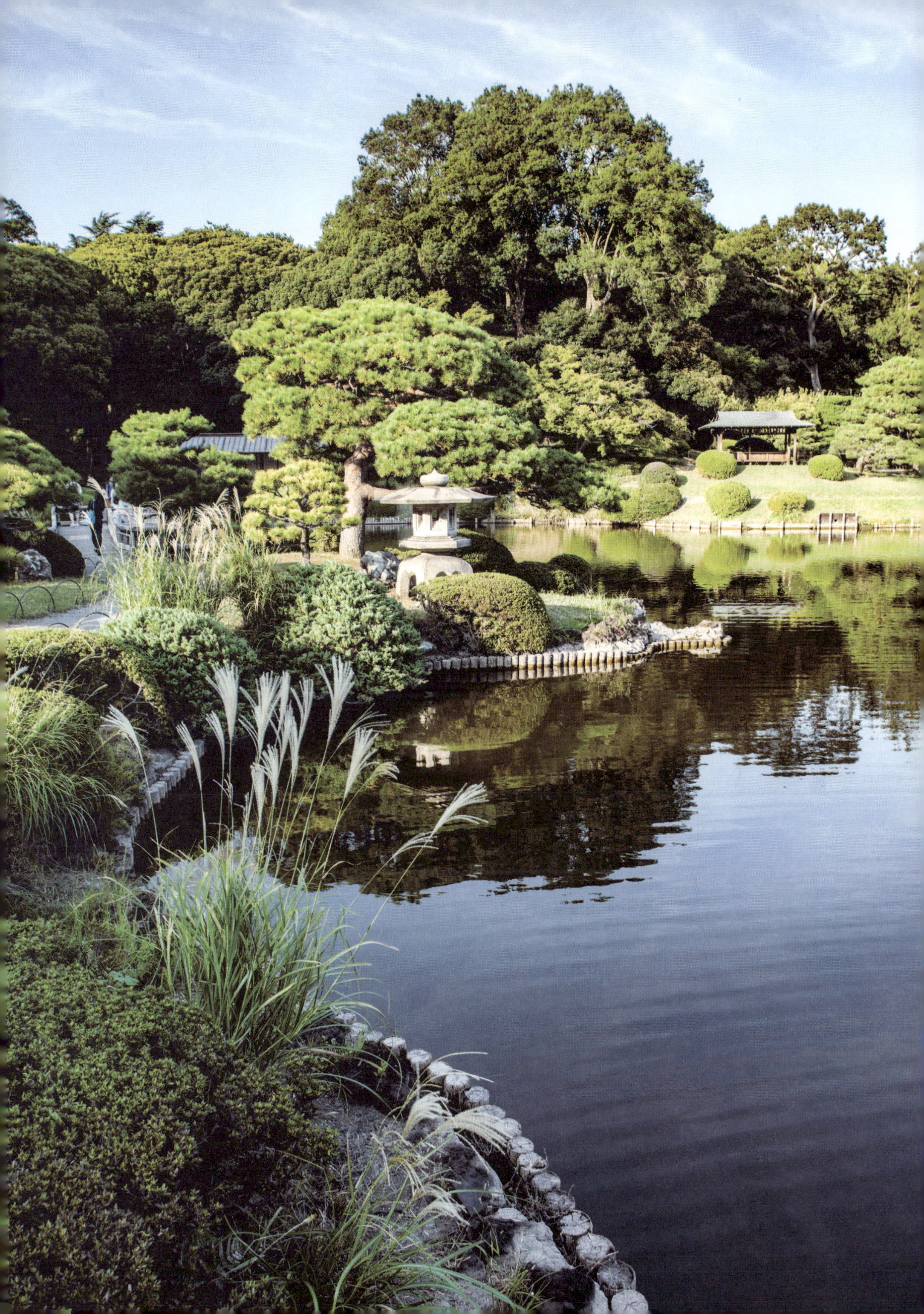

Tōkyō | SHINJUKU

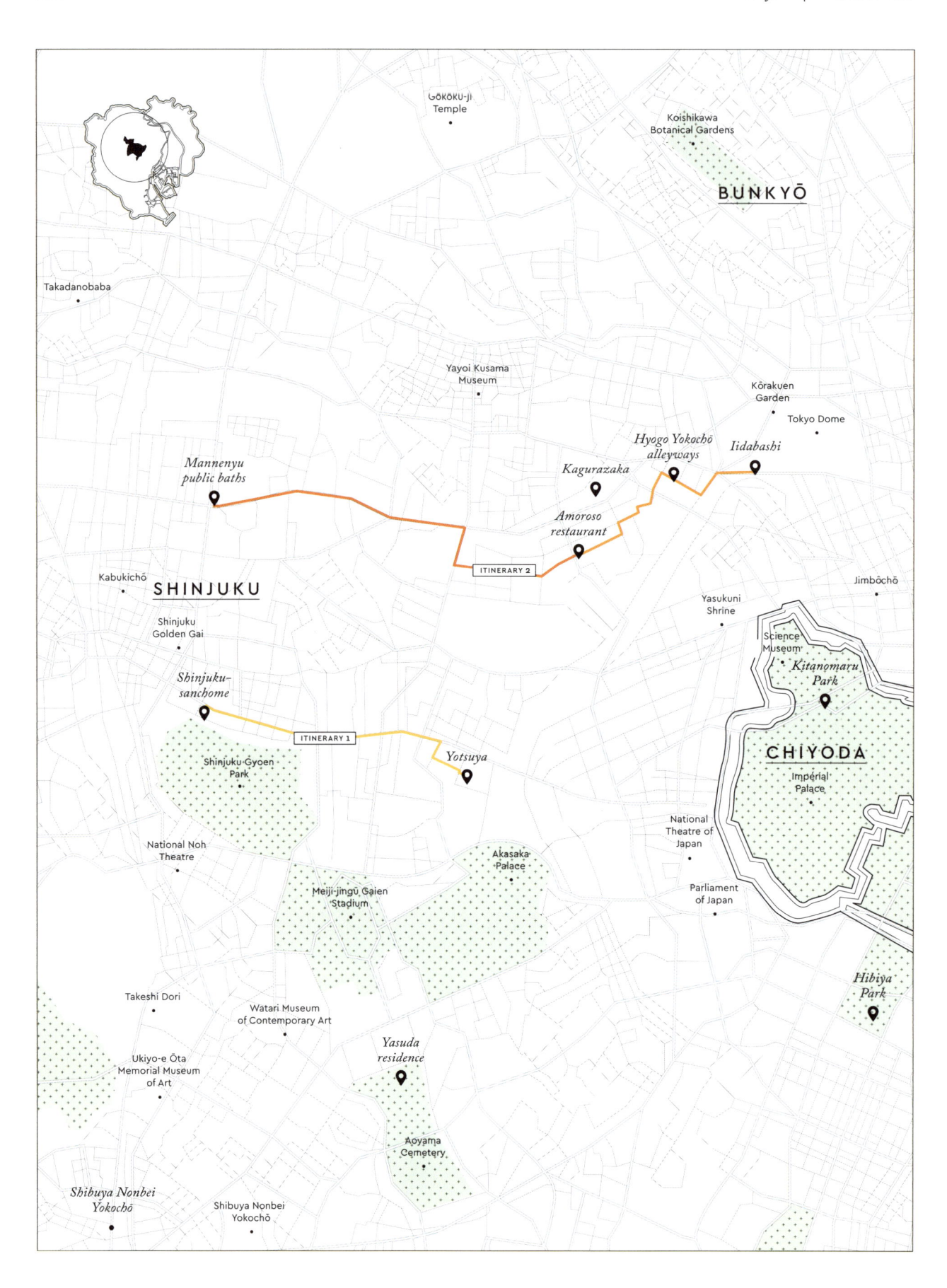

WALKING TOUR

A STROLL THROUGH KAGURAZAKA AND ARAKICHŌ

With all its glitz and glamor, Shinjuku is home to some interesting sub-districts that have developed rich and colorful cultures in the area's nooks and crannies. The alleyways of Kagurazaka (once the home of geishas) and the minibars of Arakichō are perfect examples.

ITINERARY 1: SHINJUKU, YOTSUYA AND ARAKICHŌ

Shinjuku has grown so much since the 1980s that it has to some extent replaced the district of Ginza in terms of the latest trends and consumer activity. It is now an entertainment area with excellent shopping (cheaper than the stores in Ginza), especially in the areas to the south and east of the station, and the same goes for Shinjuku-sanchōme. You will also be spoiled for choice for inexpensive lunch options. Once you have finished shopping and souvenir hunting, relax over a nice dinner in Yotsuya district, to the east of Shinjuku-gyoen, where you will find a host of unpretentious and friendly restaurants in which to round off a busy day. There are also several surprises lurking in the small streets of Arakichō in the heart of Yotsuya, as immortalized in Nicolas Bouvier's *Japanese Chronicles*, including its four hundred quirky bars and restaurants (such as the Vowz Bar, which is run by Buddhist monks), although a visit is recommended only if you have a good command of Japanese (or at least a friend who speaks the language).

ITINERARY 2: KAGURAZAKA AND SHIN-ŌKUBO

The best way to explore Kagurazaka district is to get off the train at Iidabashi Station and stroll up the street from the bridge, which is pedestrianized at weekends and on public holidays. The French embassy and the Franco-Japanese school were once located round here and there are many cafés, restaurants, and bookstores with French associations, even down to the gentle accordion music that wafts from the speakers on a Sunday. The Franco-Japanese Institute is still here and regularly puts on cultural events. Before its links with the red, white, and blue of France, Kagurazaka was historically a district for geishas. Take a right off the main drag into the alleyways of Michikusa-yokochō, for example, for a real sense of the Edo-era atmosphere that still prevails in Kagurazaka, and enjoy a delicious Japanese lunch to boot. If you decide to visit in the evening, you can expect a rather different atmosphere, with a definite whiff of nostalgia. Amoroso, a tiny restaurant near Ushigome-Kagurazaka Station, is one option for dinner. Maeda-san, the Amoroso chef, produces an exceptional range of gourmet food featuring regional Japanese products with an Italian or French twist. There's no chance of getting any of the ten or so seats at its small counter unless you book a good month in advance. Are you tempted to try some typical Korean food instead? Shin-Ōkubo district is easily accessible in about ten minutes by metro from Kagurazaka, and here you can enjoy a typical meal in one of the many restaurants in the capital's bustling "Korean Town." Or maybe you need to take it easy after a hearty dinner? Mannenyu public baths are also in Shin-Ōkubo, just a couple of minutes' walk from the station, and will guarantee you a wonderfully relaxing time.

御祈祷お札お守福銭塔婆招福猫児は總受付迄

BESIDE THE TAMA RIVER

SETAGAYA
世田谷区

Lying west of Shibuya and Shinjuku, Setagaya seems a little more discreet and secluded than its famous neighbors, but it is just as interesting. More Bohemian, closer to nature, where life flows along in rhythm with the Tama River, it attracts ever greater numbers of Tokyoites as potential residents.

P.142

Gotoku-ji Temple is renowned for its hundred or so maneki-neko, *a national good luck charm; visitors regularly bring more.*

OPPOSITE

Futako Tamagawa is known for its modern architecture but it also has plenty of streets with more conventional buildings.

Setagaya adjoins the lively districts of Shinjuku and Shibuya but has far less of their hustle and bustle. Located around the banks of the Tama River, a little farther to the west, it is a residential area of 22 square miles (58 km²) made up of a number of charming small sub-districts with distinct identities thanks to their many boutique stores, cafés, and local restaurants that few tourists would think of visiting. Setagaya is a little off the beaten track but has plenty of great surprises in store for those who take the time to investigate. The feeling that you are visiting a cute little village, less than ten minutes' train ride from Shinjuku and Shibuya, is so strong that you could easily forget that you are still in the middle of Tōkyō.

Set in the heart of Setagaya, Shimokitazawa is the star of the show; this bohemian district has a rich history but has been in the process of redefining itself over the last decade or so, and its new, ultra-modern station has indeed slightly disrupted the topography of the area, resulting in the closure of many *jazz kissaten* (traditional cafés specializing in jazz). It is still an attractive proposition, however, and the ideal place to enjoy a moment of authentic local life among its vintage thrift stores, bustling cafés, gadget stores, and concerts.

Futako Tamagawa is another area of Setagaya that is particularly popular with Tokyoites. Modern and revitalized, it boasts a wide choice of leisure activities, including parks, cinemas, shopping malls, and sports complexes. Plenty of Tokyoites would like to live here and enjoy the tranquility of life on the Tama River, and thousands come to relax on its banks, which are ideal spots to enjoy a pleasant family picnic or (in August) one of the capital's largest fireworks displays. The quiet little district of Sangenjaya, about a quarter-hour train ride from Futako Tamagawa, also has much to recommend it, with its jumble of teahouses and picturesque stores and non-conformist spirit.

Setagaya's many green spaces make it a joy to live in. These include the natural Todoroki valley, which extends for more than half a mile (1 km). The Boro-ichi flea market held in mid-December is a large and very popular event, with some 800 stands overflowing with potential finds, including crockery, secondhand kimonos, and antiques. There has been a market here for more than four centuries.

Setagaya is politically engaged and metropolitan, and in 2015 joined Shibuya as the first Japanese municipalities to vote for the introduction of a certificate officially recognizing same-sex couples that has since been adopted by twenty-five cities in the country.

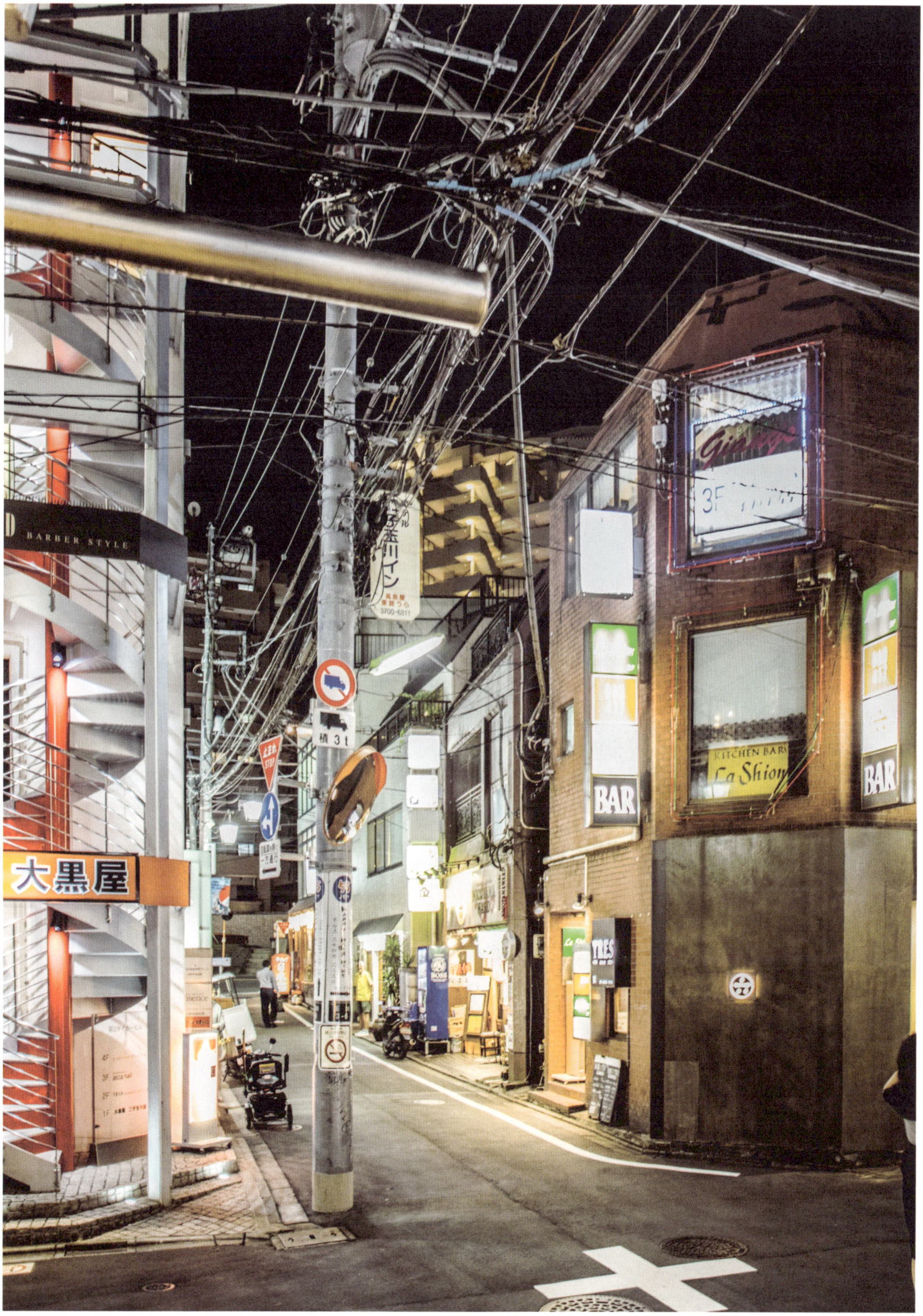
BARBER STYLE
大黒屋
積 3 t
3700-6811
BAR
KITCHEN BAR
La Shion
BAR

SETAGAYA
THE ESSENTIALS

KOMAZAWA OLYMPIC PARK

The park was built for the 1964 summer Olympics and offers a wide range of sporting activities, including swimming, soccer, running, cycling, and tennis.

30

GOTOKU-JI

This temple has found fame for its enormous collection of *maneki-neko* ("beckoning cat") statuettes that are also a good luck charm.

31

THE PLUM TREES OF HANEGI PARK IN UMEGAOKA

Hanegi Park is an ideal place for a refreshing break, and you can enjoy the sight of more than 650 plum trees in blossom here between January and March.

32

KYŌDŌ DISTRICT

A stroll round Kyōdō is worthwhile for travelers who have already tasted a little of local Tōkyō life; try some Edo-style sushi at Michelin-starred Kiraku.

33

SUSHI NO MIDORI

There is delicious sushi at unbeatable prices at Sushi no Midori in Umegaoka; the only downside is the wait, whether you have booked or not!

34

SANGENJAYA

Sangenjaya means "three teahouses" in Japanese. The district is slightly off the beaten track but has plenty of places in which to grab a drink.

35

SEIKADŌ BUNKO ART MUSEUM

This museum focuses on calligraphy and Old Japanese texts (6,500 exhibits).

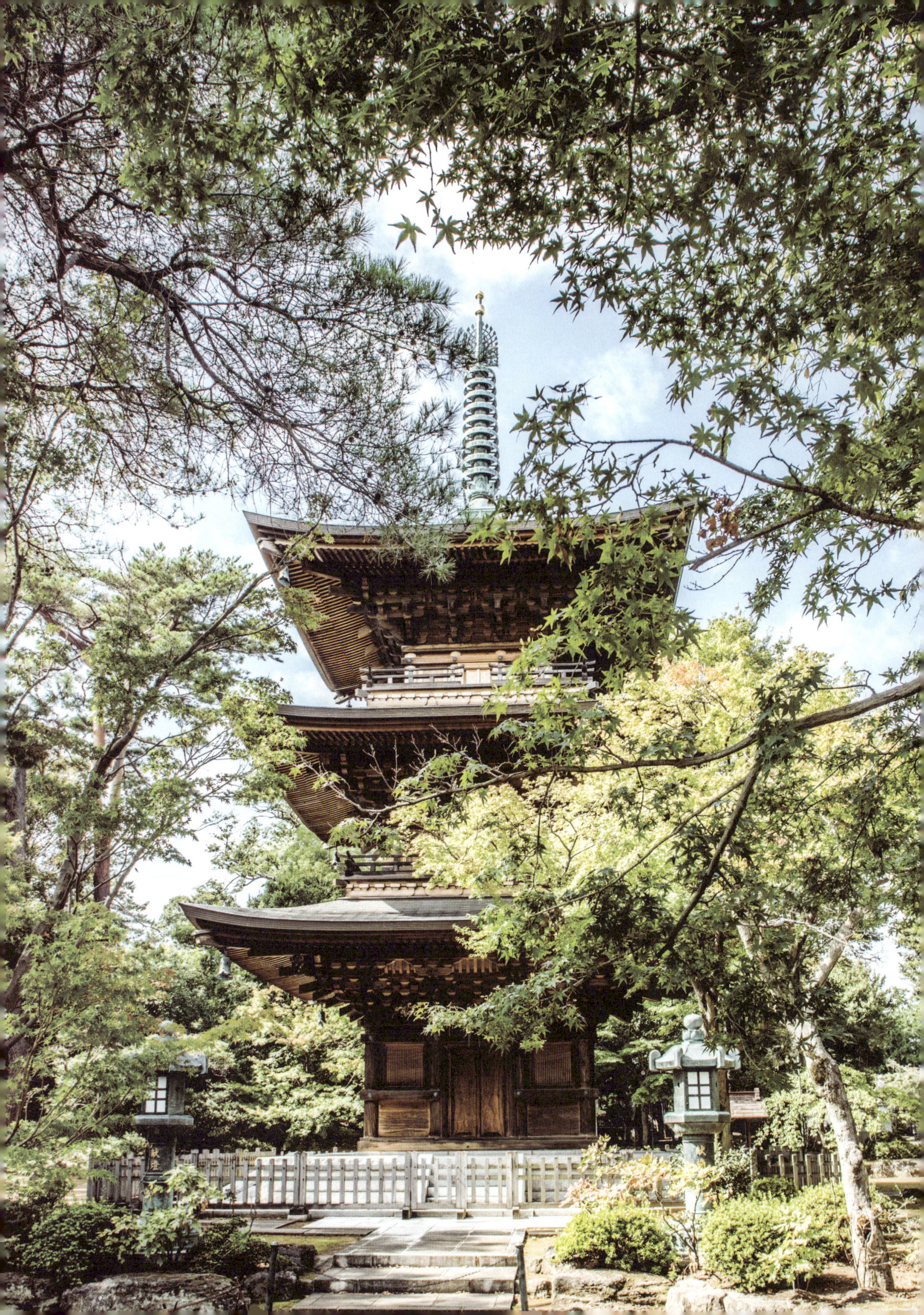

ABOVE

Tōkyō sidewalks are used by pedestrians (keep right) and cyclists (keep left). Pedestrians always obey the lights at crosswalks.

OPPOSITE

Gotoku-ji was founded as a Buddhist temple in 1480, with a main building, a Butsuden hall, and a three-story pagoda.

DEEP DIVE

SUMO

A PRAYER TO THE GODS

Sumo wrestling is much more than a sports discipline in Japan; it is intrinsically linked with the sacred and with religion. Historically, it was an offering made to the gods.

Sumo is a style of wrestling practiced in Japan for more than 1,300 years. The aim is to manhandle your adversary out of the *dohyo* (circle) or to get him to touch the ground with any part of his body, including his topknot. There are about fifty different holds. In Tōkyō, you can go to the championships held twice a year (in January and September) at the national stadium in Ryōgoku or attend an event organized in places of worship such as the shrines at Yasukuni or Meiji Jingū.

Sumo wrestling is welcomed in such places as it is considered an offering to (Shinto) gods known as *kami*, and *yokozuna* (the ultimate distinction that can be achieved by a wrestler) is equivalent to demi-god status. Because of its sacred nature, the ceremony that precedes the bout is accorded great importance, and purifying salt is scatted on the *dohyo* before every fight. When sumos vigorously strike the ground with the soles of their feet before the beginning of a bout, they do so to chase away evil spirits.

The origins of Sumo lie in Shimane prefecture, the cradle of ancient Japan, to the south of Honshū. The first fight is mentioned in the *Chronicles of Japan* (*Nihon Shoki*) and is thought to have taken place on Inasa beach by the city of Izumo more than 1,300 years ago. The term originally used was not *sumo* ("striking one another") but *tekoi*, which refers to fighting barehanded.

A wrestler is known in Japanese as a *rikishi*, *sumotori*, or *o-sumō-san*. Becoming a *sumotori* is to enter a priesthood; you join the community (*heya*) as a teenager for a lifetime of training, chores, and sacrifice in the hope of becoming a champion. A specific diet is also essential to achieve the imposing build required, in particular *chanko-nabe*, a stew made up of large quantities of vegetables, tofu, eggs, and meat. The size and weight of a *sumotori* will determine the class in which he competes.

The wrestler's outfit, which is made up of the *mawashi*, a thick, twisted loincloth, is a direct reference to the rope found at the entrance to the Izumo Oyashiro shrine (better known under the name of Izumo Taisha), one of the oldest temples in the country.

There is much debate in Sumo circles these days as ever more wrestlers (and champions) are of non-Japanese origin, and some people find it difficult to accept that they can excel in a traditional Japanese sport that is also so intrinsically linked to religious ritual. The ban on women, who have been barred from the *dohyo* for centuries as they are considered impure, is another hot-button topic; although they are allowed to train, they are denied professional status.

SOME SUMO HOLDS

YORIKIRI
(lifting out)

OSHIDASHI
(pushing out)

HATAKIKOMI
(slamming down)

SOTOGAKE
(grabbing with the leg wrapped around)

UWATENAGE
(gripping and pushing with the hand wrapped around)

TOTTARI
(twisting an arm)

The man with the black belt is the winner in the examples above.

After a walk of about thirty minutes, you will reach Todoroki Fudō temple right at the end of the ravine.

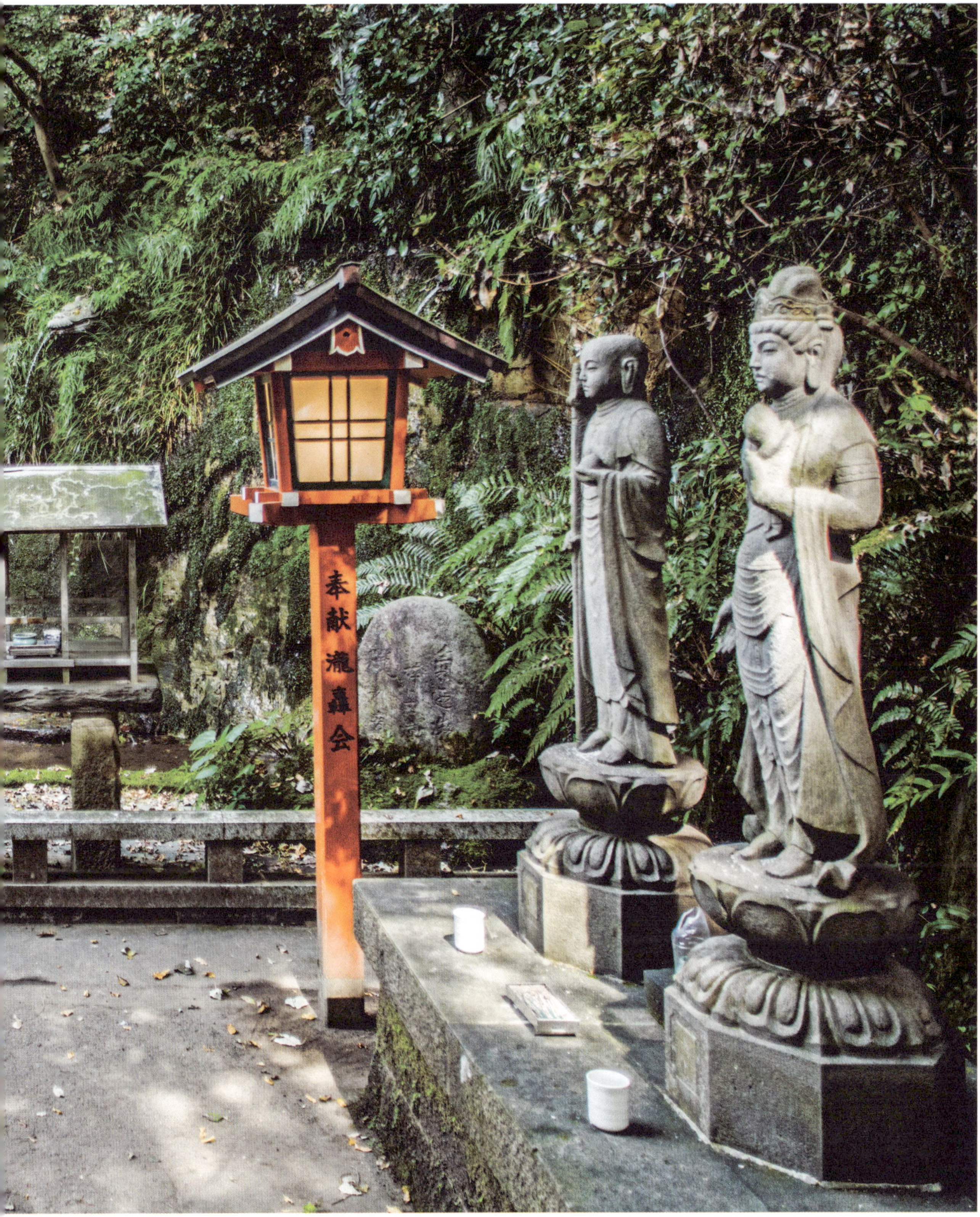
奉献滝轟会

ABOVE

There is lush vegetation in Todoroki valley even though you are still in the heart of the capital.

OPPOSITE

Enjoy a mini hiking trail of about half a mile (1 km) in the ravine.

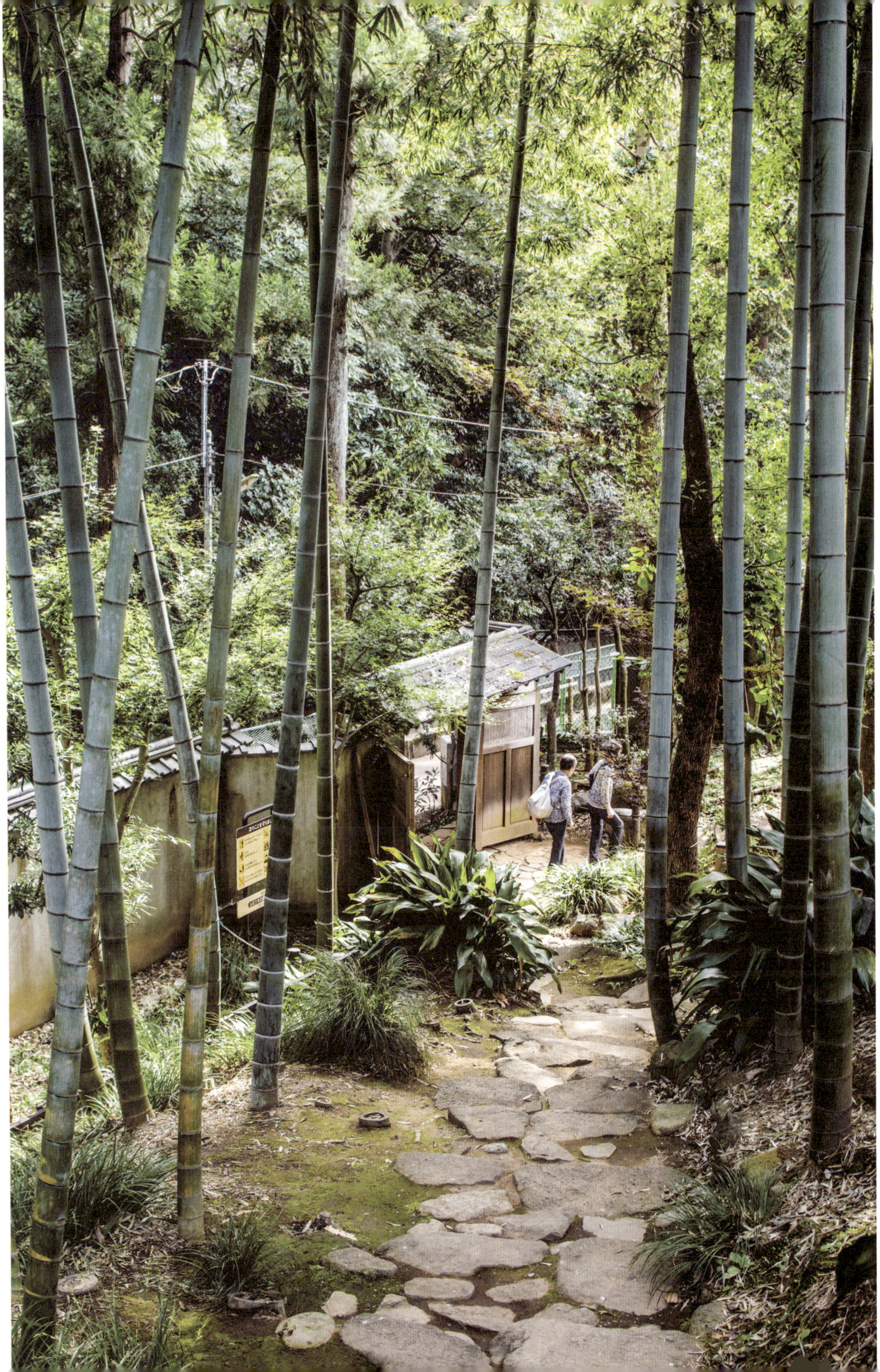

LIFESTYLE

SHIMOKITAZAWA

THE BOHEMIAN QUARTER

Shimokitazawa is home to artists, cafés, and bars at every turn.
People used to come here for its *jazz kissaten* and relaxed ambience.

Shimokitazawa was long described as bohemian, artistic, and independent, but today it is more of a residential area with a relaxed reputation that has lost a little of its soul through excess modernization. It would be a shame, however, not to acknowledge the charms of "Shimokita" (as it is known to its friends). This bustling district is indeed a hub of fashionable cafés, avant-garde boutiques, thrift stores, and bars with music you are unlikely to hear anywhere else.

Tokyoites also appreciate Shimokitazawa's preference for spreading out horizontally; there are no skyscrapers here like those found in Shinjuku, just ten minutes away on the metro. What you do find is a certain sense of gravity and an awareness of being a wealthy village. It is also a magnet for music lovers and vinyl collectors, who will discover some rare finds in the district's many stores, such as the Flash Disc Ranch. Lots of people come to Shimokita for the thrift stores; there are several outlets selling quality clothes at unbeatable prices, including Stick Out, which has a host of fashionable items on its shelves for just 700 yen (USD6.50, EUR6). Fans of surprising and unexpected souvenir gifts will not be disappointed at the Village Vanguard department store.

Extend your stroll beyond the bustle of Shimokitazawa Station's immediate surroundings to discover bars and cafés tucked away down streets that are a delight to explore. Store signs are in a constant state of flux and outlets open and close in the blink of an eye; Tōkyō is a busy place and sometimes barely has time to breathe.

Construction of the new station has somewhat disrupted the surrounding area's intimate feel, much to the regret of many of its fans. The construction site swallowed up a good many bars and homes, some of which dated back to the postwar era, but Tōkyō has few qualms about such minor details; in its eternal quest for modernity and efficiency, the capital is more than happy to demolish the old in order to build the new.

TAKE A STROLL

With its cafés, bars, and intimate gig venues, the district is the perfect place for evening excursions and all sorts of artistic and cultural exploration.

TRENDS

Shimokitazawa's thrift stores are overflowing with weird and wonderful items, often at rock-bottom prices.

ABOVE

In Japanese gardens, trees are made to look like clouds, and the branches are trimmed to form very specific shapes.

OPPOSITE

In Japanese folklore, the color red helps to ward off bad luck, driving away evil spirits and disease.

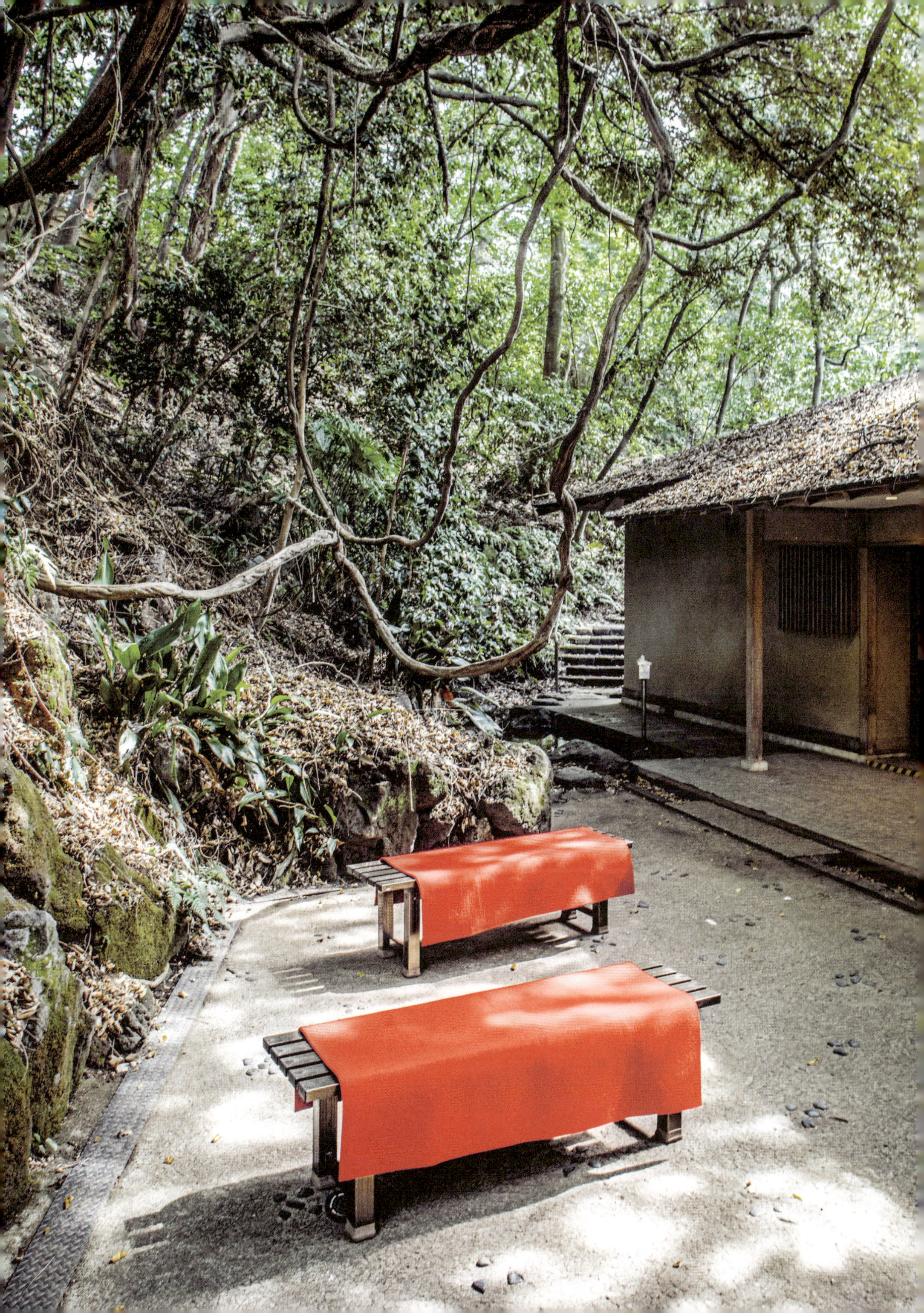

The Futako Tamagawa Rise complex just round the corner from the Tama River includes a shopping center, apartments, and a cultural venue.

Located to the west of Setagaya, Kyōdō is a district where you will find many fans of izakaya and dagashi, the candy shops of yesteryear.

The Tōkyū Setagaya line carries 58,000 passengers a day.

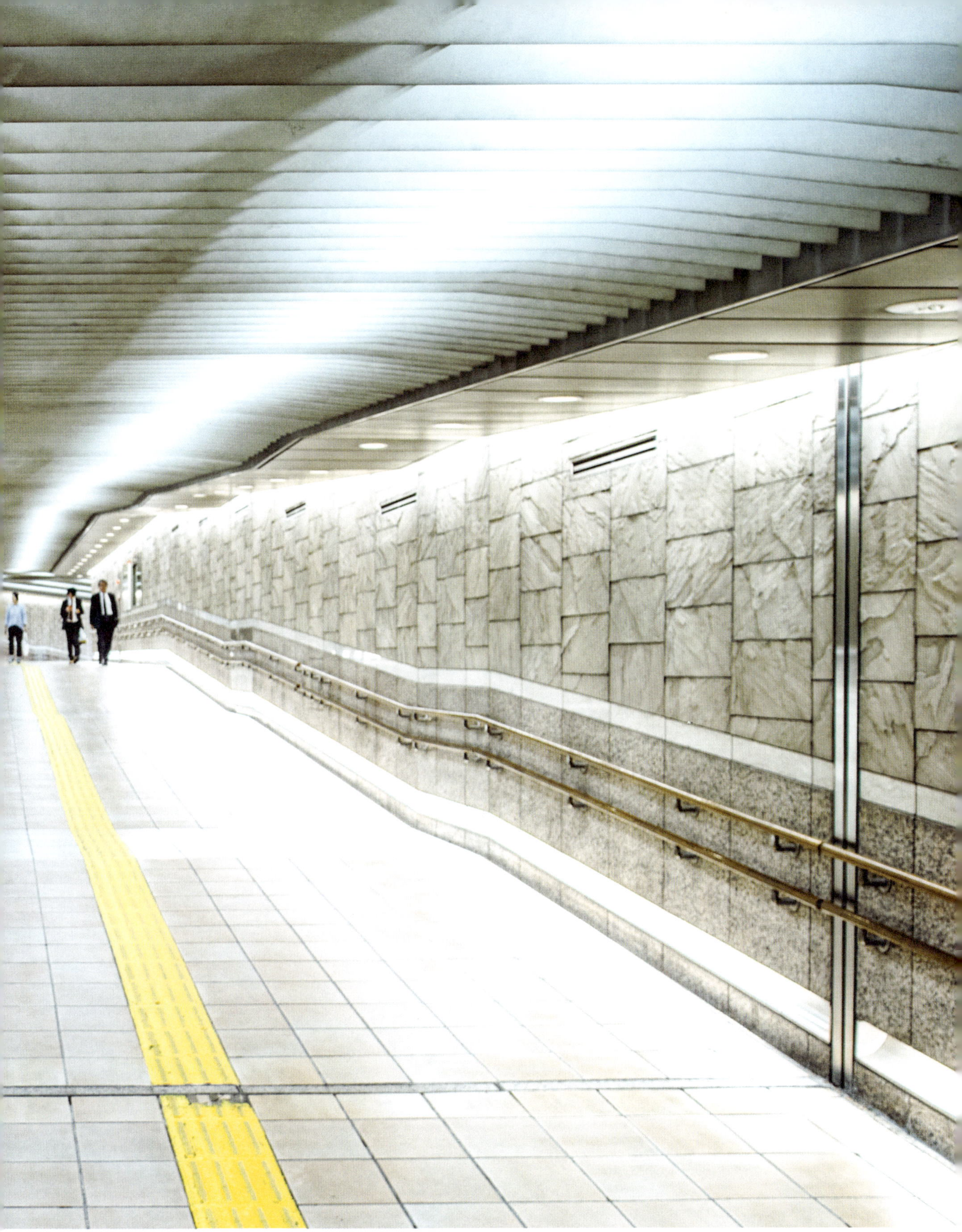

PORTRAIT

SHIRUBE

THE GENEROSITY OF HOME COOKING

For the last forty years, Shirube has been serving up Japanese home cooking in the very warm and welcoming atmosphere that only *izakaya* (a Japanese pub or tavern) can provide.

This restaurant has been operating in this small street tucked away in Shimokitazawa for forty years. What is its secret? Dishing up generous portions of simple but flavorful Japanese meals that "for Japanese people, taste like home cooking," as Ima Takehiro, the boss, is quick to emphasize.

The specialties in high demand at Shirube tend to be the plainer dishes, although the *izakaya*'s in-house recipes give them a twist. The *nikujaga*, a kind of stew of beef simmered with potatoes, is served alongside toasted crusty bread with a generous dash of garlic, while the *oden*, a winter broth full of all kinds of vegetables, tofu, and fishcake, is served at Shirube with stewed *daikon* (white radish) and seasonal produce. Fish dishes also attract gourmets in flocks: "Both our range of sashimi, which varies with the catch of the day, and *aburi shime saba*, a mackerel that we grill with a blowtorch in front of the customer and serve with a simple squeeze of lemon," explains Ima Takehiro; it's fiendishly effective.

To quench the thirst, there is beer (as there is in any good *izakaya*), and which is just the thing to wash down the establishment's deliciously spiced *edamame* (soya beans). Other signature drinks include *takezake* (sake served in a length of bamboo), *lemon sour* (a lemon-based cocktail, as the name might suggest), and *shōchū* (alcohol distilled from yams or barley). A last tasty snack to round off the meal is tofu cheese, served with bread and honey.

Ima Takehiro modestly suggests that the restaurant owes its success to the proximity of the new Shimokitazawa Station and the fact that "more and more foreign tourists are recommending it on websites." Take one look at how full this tavern is every Friday night and on weekends, however, and you begin to suspect that the contents of the plates might have something to do with it, so booking is strongly recommended. Don't forget the restaurant's extraordinary atmosphere, as the team of twenty-five willing waitstaff yell your order to the cooks from the dining room. Your table may well be a corner of the large counter that surrounds the open kitchen, conducive to companionship and conversation.

Remember also that *sake* means "alcohol" in Japanese; to order sake, ask for *nihonshu*. Shirube is part of a small chain and there are sixteen other branches (five of which are in Shibuya) all upholding the same values and the same desire to promote traditional family cooking.

The mackerel is freshly grilled and served with a squeeze of lemon juice.

Large hotplates keep dishes waiting patiently to be served warm.

The house specialty: *oden* garnished with *daikon*.

An *izakaya* is organized around its open kitchen.

Nikujaga is a kind of beef stew simmered with potatoes.

The kitchen team takes typical dishes from Japanese home cooking and reinterprets them.

Oden is a broth with a variety of ingredients, and very popular in winter.

Booking is recommended as the restaurant is really busy on Friday evenings and at weekends.

Ima Takehiro, the restaurant manager, is often in the kitchen with his team.

Tōkyō | SETAGAYA

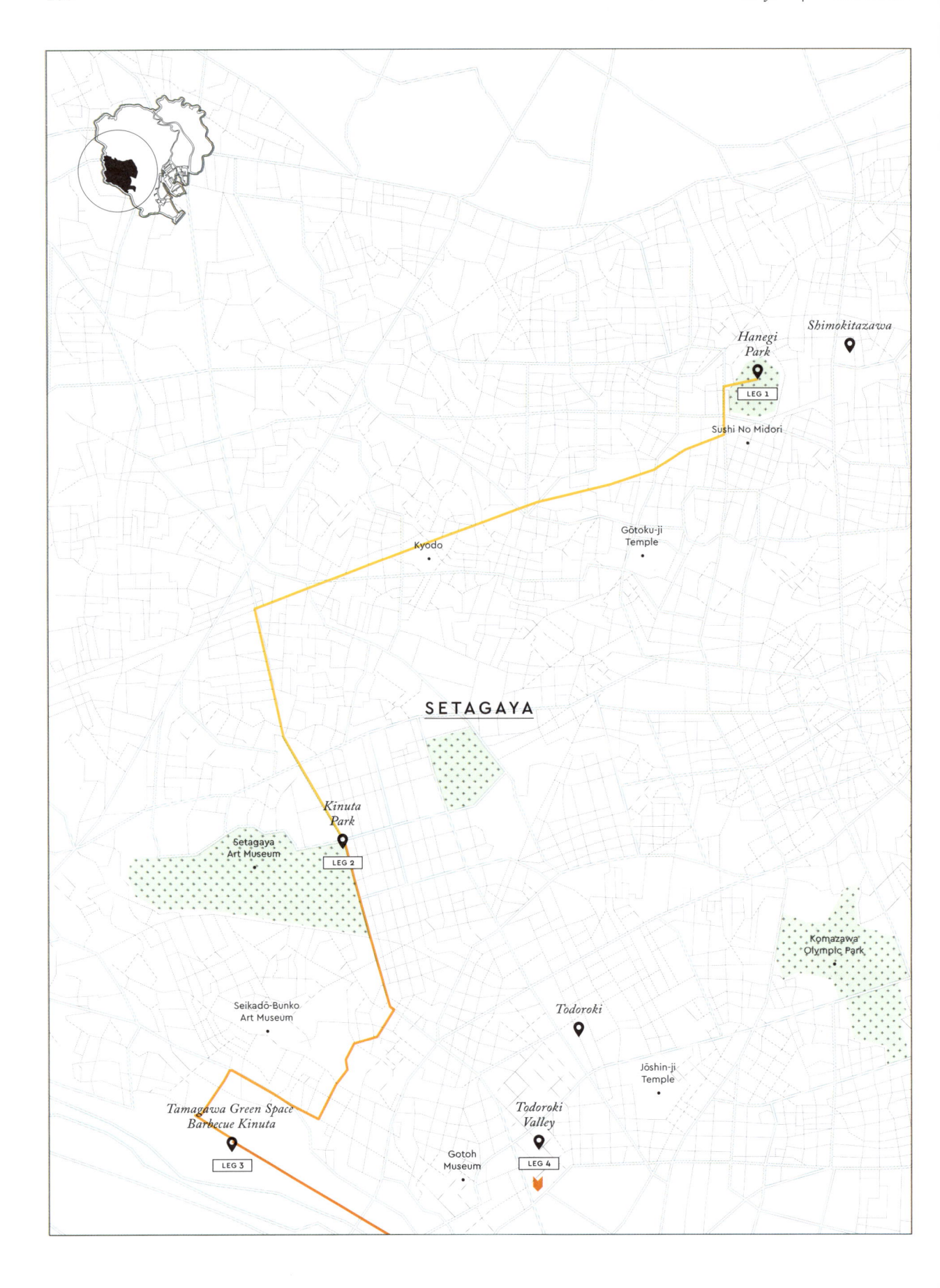

WALKING TOUR

SETAGAYA, TŌKYŌ'S GREEN LUNG

Tokyoites are particularly fond of the gentle pace of life in Setagaya, which has the advantage of combining modern infrastructure with green spaces in which to recharge the batteries and enjoy the tranquility of life on the banks of the Tama River.

LEG 1: A MORNING STROLL IN HANEGI PARK

After a hectic day in Shimokitazawa, treat yourself to the serenity of a short break and a slice of local life in Hanegi Park. Parents bring their children here for guaranteed fun as the park is particularly well equipped for kids, with a maze, sculptures, and other attractions. Sports fans jog or play tennis, while other locals walk their pets. Don't miss Hanegi between January and March, when its 650 plum trees are in blossom and a festival is held.

LEG 2: NATURE AND ART COMBINE IN KINUTA

Covering about 100 acres (40 hectares), Kinuta Park is without doubt one of the most pleasant in Tōkyō. It has the double advantage of an exceptional natural setting that is also a free open space and easily accessible, without the dense crowds you might find in Yoyogi Park (Yoyogi-kōen). You will have no problem in finding a place for a picnic in its vast expanses without feeling crammed in. There is also a baseball field, a cycle track, amusements for children, a bird sanctuary, and a pretty suspension bridge. For those keen to add a cultural edge to their stroll, Setagaya Art Museum with its temporary exhibitions of paintings and photographs is also located within the park precincts. It is home to some 16,000 works of Japanese and foreign art, mainly from the modern and contemporary periods, and the collection has a special interest in naïve art and artists with links to Setagaya ward.

LEG 3: BBQ BY THE RIVER

The Japanese love to barbecue! While this is undoubtedly one of their favorite summer pastimes, few Tōkyō residents have a home with a garden (meeting demand for outdoor space is one reason why so many restaurants in the capital have beer gardens on their roofs), so open-air green areas are extremely popular. At the Tamagawa Green Space Barbecue Area on the banks of the Tama River near Futako Tamagawa Station, you can rent everything you need for your own cookout on site (booking is strongly recommended). It also has the advantage of being open all year round, while the vast majority of the beer gardens are seasonal.

LEG 4: IN THE BOSOM OF NATURE IN TODOROKI

The Todoroki Valley is probably one of the least conventional parks in all Tōkyō. Located in the heart of Setagaya, it is perfect for a short stroll (around thirty minutes or so) through the heart of nature. It feels strange to move so suddenly from such a built-up environment to a luxuriant forest. A beautiful river flows beneath a narrow wooden path through dense undergrowth, and as you make your way along the route of about half a mile (1 km), you will see a couple of bridges, the remains of several tombs, and some plaques explaining the surrounding geology. Todoroki Fudō temple awaits at the end of the path to round off this timeless excursion.

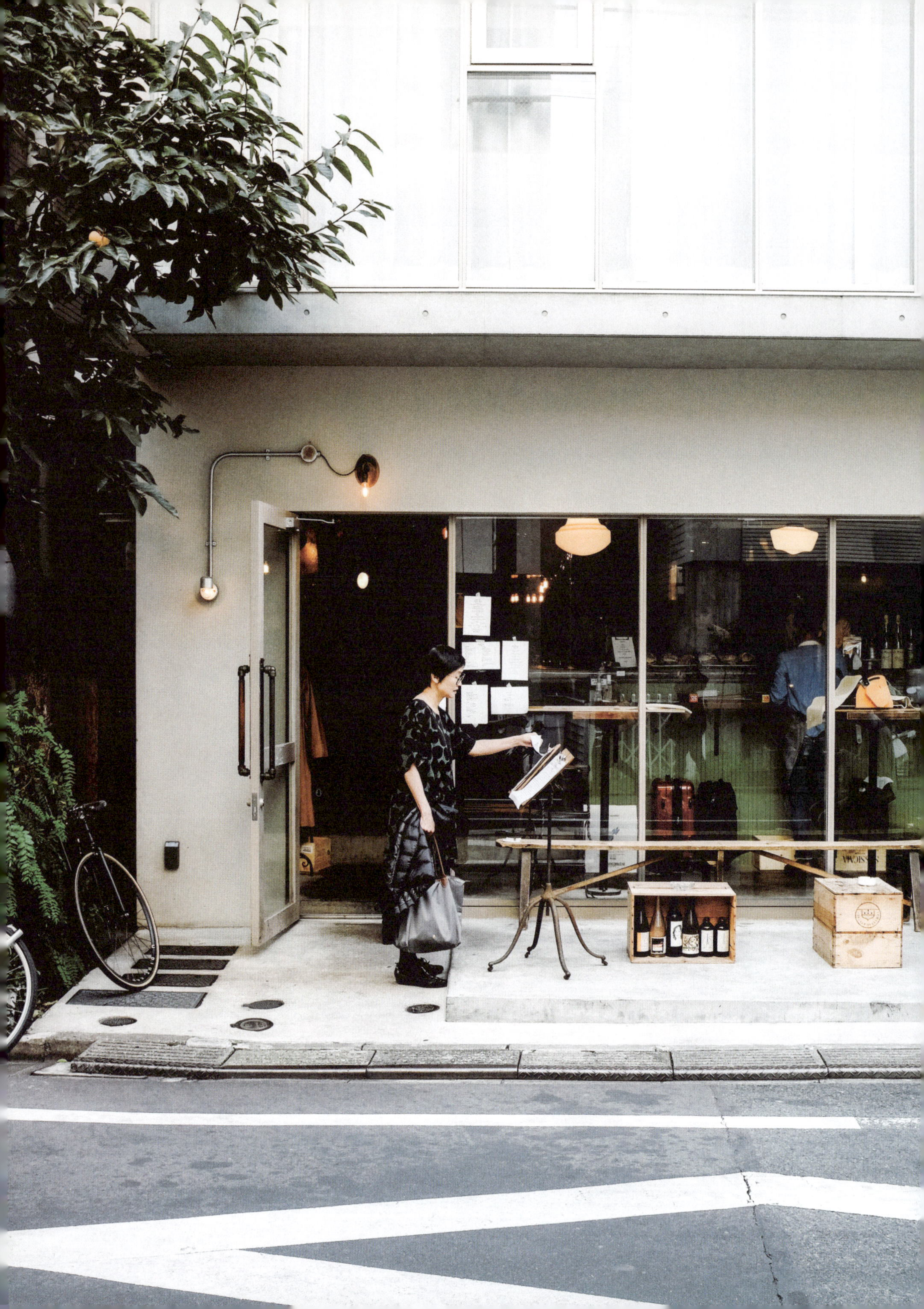

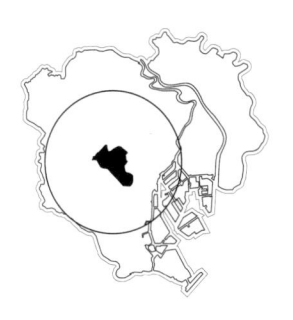

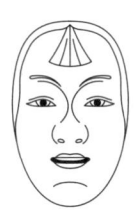

TŌKYŌ FOR NIGHT OWLS

SHIBUYA
渋谷区

Shibuya is a popular intersection and one of Tōkyō's major cultural spots.
A trendsetting hub for cutting-edge fashion and entertainment and
famous for its inventiveness and creativity, it is also loved by night owls.
The sky is the limit here.

P.168

Path is a one-stop café, wine bar, and bistro located on a bustling shopping street just round the corner from Yoyogi park.

OPPOSITE

Aoyama, at the end of Omotesandō, has a selection of cafés specializing in all kinds of Southeast Asian food (Thai, Vietnamese, etc).

Shibuya is a hub of fashion and all things cool. It's where people come for a busy, fun-filled night out. One of the liveliest districts in the Japanese capital, it is full of bustling energy. It has been attracting young people since the 1980s, who come here to party, with every kind of leisure and entertainment catered for, sometimes verging on the excessive: trendy stores, a host of restaurants, bars and night clubs, and even a hill full of love hotels. At first sight chaotic, Shibuya's famous pedestrian crossing is representative of the whole district, with a sea of people at all times of the day and night, as immortalized in many films shot in Tōkyō.

Historically, Shibuya was the name of the family that owned a castle in the area from the eleventh century until the Edo era. After the opening of the Yamanote, the railroad line that has formed a loop within Tōkyō since 1885, Shibuya gradually began to emerge as a fashionable area. As time progressed, it became a symbol of energy and frenetic activity and is home to one of the busiest railways stations in Japan. It also includes a number of famous locations such as Harajuku, a clothes shopping mecca, the avenue of Omotesandō (nicknamed "the Champs-Élysées of Tōkyō" for its luxury department store windows and museums), Yoyogi Park, which was an Olympic venue during the 1964 Games, and the majestic Shinto shrine of Meiji Jingū, tucked away in the depths of an impressive forest.

While being at the cutting edge of trends, Shibuya also boasts a cultural scene of some importance in the capital, with concert halls, movie theaters, contemporary and traditional drama, and a range of exhibitions offering a rich and varied program. It is often praised for its diversity and open-mindedness; Shibuya and Setagaya were famously the first Japanese municipalities to officially recognize gay couples in 2015.

If you need a place to meet at the end of your day in Shibuya, why not choose the statue of Hachikō. The sculpture was installed in memory of an Akita dog that was the companion of Professor Hidesaburō Ueno. Hachikō would come to Shibuya Station every evening to meet his master as he got off the train, but one evening the professor failed to return, having passed away during the day. For ten years after his master's death, Hachikō would continue to come and wait loyally at Shibuya Station. His story became famous throughout Japan when a reporter brought it to public attention in the 1930s, extolling Hachikō as a symbol of loyalty and fidelity.

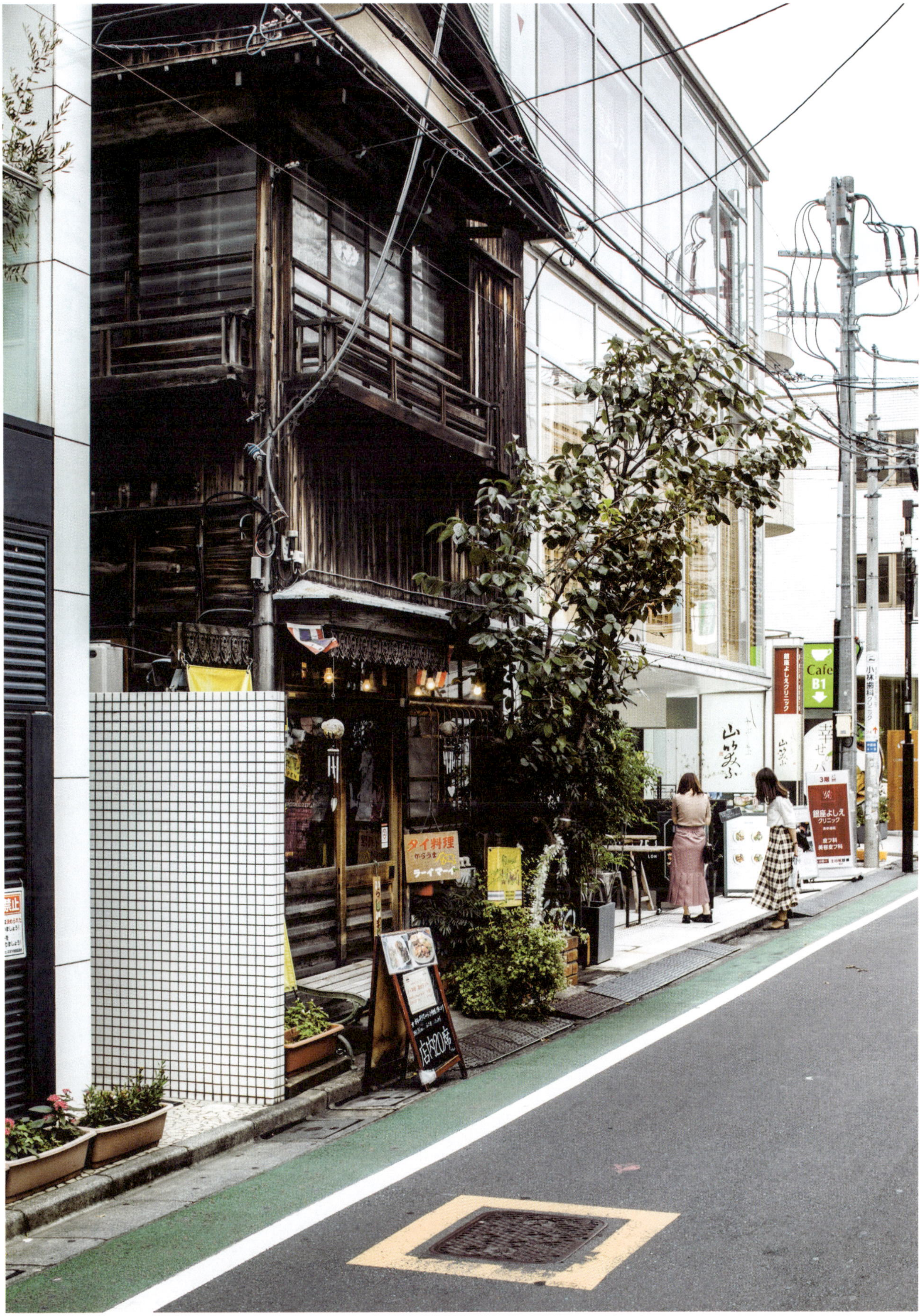
タイ料理
Cafe
B1
銀座よしえクリニック

SHIBUYA

THE ESSENTIALS

36
DOGENZAKA
This avenue beginning at Shibuya intersection leads past the Shibuya 109 department store on the way to the hill of love hotels.

37
SHIBUYA CROSSING
This is the Japanese capital's most famous crossing, immortalized in a host of films and photographs. A torrent of pedestrians crosses the intersection at all hours of the day and night.

38
AOYAMA CEMETERY
L'Aoyama-reien is an unusual place that is well worth a visit, with occasionally outsize tombstones and some celebrity residents.

39
YEBISU GARDEN PLACE
Yebisu Garden Place has been built on the old site of the Ebisu brewery, once owned by one of the main Japanese beer brands.

40
PHOTOGRAPHY MUSEUM
You don't need to be an expert photographer to appreciate the wonderful collections of images at Ebisu's top museum.

41
A CONCERT AT THE LIQUIDROOM (EBISU)
The Liquidroom is one of the more interesting gig venues in the city, thanks to a line-up of acts that tends toward rock and electro.

42

YOYOGI-KŌEN

This park was the Olympic Village in 1964 and is popular with locals who come here to relax or do sports at the weekend.

43

BUNKAMURA

This cultural center puts on theater, classical music concerts, and exhibitions, and shows films in its movie theater on the sixth floor.

44

NATIONAL NOH THEATER

Shibuya has its very own Noh theater, with performances organized on a weekly basis; they also provide small screens with translations in English.

45

TAKESHITA-DŌRI

The famous street for lovers of eccentric fashion and *cosplay*. Stop off in one of the street's *purikura*, giant photo booths that can accommodate groups.

46

NONBEI-YOKOCHŌ

"Drunkards' Alley" is lined with tiny bars that sometimes seat only four or five customers at a time; speaking Japanese is essential.

47

UKIYO-E ŌTA MEMORIAL MUSEUM OF ART

This small museum puts on monthly themed exhibitions for print-lovers alongside a permanent collection of 14,000 works by famous artists, including 12,000 that once belonged to Seizō Ōta V.

The Millennials *is an innovative concept in next-generation capsule hotels in Shibuya, with modern, comfortable amenities.*

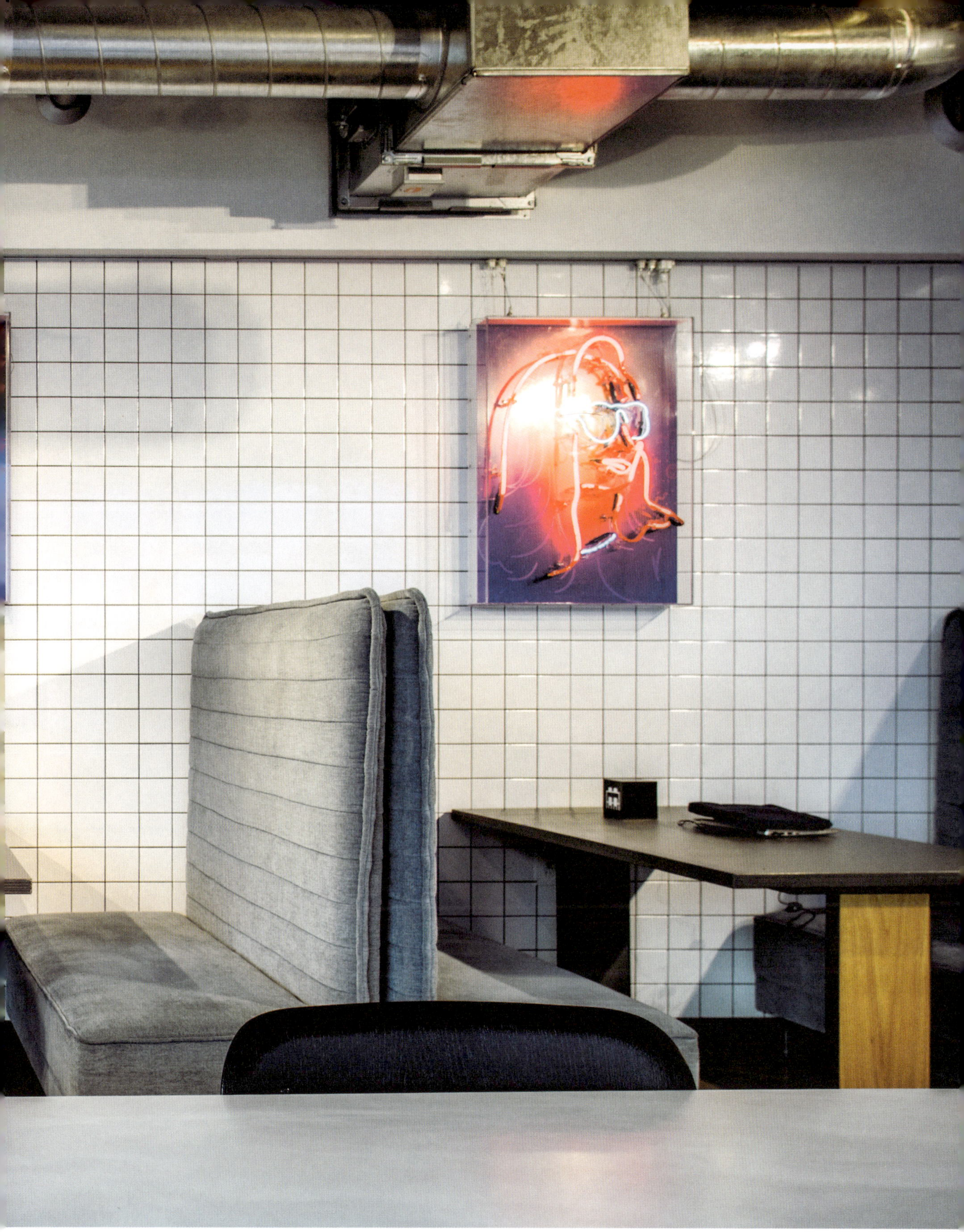

DEEP DIVE

NOH THEATER

The wide choice of culture on offer in Shibuya includes Noh, Japan's oldest form of theater, and the district also houses the theater that is the discipline's traditional home.

Noh is a major form of theater that emerged in Japan during the fourteenth century. It is not easy to get a handle on and requires a certain amount of introduction before you can master all its subtleties. The plots are based on literary stories that feature a supernatural being taking human form. A Noh performance makes use of masks, costumes, and highly stylized gestures that allow actors to interpret the gamut of emotions required to play their characters. Certain key roles such as ghosts, women, children, and old people wear characteristic masks that are instantly recognizable.

As always in traditional Japanese disciplines, Noh actors undergo a very strict apprenticeship, often handing on places from father to son (there are very few actresses) at a very early age (three years). One point to note is that it is extremely difficult to move around wearing a mask, for example, as they considerably narrow the actor's field of vision. The text requires particular pronunciation as it is delivered in Old Japanese (the language spoken from the twelfth to the sixteenth century), which is difficult enough even for a Japanese audience, and a translation is generally necessary to understand the text in its entirety.

The word "Noh" has its origins in the Mandarin *nong*, which means "skill" or "talent," and this performing art is still widely practiced throughout the country. It is a slightly more elitist theatrical form than kabuki, which has just as many sets and costumes but is more populist and is also intended to raise a few laughs from the audience.

A Noh play has two acts with dialogue and sung or danced set pieces. Its bare stage (featuring only a painted pine tree) features four categories of performers: the *shite*, the lead character who appears initially in human form and then as a ghost; the *waki*, the *shite*'s opposite number; the *kyōgen*, who acts as a kind of chorus; and finally the *hayashi*, who takes care of the musical interludes (traditional flute and various kinds of drums).

There are more than 450 masks, divided into sixty categories and five types. They may represent different genders, ages, and emotions, depending on the character appearing on the stage.

THE MAIN TYPES OF MASK

FEMALE DEMON

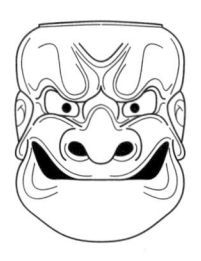

MALE DEMON

OLD MAN

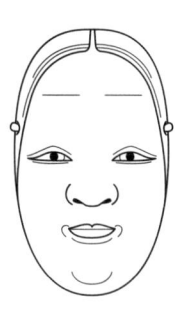

YOUNG WOMAN

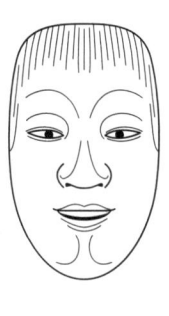

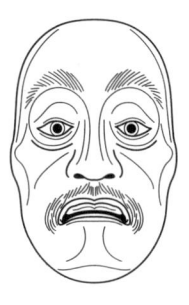

MANS

SPIRIT

There are many theater masks, but they fall into five categories: masks for spirits, men, women, demons, and old people.

ABOVE

Eel is a very popular dish in Japan, especially in summer, when restaurants make it a specialty. It is typically drizzled with a delicate, sweet sauce and eaten on a bed of rice.

OPPOSITE

Tōkyō (indeed all Japan) loves its trains, and you will commonly see many restaurants and bars located directly under the tracks, although this is also for reasons of space.

代々木商店街
ガッツソウル
3F
2F
磯丸水産
24時間
中国料理
キングスランド
代々木店
B1営業中
おしろビル
焼肉

EXCURSION
MEIJI JINGŪ
A SHRINE IN THE DEPTHS OF THE FOREST

Nestling in the depths of a vast forest of 120,000 trees, Meiji Jingū has become a major icon of Tōkyō; the shrine and its green surroundings are a particularly appropriate embodiment of the importance of nature in the Shinto religion.

This Shinto shrine located a stone's throw from the bustling district of Harajuku is impossible to miss and has become a symbol of the city. To enter Meiji Jingū, you must pass through the immense *torii*, the gate that allows access to the shrine's precincts, and then follow a majestic avenue of greenery that is like entering a benevolent and protective forest of thick foliage. The Shinto religion is not based on any one text and has no founder, appealing instead to values such as harmony with nature and *Magokoro* ("a sincere heart").

As you follow the path leading to the shrine, the forest (which covers 173 acres/70 hectares) becomes even denser; there are no fewer than 120,000 trees of 365 different species.

Some of the path is lined with barrels of sake, which are placed as offerings. Eventually, the shrine comes into view. It was built between 1915 and 1926, in the wake of the Meiji Restoration, and constructed in accordance with the traditional rules of *nagare-zukuri*, using mainly Japanese cypress for the frame and copper for the roof cladding. Meiji Jingū was badly damaged by bombing in the Second World War but was completely restored in 1958, and has recently been renovated again.

As at Nezu-jinja, visitors must make a detour before entering, passing by the ablutions basin (*temizuya*) to purify themselves by rinsing their hands and mouth. Water is drawn only once to carry out all the stages of purification (see "Nezu-jinja," page 94). Once you reach the main building, you should put a few coins in the offering box and bow twice before clapping your hands twice. You should then pray and bow a final time before leaving.

The day-to-day life of the shrine is punctuated with all kinds of ceremonies and events throughout the year and, if you are in luck, you might even spot a traditional wedding procession crossing the courtyard. Meiji Jingū also has a charming small walled garden consisting of a traditional tea house, a pond, and an area dedicated to irises, which bloom in June. To avoid the crowds and enjoy the spirituality of the place to the full, try to visit in the early morning or just before they close the doors.

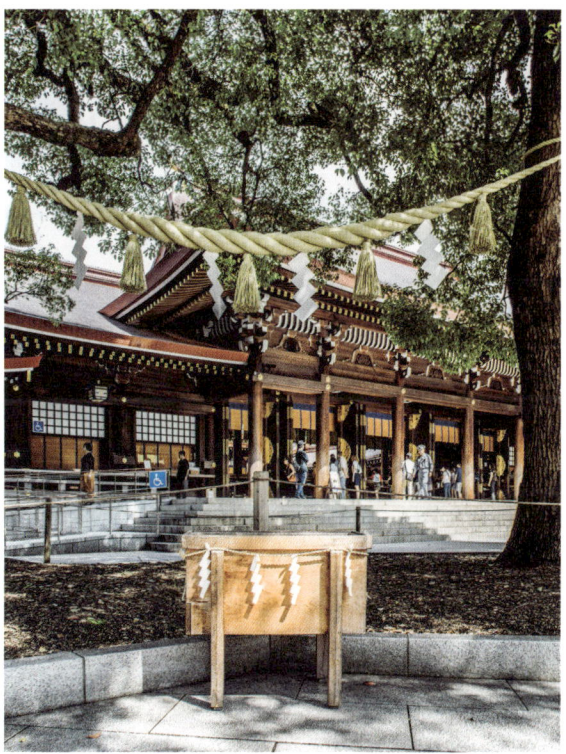

CEREMONIES

The shrine still celebrates a wide variety of ceremonies such as traditional weddings.

PRAYERS

Sumo bouts are offerings made to the gods, and on special occasions are even held within the precincts of the shrine.

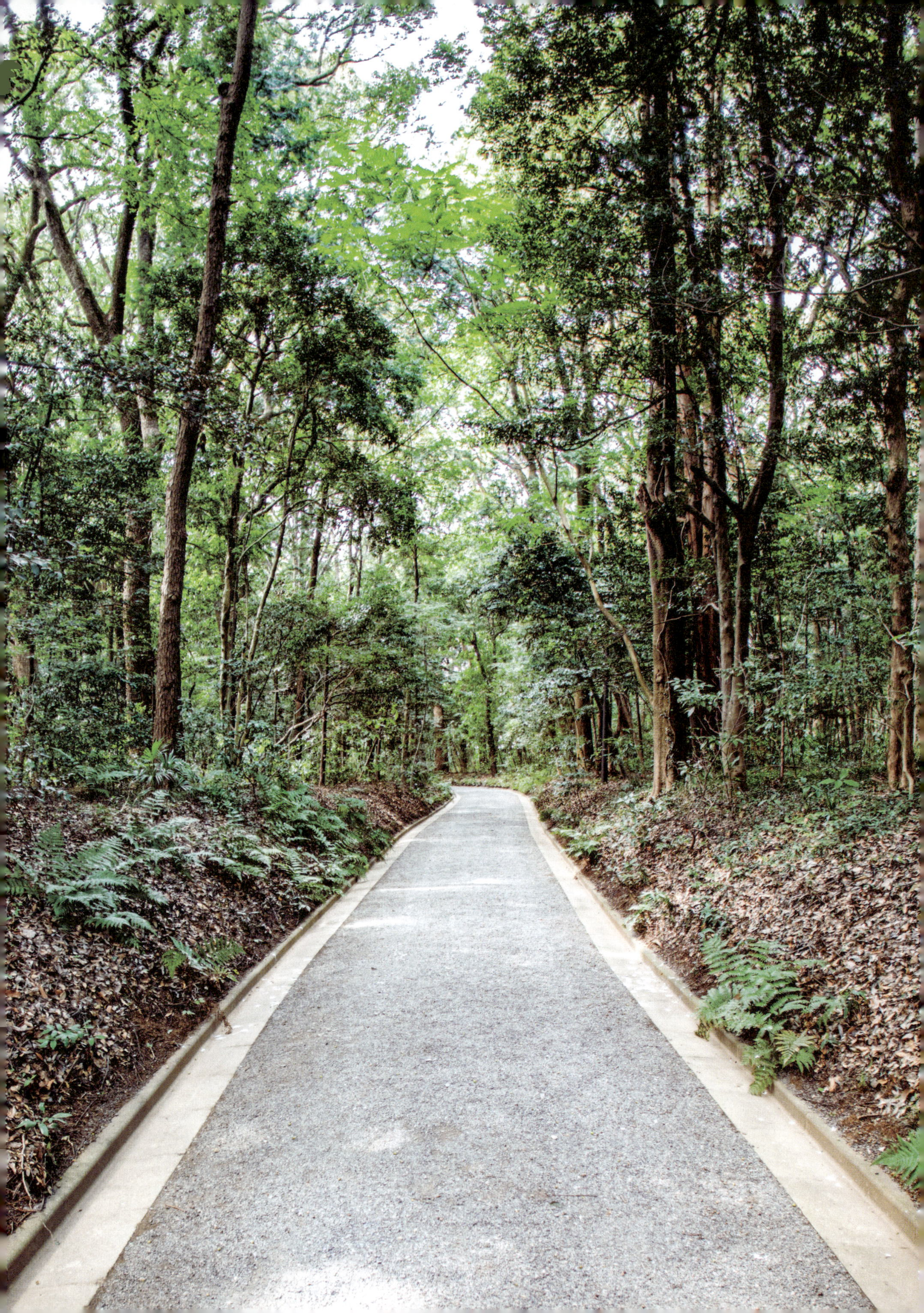

ABOVE

The Shichi-go-san festival honors children as they reach the ages of three, five, and seven, and they dress up in magnificent kimonos for the occasion.

OPPOSITE

The only way to reach the Meiji Jingū shrine is along a small asphalt path through the forest.

Tōkyō | SHIBUYA

*The impressive Shibuya intersection has found fame as the busiest in the world,
at any time of the day or night.*

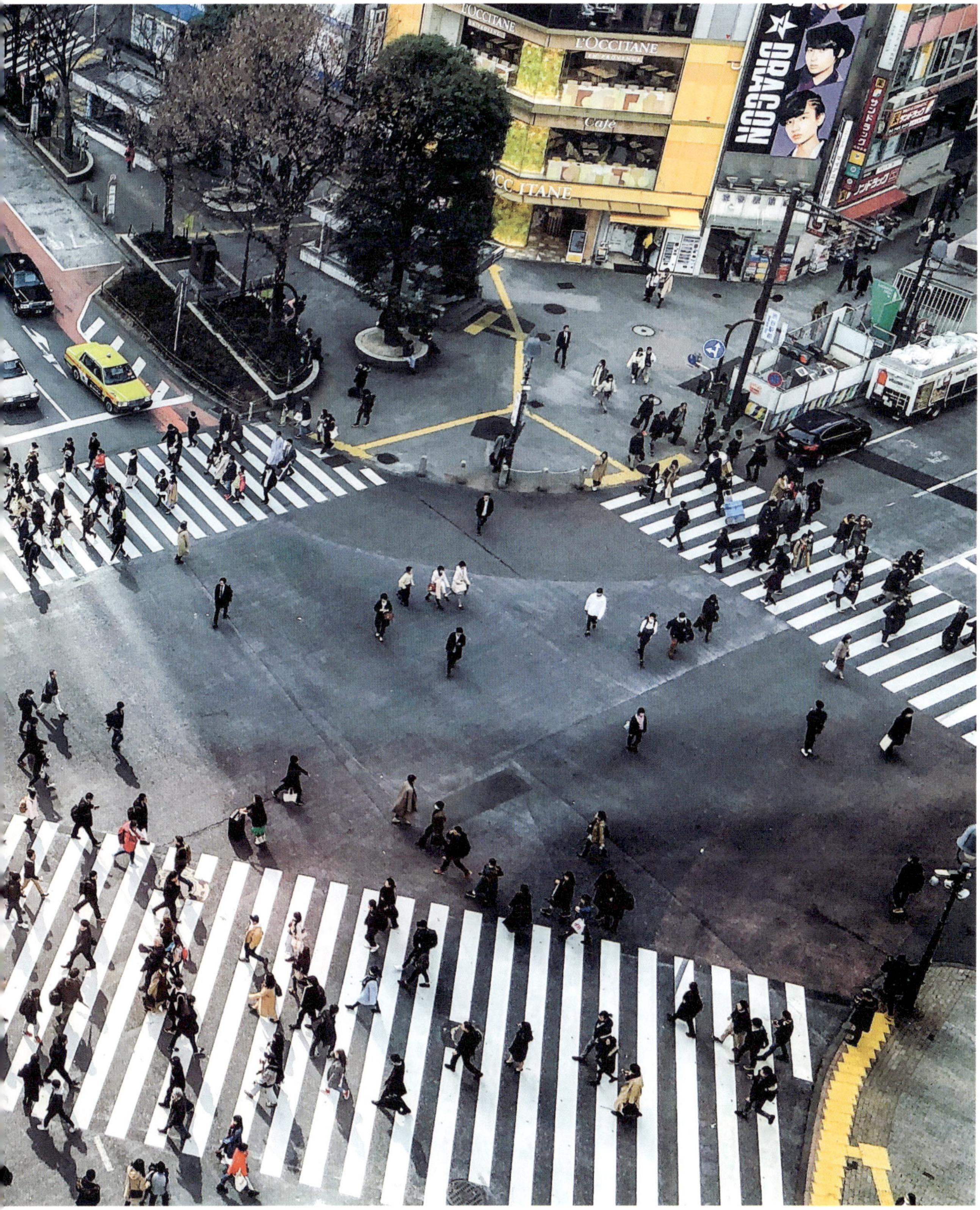
L'OCCITANE
Café
DRAGON

ABOVE

*There is a retro, film-set feel to the drinking spots in
Nombei yokochō at night.*

OPPOSITE

*Nombei yokochō ("Drunkards' Alley") is a row of small bars and
restaurants just round the corner from Shibuya Station.*

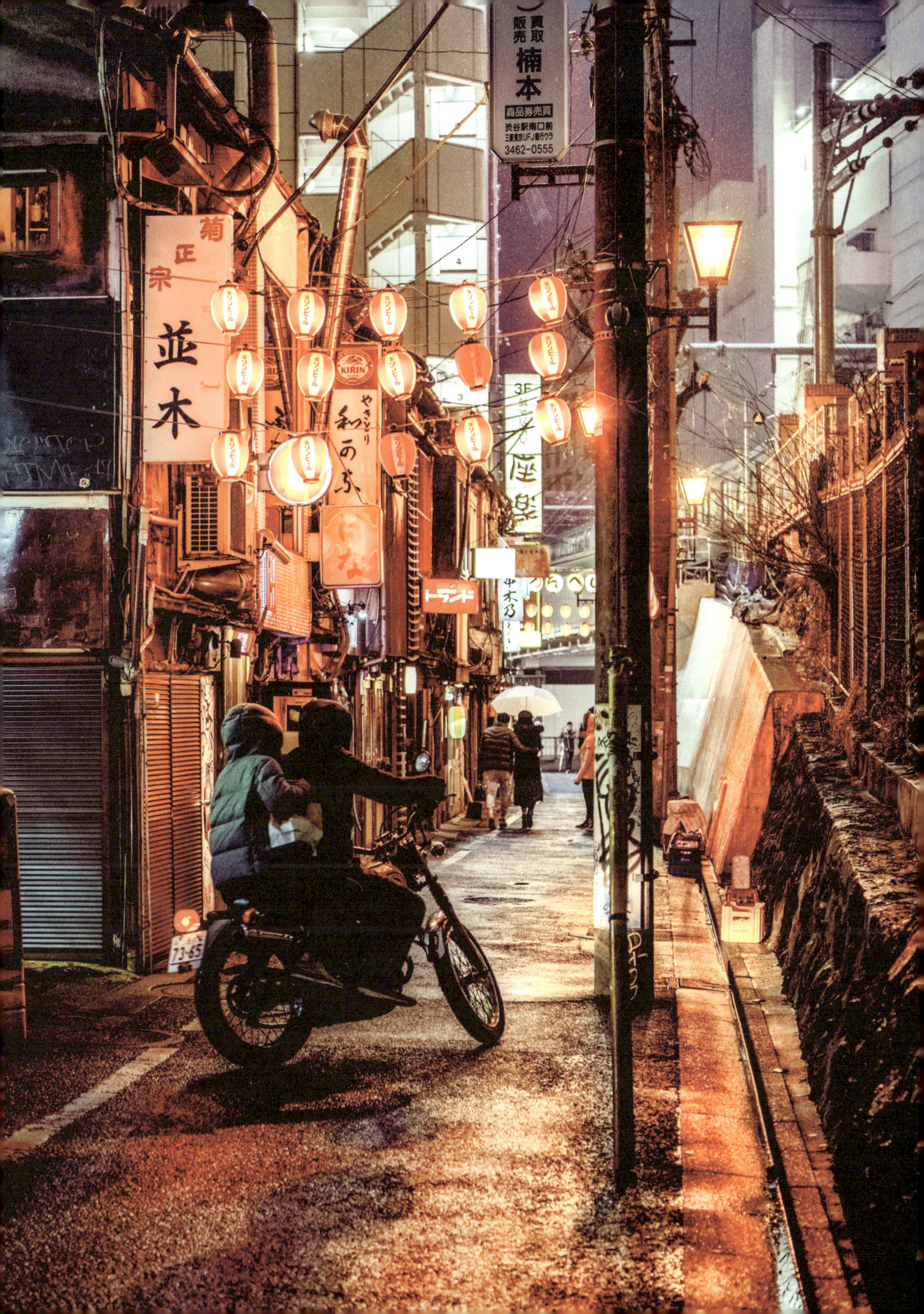
買取
販売
楠本
商品券売買
渋谷駅南口前
三菱東京UFJ銀行ウラ
3462-0555
菊正宗
並木
KIRIN

LIFESTYLE

HARAJUKU

AT THE CUTTING EDGE OF EVERY TREND

Don't miss Harajuku, the epicenter of popular culture with global appeal, and a destination for young people. It has a long reputation as an exuberant, avant-garde area but has calmed down a little recently.

Harajuku was extravagant and deliciously provocative in the 1990s but has since relaxed and changed down a gear or two, as has been documented in a column by street photographer Shoichi Aoki, the creator of *Fruits* magazine, which recorded the cutting-edge looks of young urban fashionistas for twenty years before recently closing.

Anyone taking a stroll down the famous thoroughfare of Takeshita-dōri in search of local color will a be greeted by microboutiques selling clothes in every color of the rainbow, costumes, and other *cosplay*, giant photo booths, and stores selling crêpes and other sweet treats in pastel shades.

It seems, however, that the real charms of Harajuku and the adjoining avenue of Omotesandō are now to be found elsewhere, and a more sedate Harajuku lies just around the corner from the trendsetting stores. You could even describe the area as laid-back, as it has more of a village feel, and people come here to shop in peace and quiet after exploring the cutting-edge trends in the more quirky spots. The many cafés, bars, and restaurants offer a range of original and delicious brunch menus, with a choice of hearty cuisines from various countries across Asia (China, Vietnam, Thailand) as well as Europe. Bills in Harajuku is a brunch spot with a fantastic view across the whole district from its terrace.

There are endless places to eat in Harajuku, from Japanese and Vietnamese to Thai, from *gyōza* bars to places selling burgers and pastries. Simply wander off into a side street, allowing yourself to get lost, and you will find something to satisfy your appetite. The Japanese still see Harajuku as a district for highschool girls and young people in general, and many cafés here only serve pancakes and bubble tea, which originally came from Taiwan.

The Spiral Café in Omotesandō is also worth a visit for its location within a museum and for its excellent lunches.

DISPENSING SURPRISES

Gashapon are very popular with children; drop a coin in the vending machine slot and you will be rewarded with a gadget toy in a capsule.

THE CANDY QUARTER

A mecca for those with a sweet tooth and teenagers who come to Harajuku to enjoy bubble tea or crêpes.

The streets of Harajuku and Shibuya are lined with food trucks selling drinks and lunchboxes.

Omotesandō Avenue's luxury department stores have earned it the nickname "the Champs-Elysées of Tōkyō" and large crowds turn up at weekends to enjoy a day of shopping.

FOOD & DRINK

A COCKTAIL AT THE SG CLUB

BARMAN

Shingo Gokan, the manager of the SG Club and three other bars in Shanghai, has lived in Tōkyō for more than thirty-five years and is one of the most famous barmen in the world. All the cocktails here are mixed to original recipes.

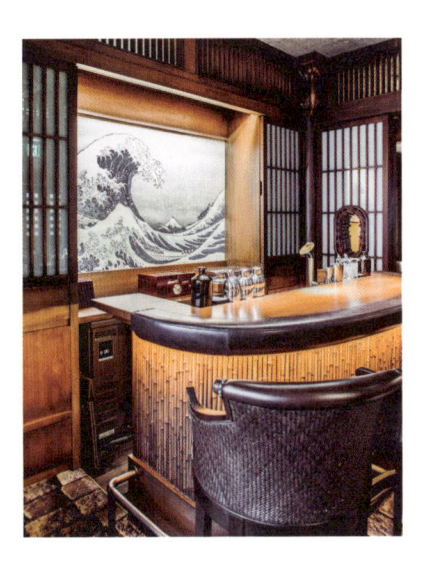

PRIVATE ROOM

There is even a space upstairs where you can enjoy a cigar with your cocktail.

DETAIL MATTERS

The attention to detail so typical of Japan is particularly charming.

DÉCOR

The esthetic here is reminiscent of the first Western-style bars that were founded by samurai after a trip to New York.

HISTORY

This unusual establishment reproduces the atmosphere of bars in Tōkyō during the 1900s.

FLAVORS

Japanese drinks vie with Western spirits to produce extraordinary cocktails.

BOURBON

This bourbon-based cocktail is served with a slice of dried wagyu.

COCKTAILS

Whether sake or *shōchū*-based, or even enhanced with Parmesan liqueur, every cocktail promises a unique and surprising blend of flavors.

DISTINCTION

The SG club in Shibuya was ranked among the fifty best bars in Asia in 2023. Blending the sophistication and finesse of Japanese cocktails with a touch of Western style, it offers a unique experience.

SHIBUYA

Tōkyō

WALKING TOUR

DAIKANYAMA
A TRANQUIL BREAK

The elegant district of Daikanyama, to the south of Shibuya, is an ideal place for a quiet break among the terraces, cafés, and bustling boutiques in its maze of tiny streets. Tokyoites are also drawn to Daikanyama by its architecture and one of the city's most beautiful bookstores.

LEG 1: EXPLORING A TRADITIONAL HOME

The Kyū Asakura House, located five minutes' walk from Daikanyama Station, was built by its owner Torajiro Asakura in 1919. This historic building is one of a kind in Shibuya and notable for having a garden with the esthetic of a *rōji*, the kind of garden laid out on the approaches to a tea house. The house was designated "Cultural Property" in 2004 and opened its doors as a museum to the public the same year.

LEG 2: NO-WASTE LUNCH

While every item in a Tōkyō supermarket must be perfect and laid out neatly in identical rows, the Japanese philosophy of *mottainai* is based on the principle of using everything and wasting nothing, and a few restaurant owners in Daikanyama are trying to revive a practice that is so dear to the Japanese (but sometimes forgotten by the capital). The Lupicia Bon Marché store is a good example, selling fresh and dried products at reduced prices due to their approaching sell-by date.

LEG 3: FOR BOOKWORMS

Daikanyama T-Site is ranked among the twenty most beautiful bookstores in the world and has won awards from the World Architect Festival; it is undoubtedly one of the district's main attractions. This ultra-modern building designed by the architect Klein Dytham houses Tsutaya, an elegant bookstore and a brand known throughout Japan for its wide selection of books and for its CD and DVD hire services. Daikanyama T-Site (nicknamed the "book store in the woods" as its premises open out onto the garden) has three wings and six different book departments. The façade is decorated with a T-shaped white mesh and features large, blue-tinted windows. The airy and spacious bookstore appeals to readers of all ages.

LEG 4: READY FOR ACTION AT A CONCERT?

The Daikanyama Unit's rich and varied progam of events is particularly cutting-edge and one of the places you are likely to discover new artists from Japan and overseas. The generous size of the room allows you to relax and enjoy the gig without feeling hemmed in by a crowd.

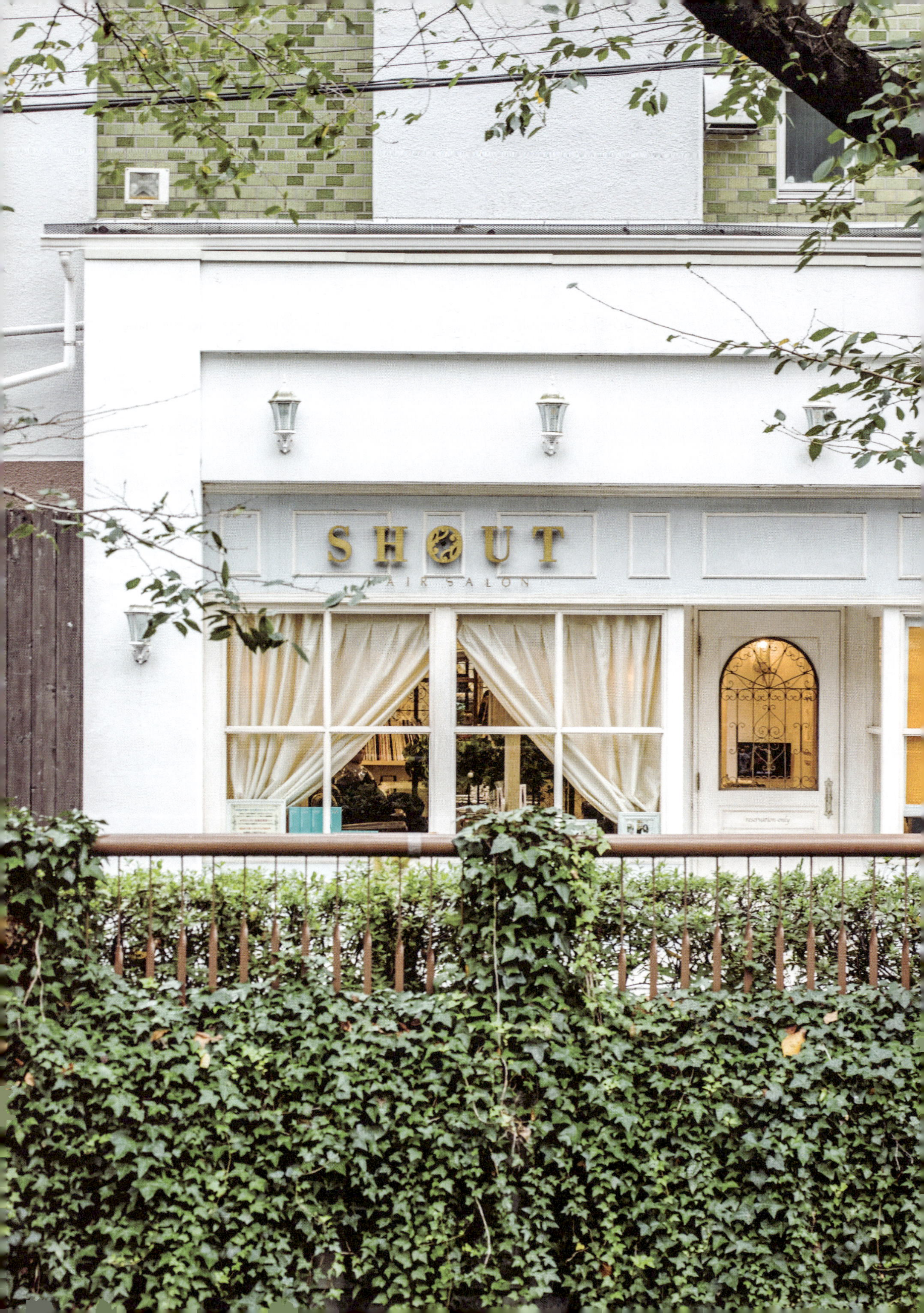
SHOUT

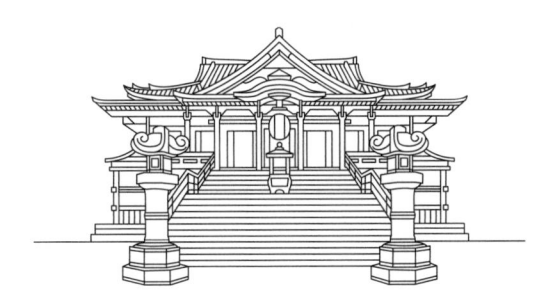

HISTORIC AND AVANT-GARDE

MEGURO
目黒区

Meguro was named for its temple, Meguro Fudō. It was the birthplace of the capital and has preserved many remnants of its past, providing unique insights into prehistoric life. Meguro also boasts a canal and a vibrant and influential artistic scene thanks to the trendy districts of Nakameguro and Jiyūgaoka.

P.196

*Hair salons and fancy patisseries line the banks of
Meguro's Nakameguro canal.*

OPPOSITE

*The dazzling spectacle of the cherry trees in blossom along the Nakameguro canal
is at its best during late March and early April.*

Meguro appears at first to be a quiet, tranquil residential district, perhaps even slightly underwhelming when compared to flamboyant Shibuya to the north. If you take time to explore it, however, it will reveal its many charms and a complex and unique personality that is deeply rooted in the history of Tōkyō; Meguro is just as assertive and even avant-garde as its famous neighbor.

In Japanese, *meguro* means "black eyes," a reference to the Meguro Fudō temple (Ryūsenji) dedicated to the god Fudō Myōō, also known as Acala, one of the five "Kings of Brightness" protecting the Buddha. This major figure in the Buddhist pantheon is also venerated by many *yakuza* (members of the Japanese underworld). Despite his terrifying appearance, he is a powerful, passionate, and protective divinity who consigns to the flames anything that might stand in the way of enlightenment. Meguro Fudō temple is guarded by five statues, each with eyes of a different hue, a reference to the five colors of the five levels of consciousness in Buddhist philosophy. These sentinels have kept careful watch over the temple for more than four centuries; Ryūsenji is the oldest Fudō temple in Japan and one of the three largest on the archipelago.

There are also unique prehistoric remains in Meguro that provide clues to life in the region during the Neolithic (the Jōmon period, around 7,500–300 years BCE), the Yayoi period (300 BCE to 300 CE) and the era of tumulus-building (*kofun*, the third century) and there are signposted walks for history buffs keen to explore the district in new and fascinating ways. The Higashiyama hills are a remarkable archeological site housing numerous traces of human activity (worked shells, food remains, evidence of hunting expeditions) when the population was still nomadic. Meguro has also preserved several impressive aristocratic homes, some of which are open to the public. Meguro lies in the former province of Musashi, a major region of medieval Japan, now fallen into abeyance, but it has clearly left its mark in this part of the capital.

Despite its deep historical roots, Meguro embraces its present and is home to trendy boutiques, bijou cafés, and the Nakameguro Canal. The canal is an unforgettable and unmissable sight when the cherry trees are in blossom, while Jiyūgaoka, near the Tama River in the very south of Meguro, is a favorite with strolling groups of Japanese seeking French-style patisseries and café terraces.

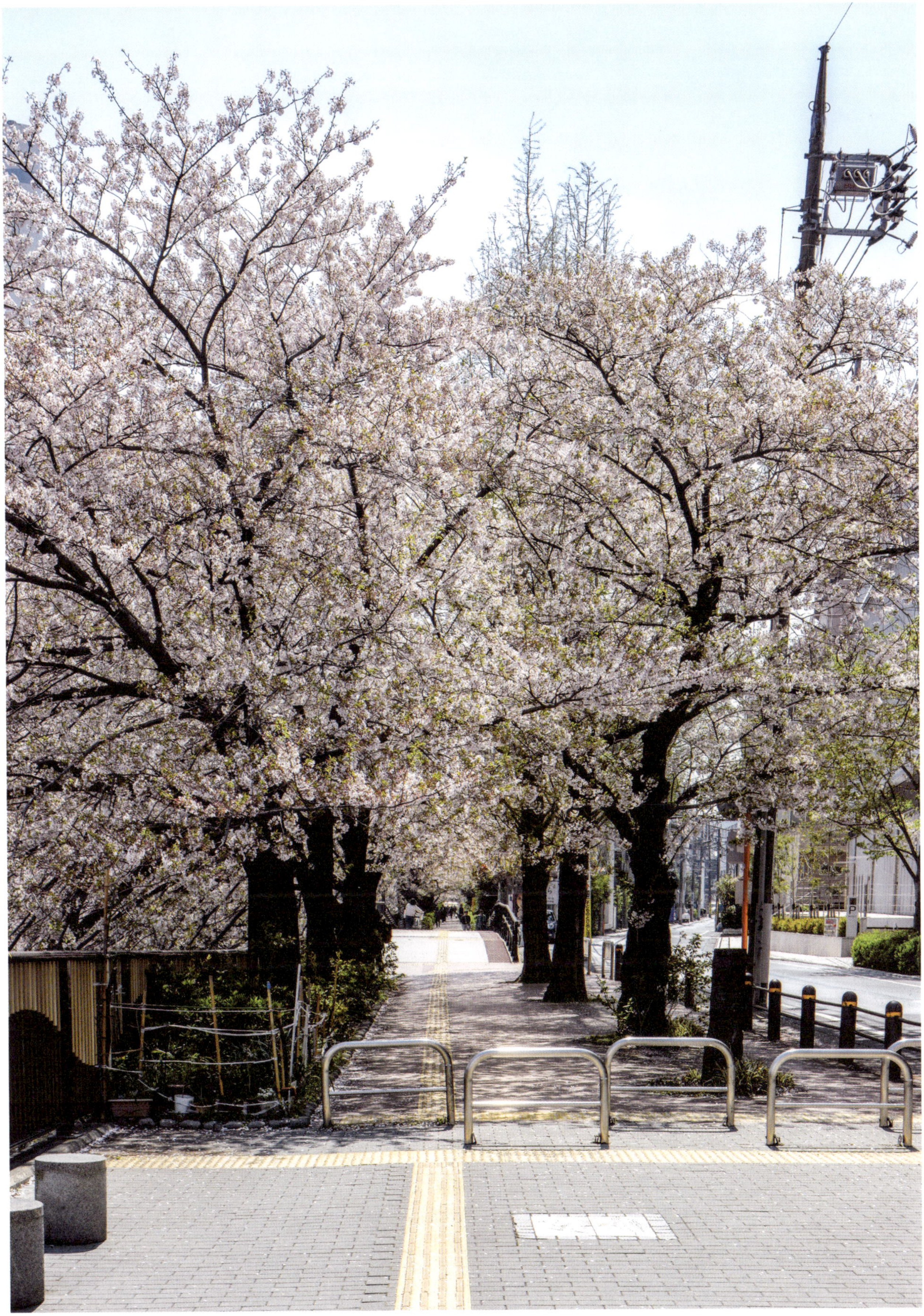

MEGURO
THE ESSENTIALS

MAEDA HOUSE

The Maeda were once one of the most powerful aristocratic families in the Tokugawa shogunate.
Their house was built in Komaba Park in 1929.

49

MEGURO ART MUSEUM

This museum was created by the Nihon Sekkei architectural design firm and exhibits artists who have created works since the Meiji era.

50

MEGURO SKY GARDEN

There are more than 1,000 trees in this circular garden. On a clear day, you can see Mount Fuji.

51

TOKYO METROPOLITAN TEIEN ART MUSEUM

The Art deco-inspired home of Prince Asaka boasts a delightful garden and has been a museum since 1983.

52

MEGURO FUDŌ

The tomb of lovers Hirai Gonpachi and Komurasaki, whose romance has inspired a host of kabuki plays, lies in Ryūsenji temple, also known as Meguro Fudō.

53

THE JAPAN FOLK CRAFTS MUSEUM

Fans of ceramics and pottery will enjoy the collections in this museum founded by Sōetsu Yanagi.

54

MUSEUM OF CONTEMPORARY SCULPTURE

The Watanabe collection curates 200 sculptures by 56 contemporary Japanese artists.

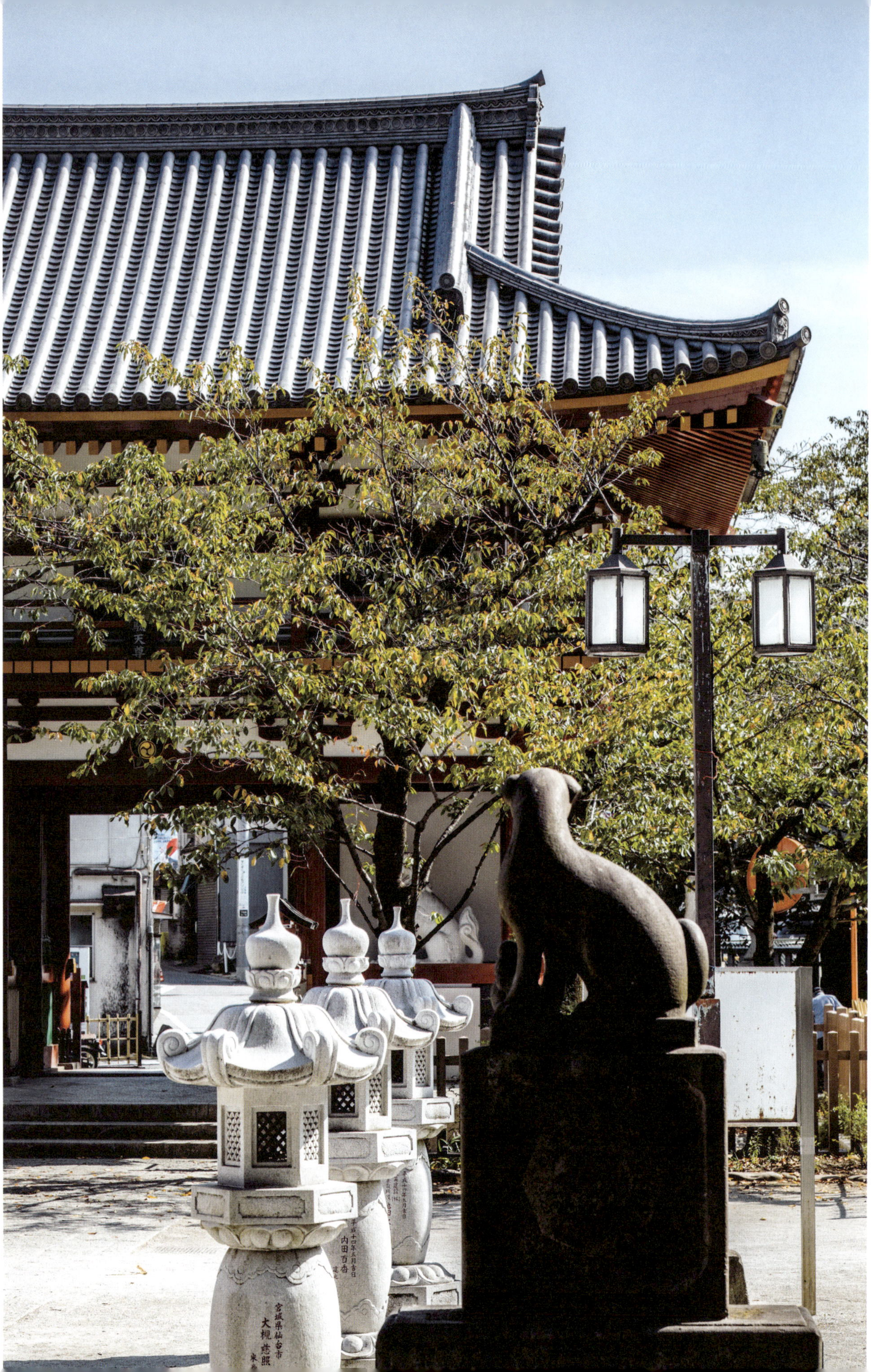
宮城県仙台市
大槻慈照
内田百香

ABOVE

Dreams and wishes are written on a piece of paper and hung up in the hope they will come true; you can also write predictions for the future.

OPPOSITE

The stone lanterns found in Japanese temples (and sometimes in gardens) are known as tōrō. When lit, they are considered an offering to the Buddha.

Meguro Fudō is also known as Ryūsenji and it is here that Hirai Gonpachi and Komurasaki, who have since become main characters in many kabuki plays, were laid to rest.

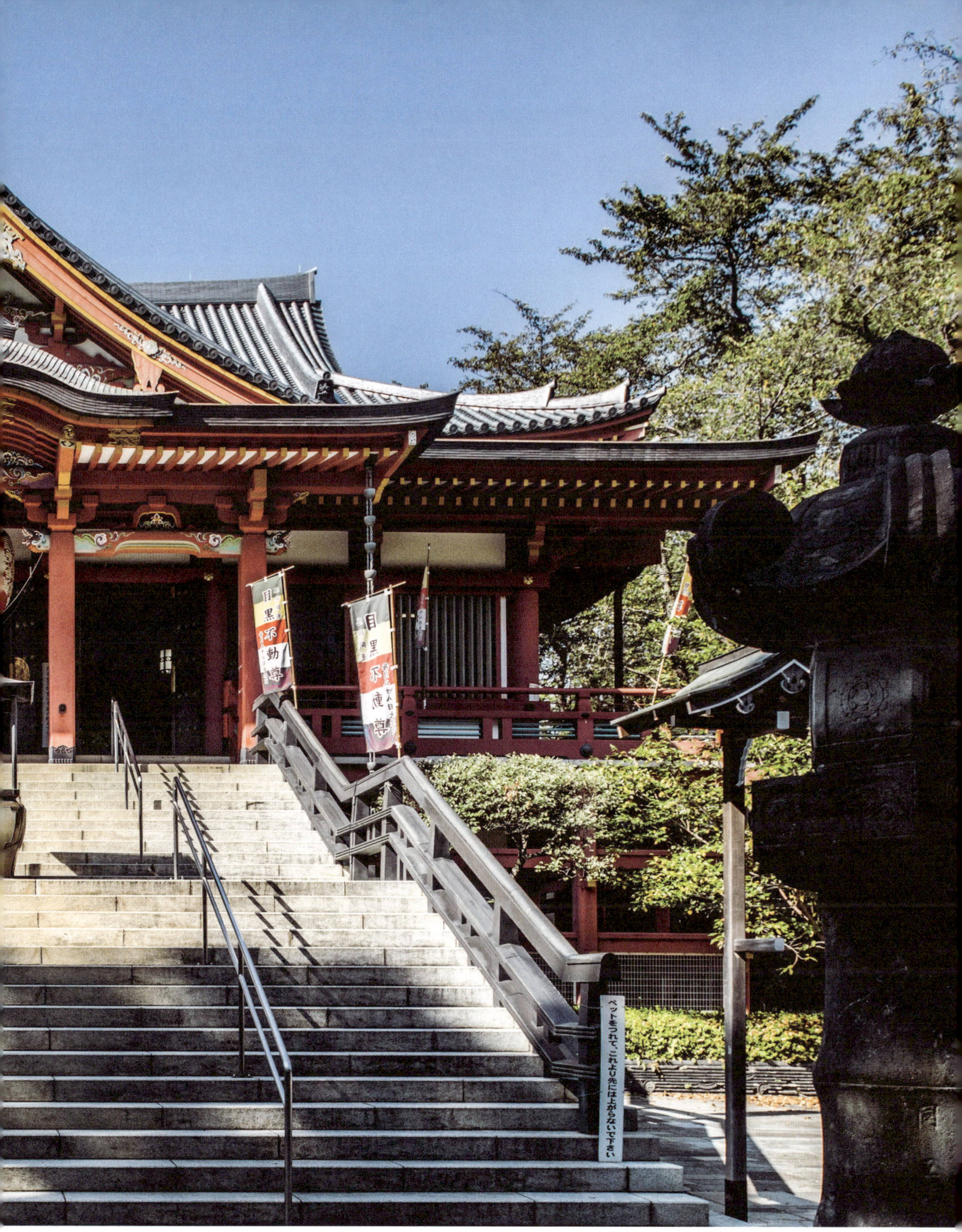
目黒不動尊
ペットをつれて、これより先には上がらないで下さい

ABOVE

It is customary to toss a coin into the collection basin after making a wish or a saying a prayer in a temple.

OPPOSITE

The Niomon at Meguro Fudō temple, the gate marking the entrance to a Buddhist shrine, is flanked by two stone lanterns (tōrō).

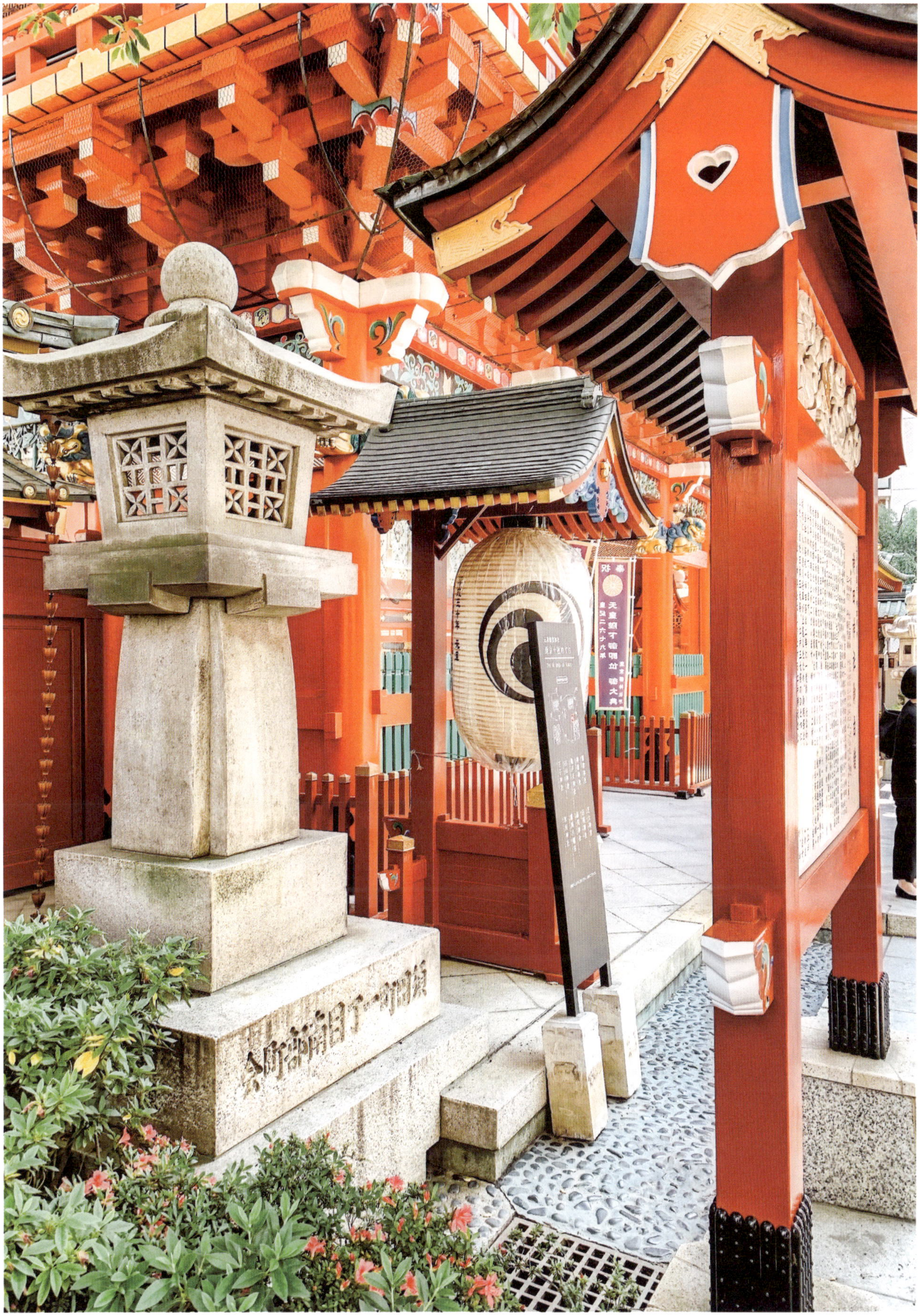

DEEP DIVE

TŌKYŌ

AN ARCHITECTURAL OVERVIEW

The urban landscape of Tōkyō has suffered many different natural events and disasters, and its architecture bears witness both to its scars and to the resilience that the Japanese capital has shown throughout its long history.

The architecture of Tōkyō has adapted to its history. The city has undergone two rounds of massive destruction (during the Kantō earthquake of 1923 and the bombing of the Second World War), with the capital reduced to rubble on both occasions and requiring rebuilding. As a result, Tōkyō's skyline is a modern one of contemporary constructions and a distinct lack of older buildings.

The city used to prefer horizontal urban development of generally low-rise buildings, but this seems no longer to be the case; Tōkyō's towers are rising ever higher as the city seeks to make better use of space and meet the needs of a constantly expanding population. The upper floors of residential towers are also generally more popular with Tokyoites, mainly because of a fear of flooding.

Ginza is one of the most expensive shopping areas in the world and the department stores defy gravity as they reach for the sky. Architects have to be ingenious and daring to meet the increasing need to exploit every last square foot to the full and sell them at the highest price. In order to incorporate some green space that is otherwise distinctly lacking in Ginza, the architect Shigeru Ban created the hanging garden in the Nicolas G. Hayek center, rising from the floor to the ceiling of a 184-ft/56-m tower block.

Green roofs are cultivated on top of skyscrapers to bring residents a small slice of nature in the heart of the city. The rooftops of Miyashita Park in Shibuya and the forty-seven stories of Shibuya Scramble square provide much needed green spaces and a breath of fresh air for Tokyoites.

As outlined, old buildings tend to be few and far between in the Japanese capital, but a few remain, such as the residence of Prince Akasaka in Meguro district, which was turned into an art museum in 1983. The house was built in 1933 and belonged to Prince Asaka Yasuhiko and his wife Nobuko, who had lived in France at the height of the Art deco period. Fascinated by the style, they introduced it to varying degrees in the architecture of their residence, which was designated as "Cultural Property" ten years after its transformation into a museum.

REACH FOR THE SKY

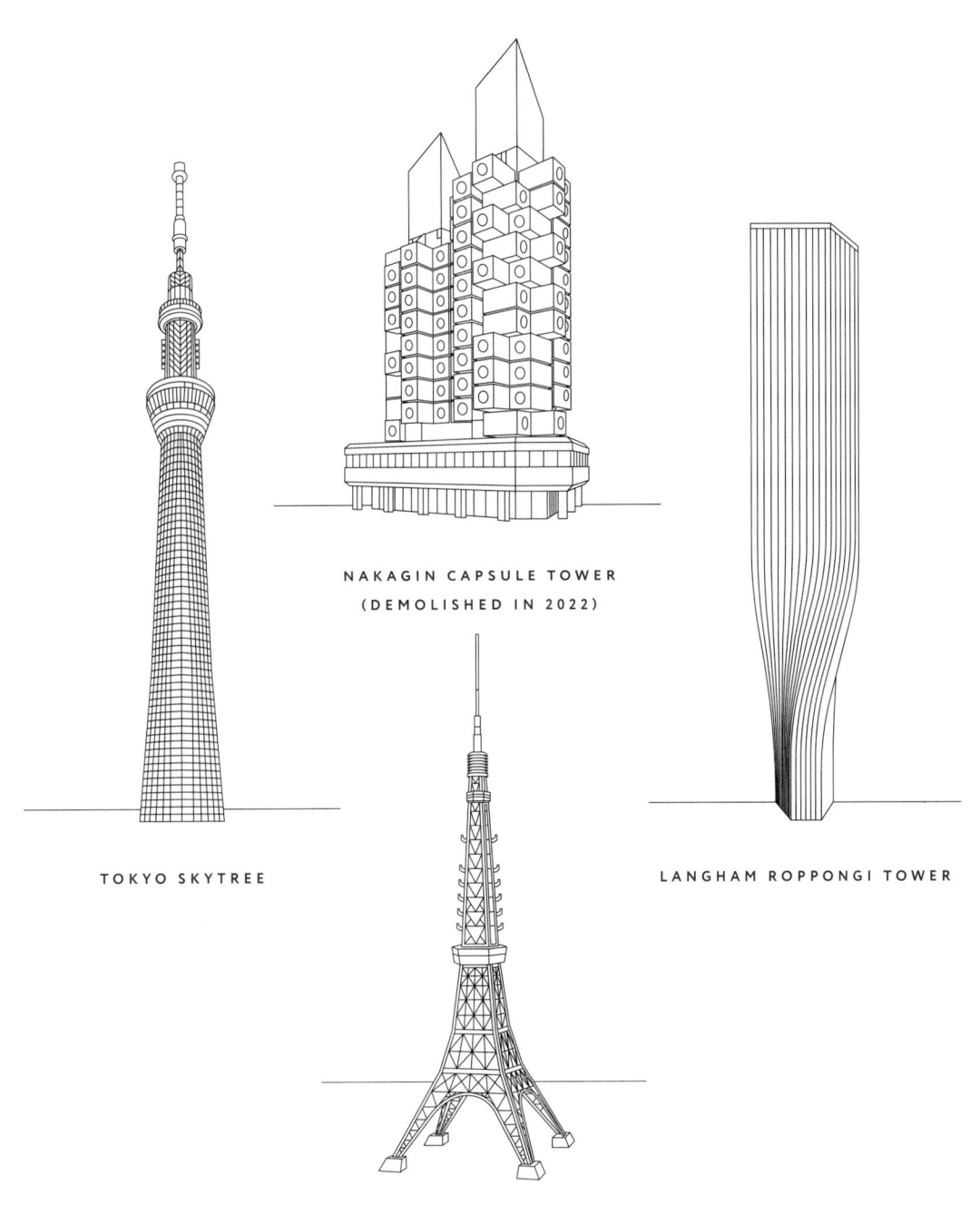

NAKAGIN CAPSULE TOWER

(DEMOLISHED IN 2022)

TOKYO SKYTREE

LANGHAM ROPPONGI TOWER

TŌKYŌ TOWER

HIGHER AND HIGHER

Seventeen of Japan's twenty-five tallest buildings are in the city of Tōkyō, including the 2,080-ft/634-m Tokyo Skytree and the 1,092-ft/333-m Tokyo Tower.

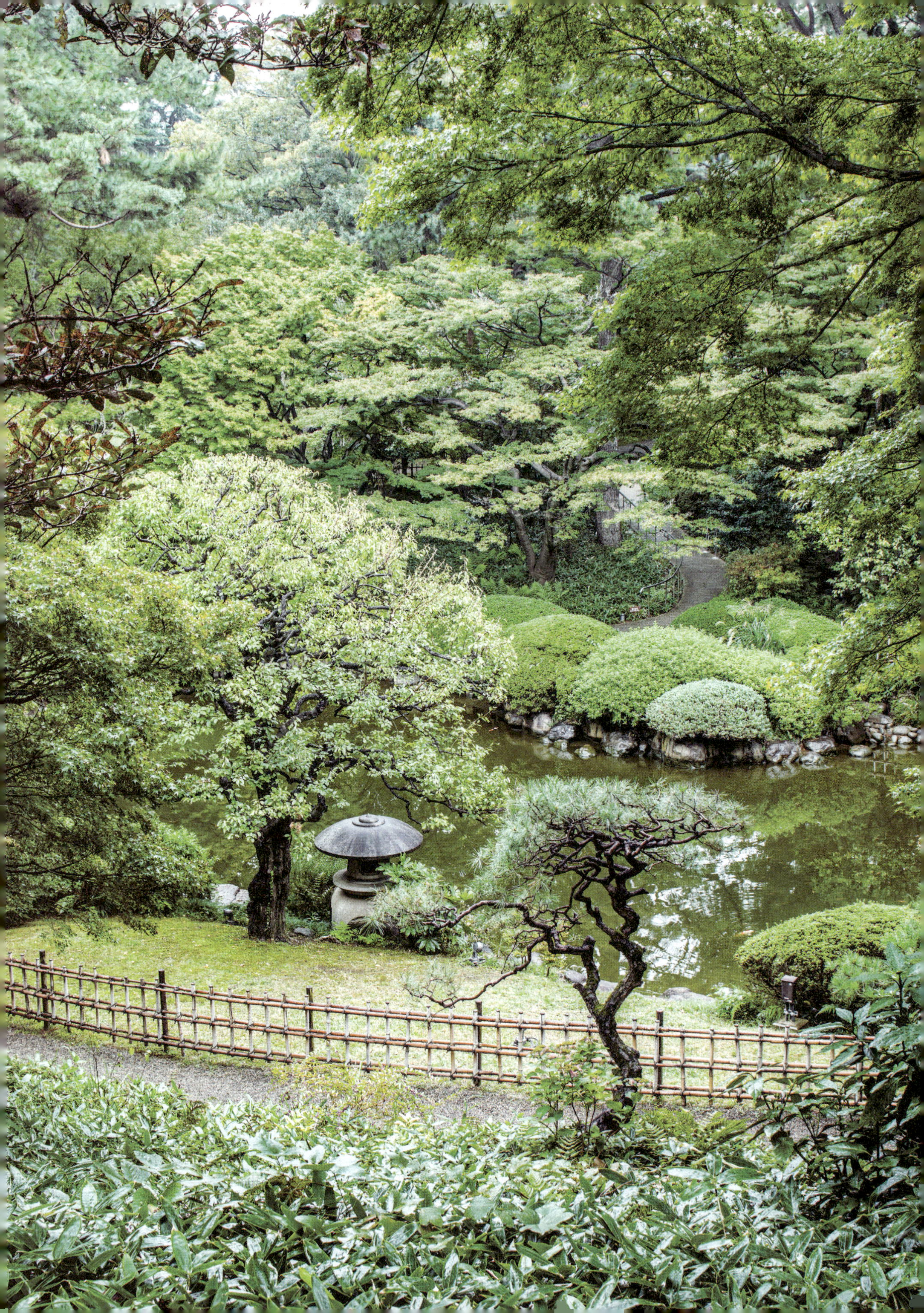

ABOVE

The Tōkyō Metropolitan Teien Art Museum was once the residence of Prince Akasaka and features some surprising architecture and Baroque touches.

OPPOSITE

The Tōkyō Metropolitan Teien Art Museum is also worth a visit for its magnificent garden, which changes dramatically with the rhythm of the seasons.

LIFESTYLE

GAJOEN TOKYO

THE "PALACE OF THE DRAGON GOD"

The majestic Hotel Gajoen Tokyo has looked out over the city since 1935, and fans of architecture and art will be fascinated by the "Palace of the Dragon God," with its walls lined with paintings and wooden sculptures and decorated with mother-of-pearl inlay that transform the place into a work of art.

Hotel Gajoen Tokyo is so astonishing and extravagant it has been nicknamed the "Palace of the Dragon God of the Shōwa era" (*Ryugujyo*). Its story began in 1928 when Rikizo Hosokawa, the owner of the site, decided to turn the original restaurant into a hotel fitted out with banqueting halls intended for various ceremonial functions. Gajoen has become the capital's most sought-after venue for society weddings, but this five-star palace, the pride of the capital, is not reserved for resident guests only.

With a history going back ninety years, Gajoen is a museum-hotel that can be visited by the public much like an exhibition. Its sixty rooms are all suites and its four restaurants are open to non-residents. There are several banqueting halls, each a work of art in its own right and different from the last. The murals recount the history of the Edo period along with tales from Japanese mythology, depicting beautiful women in monumental portraits and showcasing sculptures, paintings, and precious materials such as mother-of-pearl.

Fans of architecture and art will enjoy this unique venue, which is so much more than a luxury hotel. Gajoen is such a slice of history that it has been designated part of Tōkyō's "tangible cultural property," in particular for its Hyakudan Kaidan (wooden staircase with a hundred steps), leading to seven wonderfully sumptuous rooms of extraordinary artistic quality that are open to the public (such as the Jippo room, for example, which was named in homage to the painter Araki Jippo who decorated the space). Note the meticulously worked mother-of-pearl (*raden*, in Japanese) on the ceiling beams. The stand-out features of the Gyosho room are the two pillars supporting the ceiling, adorned with magnificent sculptures, the trunks of 300-year-old cedar trees. In the Seikou room the painter Seikō Itakura has depicted the four seasons of the year in vivid color. The famous staircase with its hundred steps in fact only has ninety-nine, symbolizing both how there is no such thing as perfection and how we should remain in a state of perpetual striving.

GARDEN

The hotel bar looks out through a bay window onto a Japanese garden where you can take a stroll. You also don't need to be a hotel guest to eat at the restaurants.

WORKS OF ART

Artists have decorated all the hotel rooms, with painted murals or sculptures carved directly into the wood of their structure.

At the end of March and the beginning of April, the canal is completely covered in cherry blossom.
Lights are installed so the spectacle of the trees in full bloom can be enjoyed in the evening.

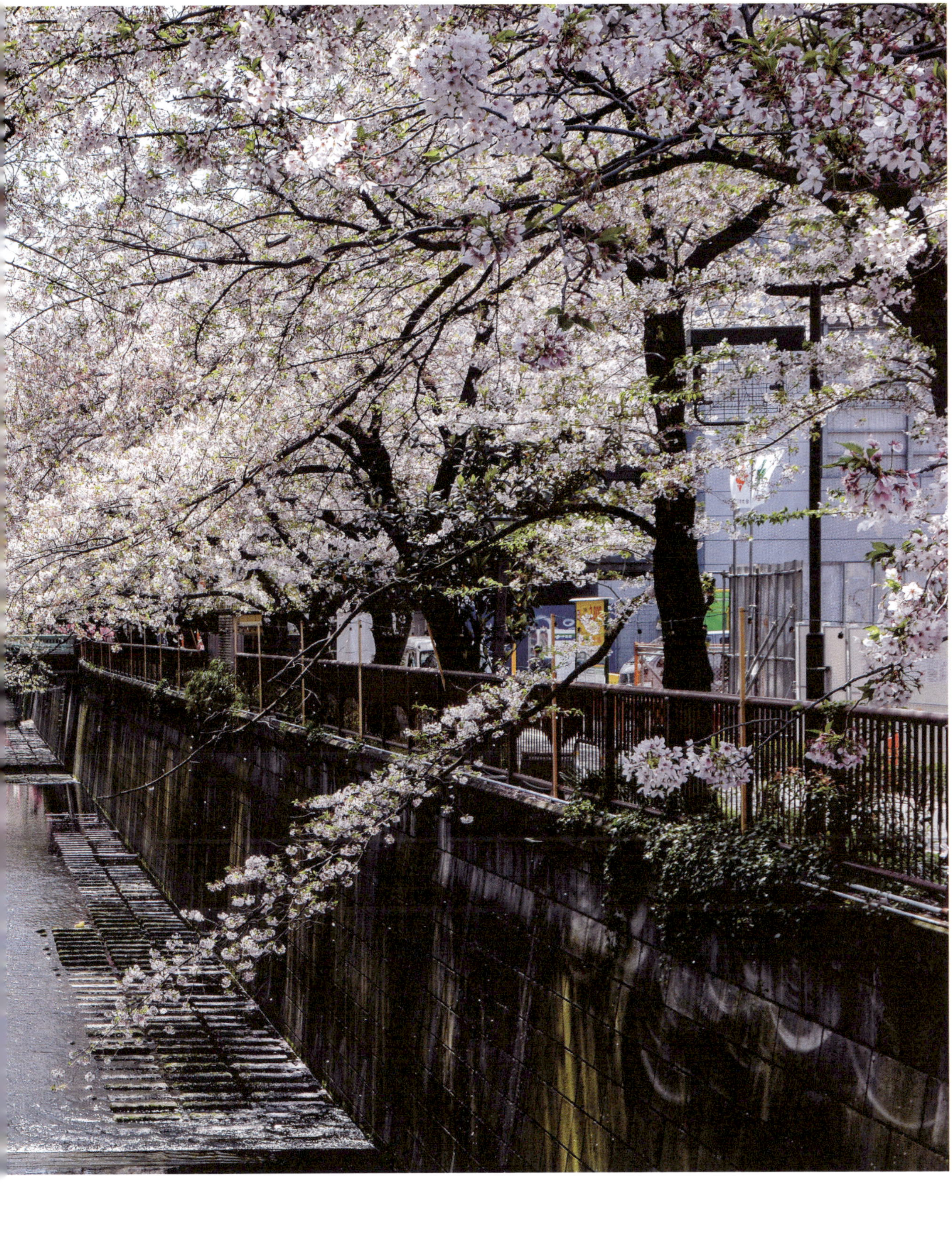

LIFESTYLE

NAKAMEGURO

AND ITS CANAL

Pleasure-seeking visitors are naturally drawn to the banks of this charming canal lined with cafés and trendy boutiques, but Nakameguro is at its most stunning in spring, when all its cherry trees suddenly explode into blossom.

Nakameguro is a popular destination for Tōkyō residents hoping to see ornamental cherry trees in full bloom (*sakura*), and the charms of the capital's iconic canal are at their height in spring, when the cherry trees burst into great clouds of white and pink petals. It is such a wonderful sight that the area is mobbed by locals during the peak weekends of blossom between the end of March and mid-April, and crowd management unfortunately overshadows peaceful contemplation. The sea of blossom that seems to hover in space over the canal is certainly worth it, however.

Traders also waste no time in setting up outdoor stands and stoves at this time of the year, serving the crowds snacks, beer, and other carbonated drinks. Blue tarpaulins are also spread out on the ground so strollers can picnic and, as evening falls, lanterns are lit so that visitors can admire the cherry trees in a different light and enjoy the cool night air.

Nakameguro's attractions are not limited to spring, however; this tranquil residential area reveals its character as soon as you leave the station and offers everything you could hope to find: trendy stores, original small cafés, bistros, and European-inspired patisseries. Foodies and lovers of subcultures and cool spots won't be disappointed. The district boasts bars that serve craft beer throughout the year, cafés that roast their own coffee, restaurants blending Japanese food with flavors from other countries, antique stores that spill out onto the street, fashion boutiques, and bookstores that line the waterfront right up to the metro station. Nakameguro is young, hip, and cool and knows it, and that is why people come here.

A ten-minute stroll takes you to Daikanyama (see page 194), another of the capital's elegant districts full of food spots, designer boutiques, and bookstores that double up as art galleries.

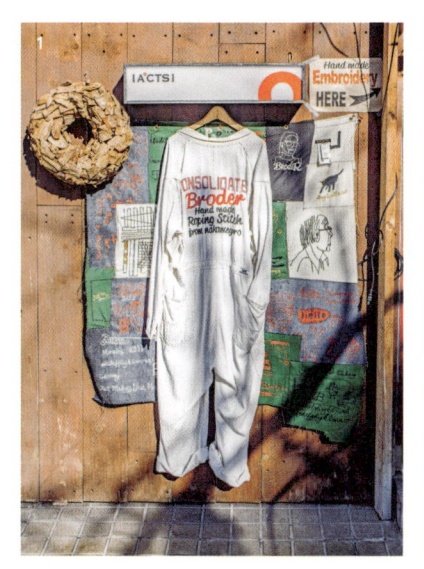

1 / VINTAGE

Tokyoites love to hunt for clothes at the retail outlets and thrift stores in this trendy district.

2 / UNIQUE

With its hair salons, bike stores, cafés, and chic pet stores, Nakameguro is a one-off.

3 / BRIDGES

There are several bridges over the canal, including Nakano-bashi, which offers a superb vantage point when the trees are in blossom.

4 / CAFÉS

The canal is lined with boutiques and cafés that include the famous Starbucks Reserve Roastery designed by Kengo Kuma.

5 / BOUTIQUES

Crockery, tea utensils, antiques: Nakameguro has a vast array of useful and ornamental items on sale.

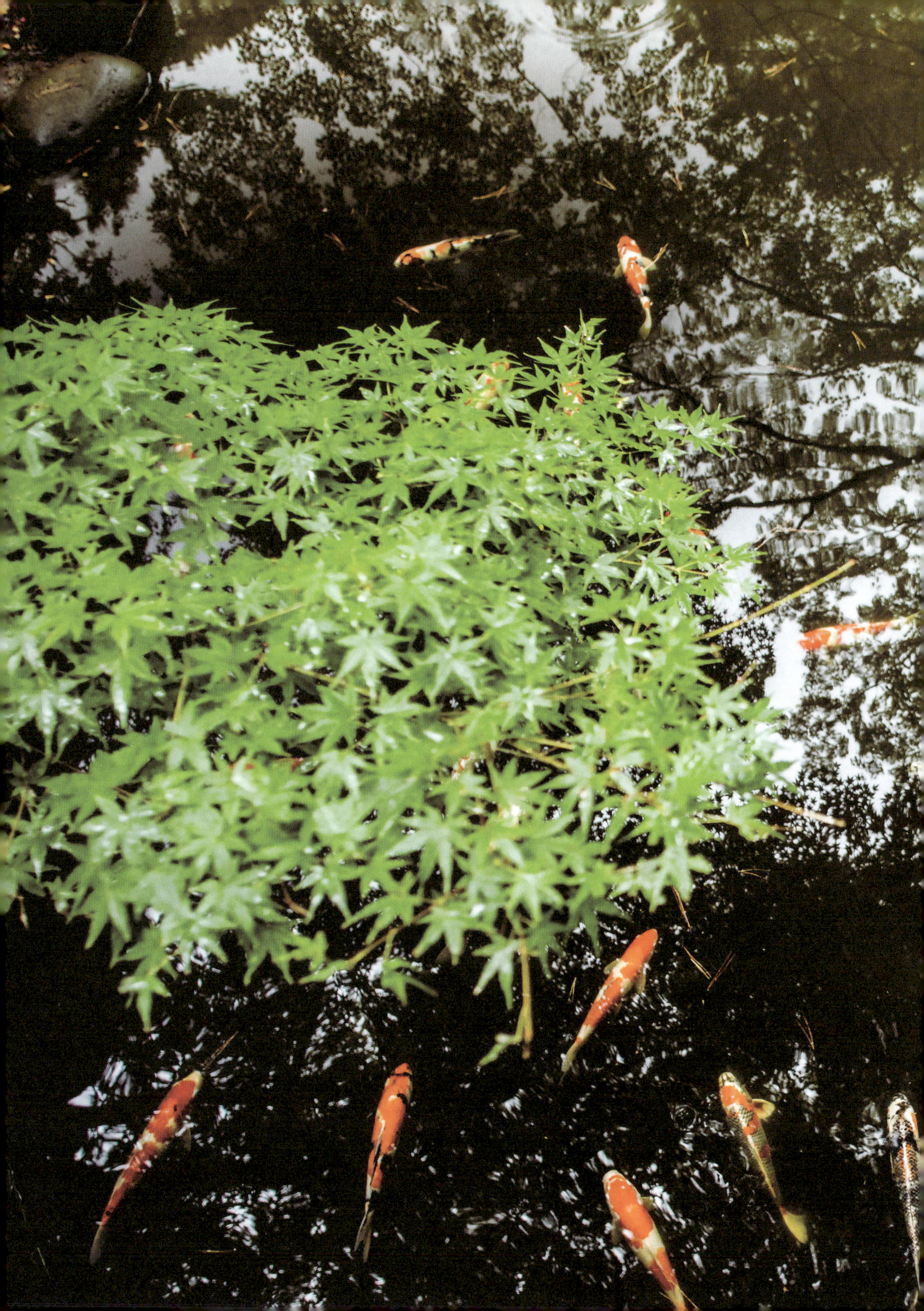

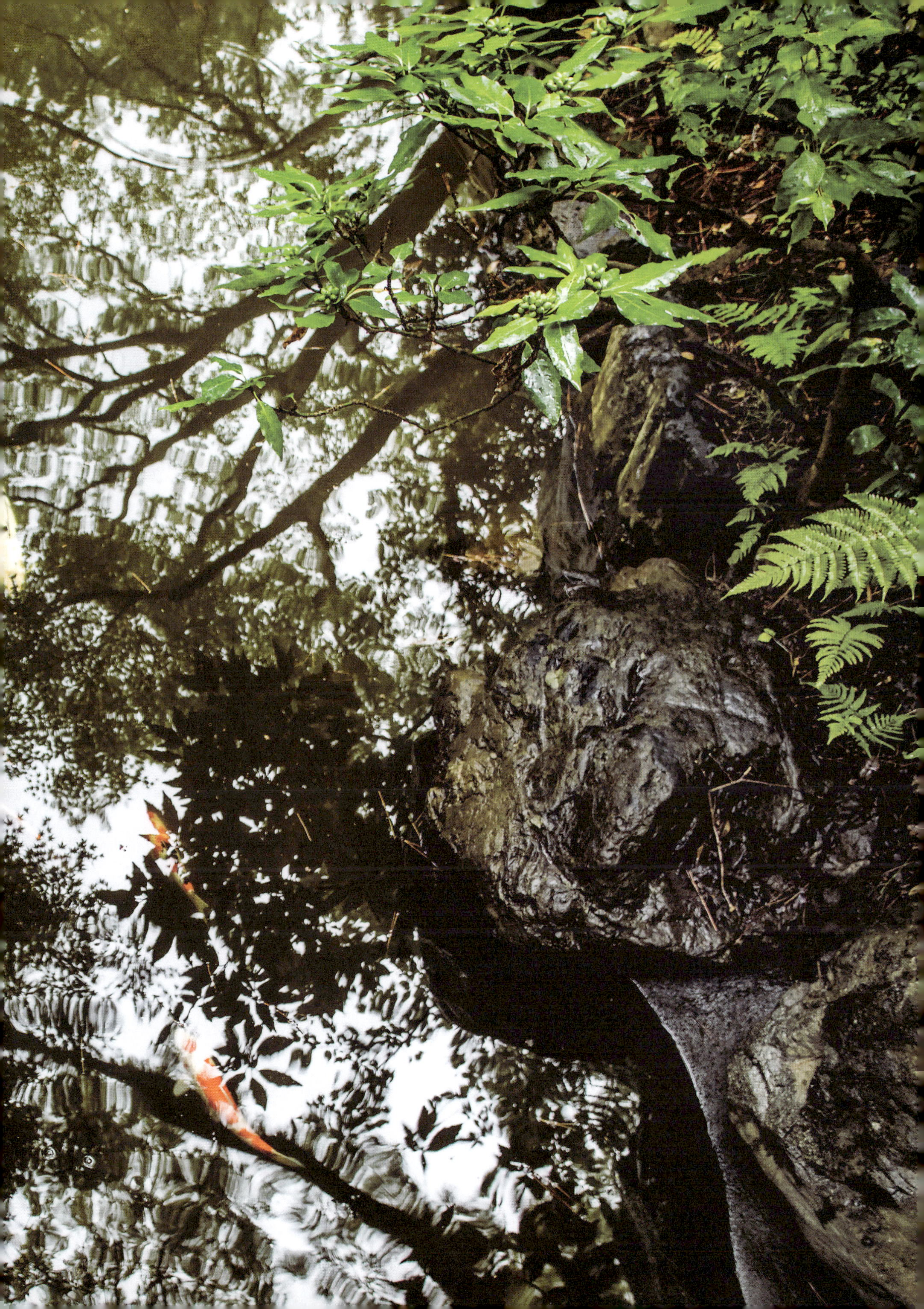

Tōkyō | MEGURO

LIFESTYLE

JIYŪGAOKA LITTLE EUROPE

CHIC

Tokyoites love the exotic and chic aspects of the sophisticated district of Jiyūgaoka ("Liberty Hill").

LA DOLCE VITA

You don't need to go to Venice to enjoy canals and gondolas; everything you need can be found at La Vita in Jiyūgaoka.

BOOKS, BOOKS, BOOKS

The bookstores and second-hand booksellers on Marie-Claire Promenade are reminiscent of Paris.

INFLUENCES

The district's many references to the West in its architecture have earned it the nickname "Little Europe."

HISTORY

The Kosoan house, which dates from the Taisho era (1912–1926), is open to the public and you can even take part in a tea ceremony.

DESIGNERS

The many homeware stores offer unique designer items.

URBAN DEVELOPMENT

The district took on a decidedly European flavor in the 1970s.

UNUSUAL

Jiyūgaoka is chic but not snobbish, a perfect destination off the beaten track.

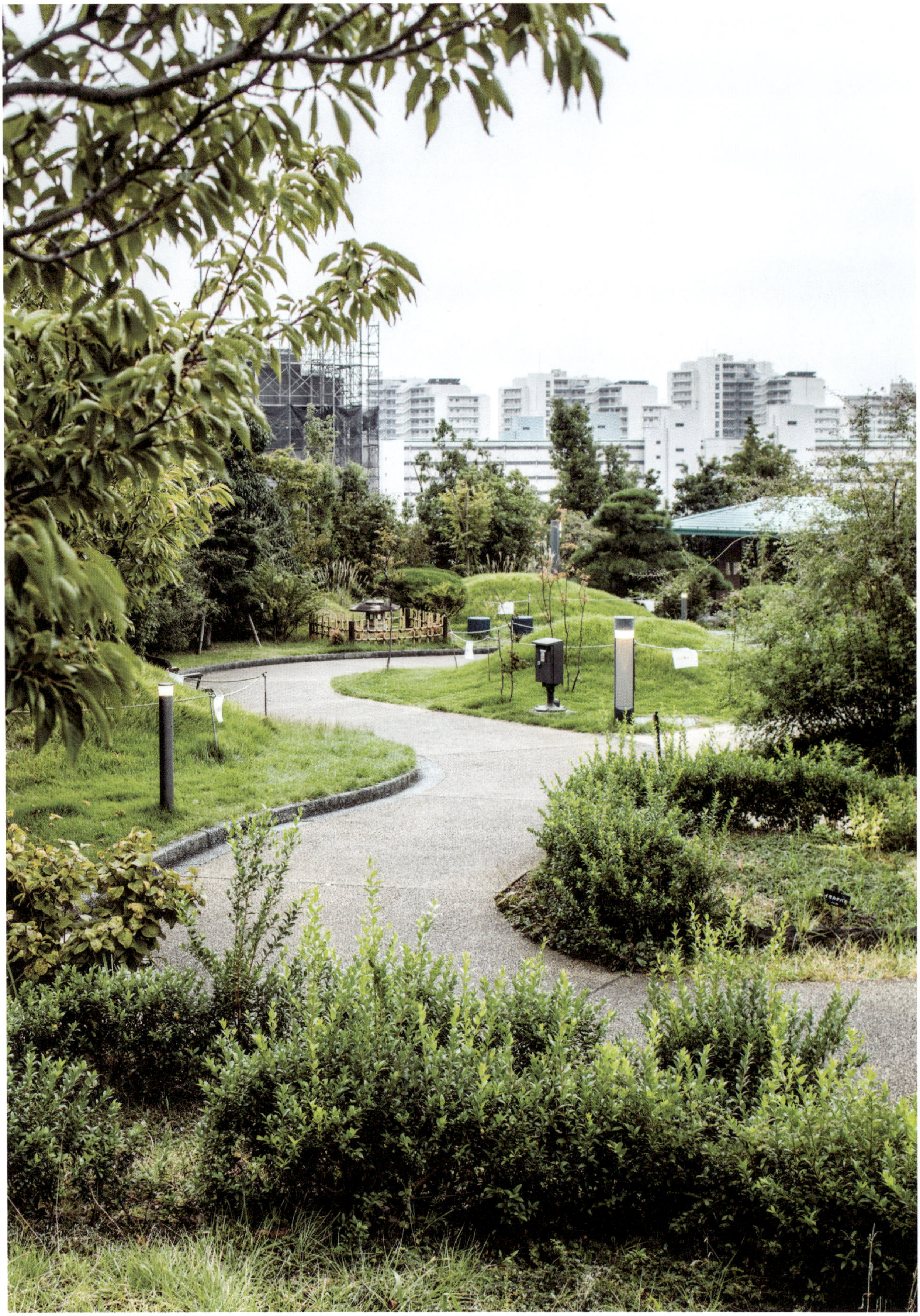

ABOVE

You can always spot Tōkyō postal workers by their red mopeds.

OPPOSITE

Meguro Sky Garden is a 1¾-acre (7,000-m²) rooftop promenade, built to hide the junction of two expressways.

P.218-219

Carp in the garden of the Tōkyō Metropolitan Teien Art Museum.

224 Tōkyō | MEGURO

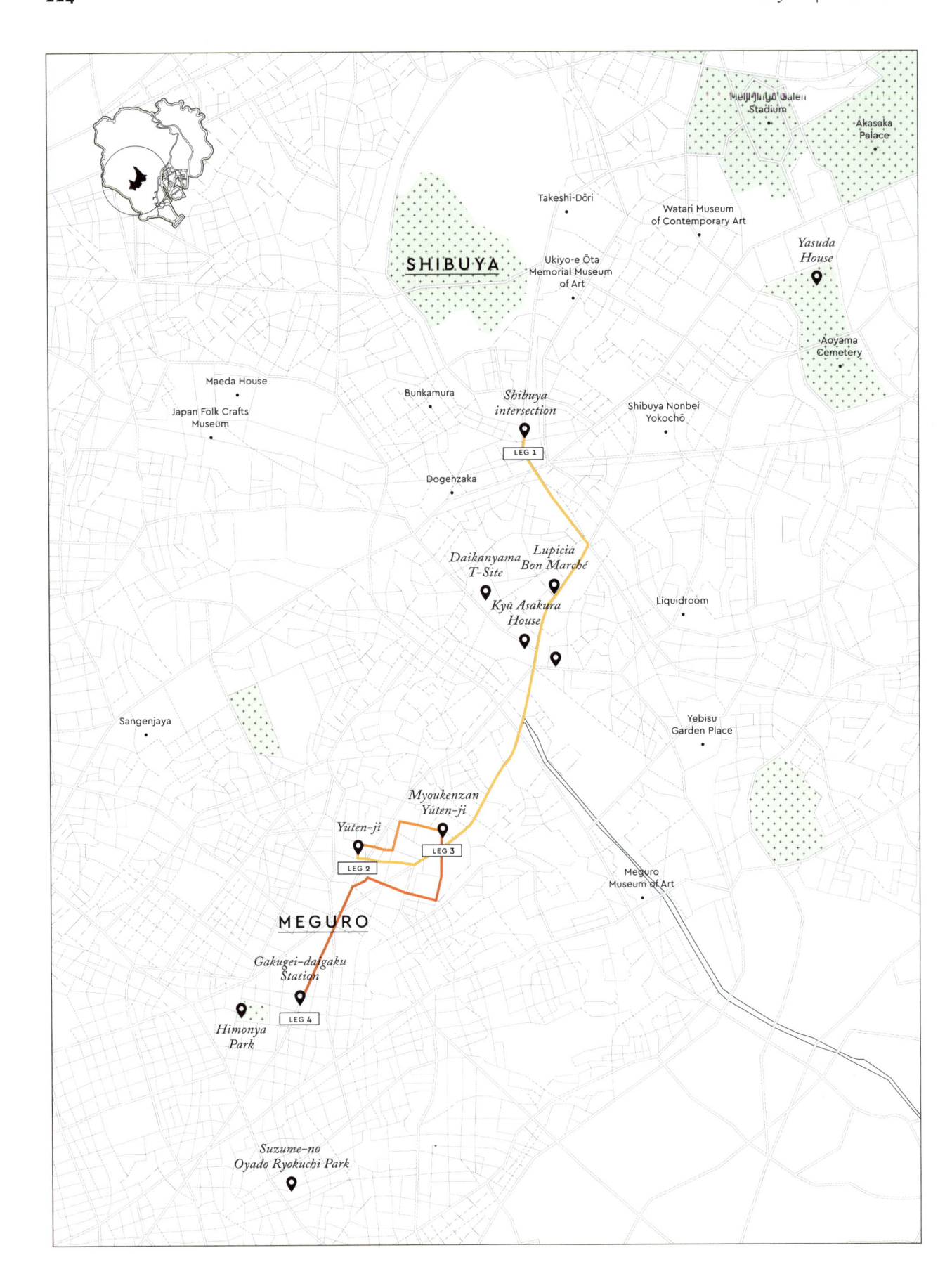

WALKING TOUR

YUTEN-JI TEMPLE AND *SHOUTENGAI*

Yūten-ji, a small and quiet district that shows a very different side to the capital, lies just six minutes' train ride from bustling Shibuya. Yūten-ji and its Buddhist temple are like a tiny village lost in the heart of the megacity.

LEG 1: FROM SHIBUYA TO YŪTEN-JI

It's hard to imagine that this is so close to the hustle and bustle of Shibuya (a forty-minute stroll away) as the atmosphere of Yūten-ji is so different. Make your way over the famous pedestrian crosswalk in Shibuya and leave the frenetic young people and night owls behind as you stroll slowly to Daikanyama; Yūten-ji is just a few paces away. It's all about the simple, fuss-free life here, and there are more bikes than cars.

LEG 2: A VINTAGE SHOPPING SPREE IN YŪTEN-JI

Yūten-ji has a more local feel and seems more rooted in the day-to-day life of the district's residents. Come here to enjoy a simple lunch of rice, fish, and miso soup. In the afternoon, try some *an-mitsu*, a traditional dessert made of red bean paste, washed down with green tea. Stroll down the narrow shopping streets (*shoutengai* in Japanese) and it will feel like time has stood still in the agreeably old-fashioned stores. There are no signs of the garish boutiques of Ebisu and Daikanyama; you are more likely to rummage through crockery or chance upon a vintage kimono worn for generations.

LEG 3: EXPLORING THE MYOUKENZAN YŪTEN-JI

People also come to Yūten-ji because of Myoukenzan Yūten-ji, its Buddhist temple, which was built in 1723 and has remained particularly well preserved, even surviving the bombing during the Second World War. The temple boasts 300 years of history and is dedicated to the Jōdo (Pure Land) school of Buddhism. There are several exceptional rooms to explore, such as the Jizodo hall which pays homage to Jizo Bodhisattva, or the *shorondo* (belltower), built in 1729 and donated by Teneiin, the widow of Tokugawa Ienou, the sixth shōgun. Nowadays, the bell is rung at six every morning and on New Year's Eve, when crowds gather to celebrate the incoming year. The temple organizes its traditional big summer festival in mid-July and this is particularly popular with the locals, who don a *yukata*, a light, cotton version of a kimono, and gather to watch the music and dancing and sample the food from stalls set up for the occasion.

LEG 4: TAKE A BREAK IN NATURE AT GAKUGEI-DAIGAKU

If you feel the need to get back to nature, continue to the next station, just fifteen minutes' walk away. Gakugei-daigaku (known as Gakudai to its fans) is a great spot to enjoy a *bentō* box, a packed lunch you can buy in advance from one of the stores in Yūten-ji or in Suzume-no Oyado Ryokuchi park, which also has a bamboo grove that is 200 years old. Parents of young children will be glad to learn that Himonya Park, which is also just around the corner, has pony rides, playgrounds, and boats you can rent to get about on the lake. As evening falls, there are bars and other *izakaya* to enjoy at prices that are significantly lower than those of Shibuya or Nakameguro.

国会正門前
The National Diet Main Gate

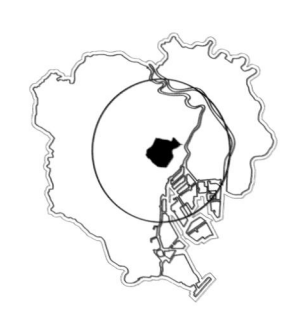

THE CRADLE OF TŌKYŌ

CHIYODA

千代田区

Chiyoda is a district for trade and official business, with the fewest inhabitants at night but accommodating more than 900,000 employees during the day. It was also here that Tōkyō (or Edo, as it was known back then) first began.

P.226

The National Diet, the Japanese parliament, is open to the public (booking required) with English-speaking guides.

OPPOSITE

Hibiya Park, the green lung of this built-up area, changes color with the seasons.

Chiyoda ("field of a thousand generations") is the political heart of Tōkyō. Its name comes from Chiyoda castle (also known as Edo castle), once located on the site of the current Imperial Palace. Its geography also reflects the complexity of the Japanese capital in the sense that it symbolizes the invisible border separating Yamanote (the "upper town") from Shitamachi (the "lower town"). Kanda district, home to Kanda Myōjin temple, is the heart of Shitamachi, Tōkyō's true birthplace.

Chiyoda is not only the location of the imperial seat but also home to most government buildings, including the National Diet (Japanese parliament), many ministries, the official residence of the prime minister, and the Supreme Court, along with fifteen or so embassies. To the east, you will also find flamboyant Tōkyō Station, instantly recognizable for its unique architecture in red brick. To the south, beyond the business district of Yurakuchō and Hibiya Park, where a sea of *salarymen*, Japanese executives, moves in an eternal ebb and flow, Minato special ward is home to the Tōkyō Tower, Nezu Museum, and the French embassy. There are more than 36,000 companies based in Chiyoda, with nearly 900,000 employees.

Chiyoda loves to reach for the sky and a survey carried out in 2001 established that 6,572 of the buildings in the area had four floors or more. With so many institutions and corporate offices, it comes as little surprise that Chiyoda is the least populated of Tōkyō's twenty-three wards. In addition to its size and official aspects, Chiyoda is also a major cultural center, with its traditional theaters (Noh, kabuki) and art museums complemented by the extravagance of Akihabara district, a favorite haunt of video game, manga, and IT hardware enthusiasts.

The Imperial Palace has always been a symbolic place for visitors to the capital. Although the building itself is open to the public only by appointment with the imperial office, the three gardens, including Kitanomaru-kōen with its various museums, are open all year round and you can explore a different side to the area here. A stroll is also a pleasant way to soak up its unique and particular atmosphere. If you are very lucky, you will be there on one of the two occasions the Imperial Palace opens its doors (January 2, when the emperor presents his good wishes to the people, and February 23, his birthday). When the cherry trees are in blossom, the Imperial Palace is swathed in thousands of pink petals, an incredible spectacle.

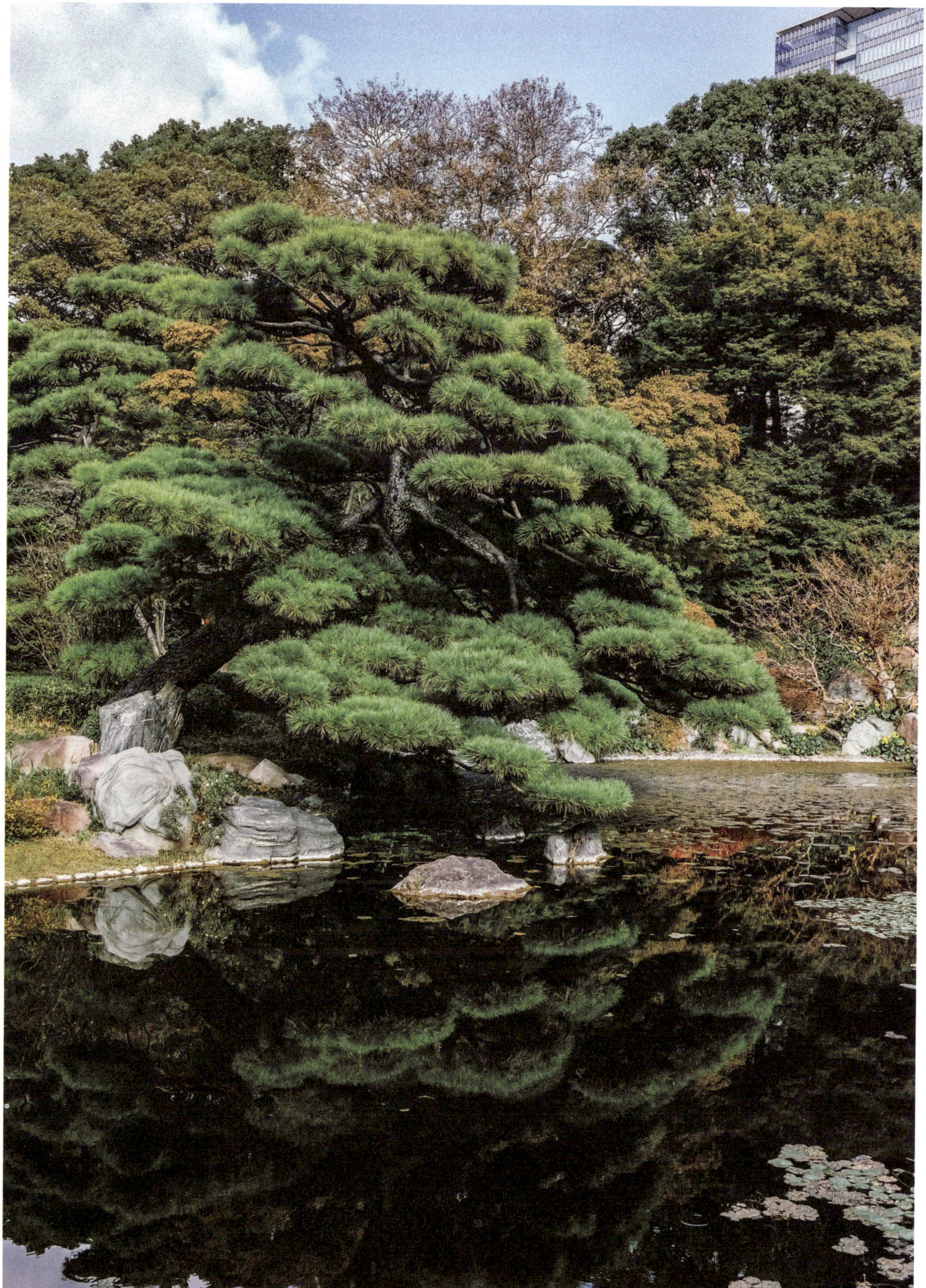

CHIYODA

THE ESSENTIALS

TŌKYŌ STATION

Tōkyō Station was built in 1914 and is one of the largest in the country (3,000 trains daily).
Its red-brick façade has become a symbol of the city.

56

VISITING THE NATIONAL DIET

The National Diet is the Japanese parliament and is open to the public several times a week (book in advance).

57

SCIENCE MUSEUM

The Science Museum, located northwest of the Imperial Palace in Kitanomaru Park, offers fun and education. Its director was awarded the Nobel Prize for chemistry in 2001.

58

IMPERIAL PALACE

The Imperial Palace is not open to the public except on special occasions. It is a wonderful sight when the cherry trees are in blossom.

59

YASUKUNI SHRINE

Yasukuni, which turned 150 in 2019, is renowned for its Mitama festival, during which 30,000 lanterns are on display. The shrine has attracted some controversy as its 2.5 million *kami* also include deified war criminals.

60

JIMBŌCHŌ

Jimbōchō is a mecca for bookworms, with some 200 bookstores and antiquarian sellers based in the district benefiting from close proximity to several universities.

61

NATIONAL THEATER OF JAPAN

The National Theater of Japan is located southwest of the Imperial Palace gardens. Kabuki performances can be watched in various languages using audio guides.

The unique red bricks of Tōkyō Station in the heart of the Marunouchi district are instantly recognizable and reminiscent of Amsterdam Centraal Station.

EXCURSION

KANDA-MYŌJIN

A SHRINE THAT HAS BEEN REBUILT SEVERAL TIMES

The Shinto shrine at Kanda-Myōjin is 1,300 years old and a precious remnant of historic Tōkyō. Hidden away in a highly developed area, it is a destination for locals seeking to recharge their batteries or purchase a protective amulet.

Kanda-Myōjin shrine was founded in 730 CE and has lived several lives already; after being relocated in 1603 to allow the expansion of Edo castle, it moved to its current location in 1616. Having suffered several fires and earthquakes, in particular the devastating upheaval of 1923, it has been rebuilt several times and the current concrete structure dates from 1934. The original Kanda Myōjin shrine was erected in Shibasaki, a village that has since been subsumed into the Japanese capital. With Akihabara (a district for electronics freaks) just a stone's throw away, it's difficult to imagine these rural roots when you visit today.

Kanda-Myōjin has retained an atmosphere of particular calm and tranquility despite its highly urbanized surroundings, and locals would come here to pray to three divinities (*kami*): Daikokuten, the god of good harvests and marriage, Ebisu, the god of fishermen, trade, and business (these are two of the Seven Lucky Gods), and Taira Masakado, a tenth-century feudal lord who had been elevated to the status of a demi-god. The latter was stripped of his divinity during the Meiji Restoration (1868) as he had led a controversial insurrection against the government in power during his lifetime, and the spirit of this fallen god is said to have wandered the precincts of the shrine ever since.

Kanda Myōjin is also known throughout Japan for the major public festival it has organized since the seventeenth century, one of the three largest celebrations in the capital. The Kanda Matsuri festival, held in mid-May on alternate years, is an opportunity to see a massive parade of dancers, floats, musicians, and nearly 200 *mikoshi* (altars) that are carried through the assembled throng. Interestingly, the shrine also owes its popularity to its large range of talismans and other amulets, which draws crowds of Tokyoites wanting to attract good fortune to their homes (especially at New Year). In 2018, a very modern building where shows can be performed was unveiled in the shrine, along with several gift shops honoring the Edo period of which it is a worthy heir.

PRAYERS

Small lanterns are lit to pay homage to the dead. Cremation is compulsory in Tōkyō and the rate throughout the country is close to a hundred percent.

GOOD LUCK CHARM

People pray in the shrines and place five-yen coins, which are considered lucky charms, in the *saisen-bako* (offering box).

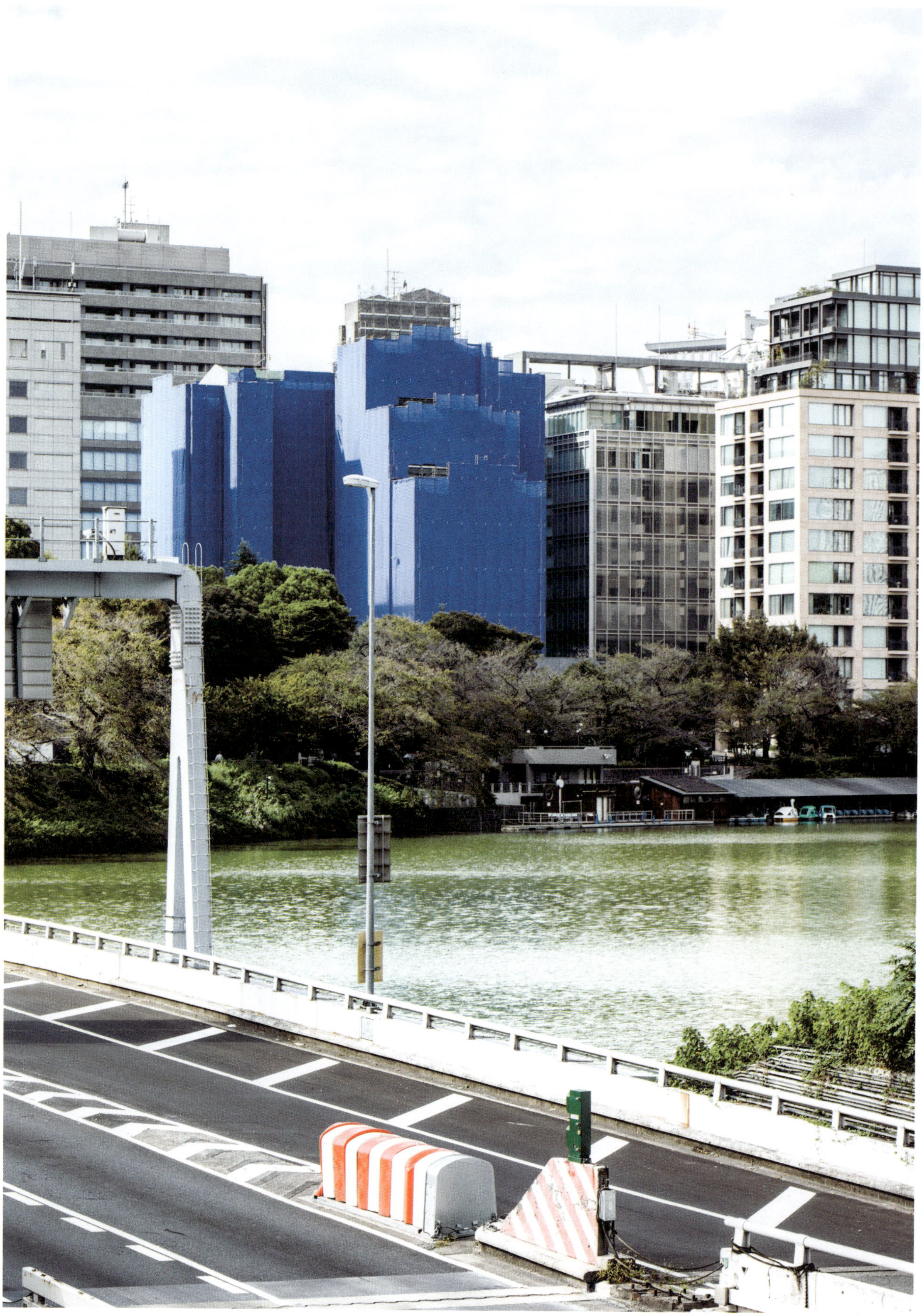

ABOVE

This area is the city's political center, with a hub of official buildings and government offices.

OPPOSITE

Modern bridges now span the Imperial Palace moat, as here near the Chidorigafuchi walkway.

P.238-239

Chiyoda has more businesses and employees than residents.

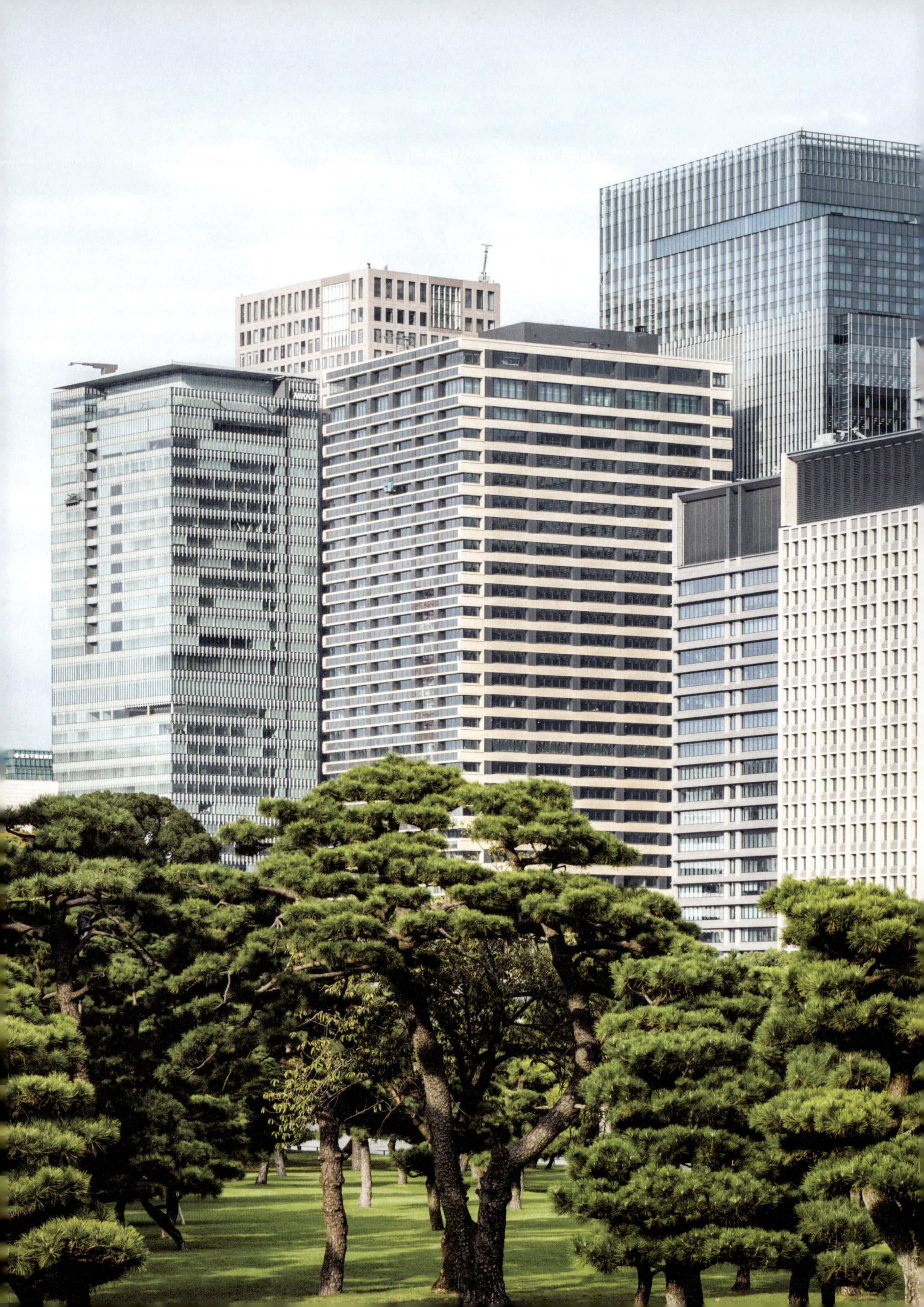

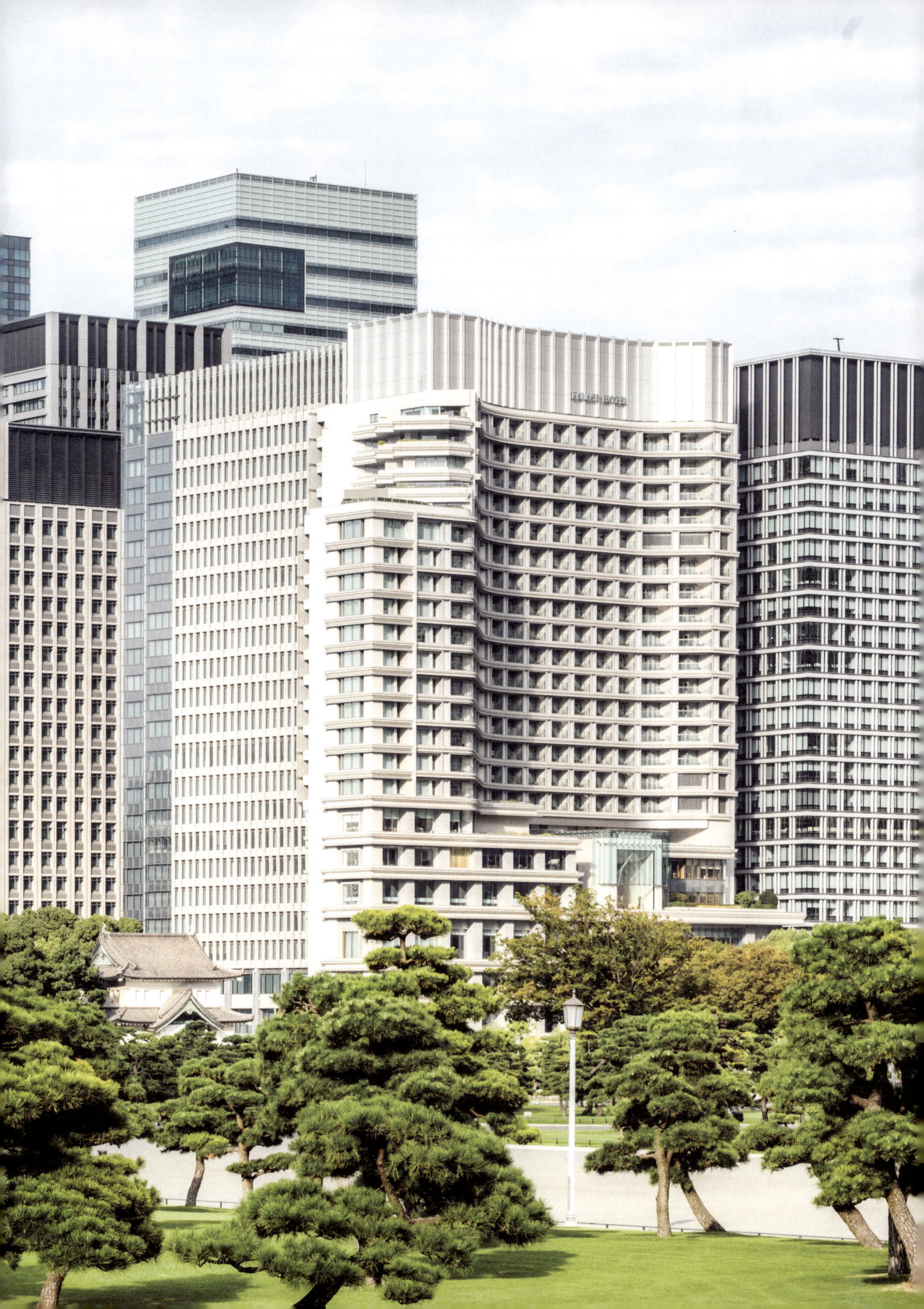

PORTRAIT

SHOUKEI MATSUMOTO

THE MONK WHO LAUNCHED THE "WAY OF CLEANING"

Shoukei Matsumoto, a Buddhist monk at Tōkyō's Kōmyō-ji temple, is known throughout Japan as the author of books dedicated to the "way of cleaning." In Buddhist belief, cleaning is an act of purification.

"According to Buddhist principles and from a spiritual perspective, cleaning your house has always been of great significance in Japan," the monk Shoukei Matsumoto reminds us. "It is not just about removing dust, it also involves bringing order to your inner life." Shoukei Matsumoto is in his forties and a Hongan-ji monk, one of the schools of Buddhism known as "Pure Land." He entered Kōmyō-ji as a twenty-three-year-old philosophy graduate and is now married with two children. Head shaved and wearing the traditional blue *samue*, he rises daily at dawn, with each morning beginning the same way, with cleaning and tidying. For him, this involves "relearning how to live in the frenzy of the present, just as monks do. Happiness is in the moment," he confides.

His method, known as *osojidō*, the "way of cleaning," has been outlined in books sold in their thousands up and down the archipelago, with translations appearing in English and in more than fifteen languages. In Japan, "Learning how to clean is done in groups from the earliest age," he explains; schoolchildren are regularly asked to clean their classrooms together at the end of a lesson. "The Japanese have long known that cleaning is much more than a thankless chore; removing dirt involves bringing order to one's inner life and cleaning is in itself an important Buddhist purification ritual and one of the paths to Enlightenment. Sharing household chores in the morning is a very important part of leading an ascetic life—dusting equates to purifying the heart of its passions and removing the attachments that encumber us."

Shoukei Matsumoto took the idea a step farther by organizing twice monthly cleaning sessions in his temple in the heart of the Kamiyachō business district; anyone can drop by and apply the monk's principles in practice before heading off to work. Some people find that cleaning the temple "is also a way of breaking through their loneliness." Other Buddhist monks from Kyūshū to Hokkaidō, from Nara and Ōsaka to Nagoya, have been inspired by *osojidō* and are organizing their own "temple mornings." For some, it is a place to talk that they can find nowhere else.

1 / CLEANING AND MEDITATION

Shoukei Matsumoto opens his temple to the public once or twice a month to initiate the purification of his spirit with "the path of cleaning."

2 / CONTEMPLATION

A large cemetery looks out over Kōmyō-ji temple in the heart of Toranomon district.

3 / PURIFICATION

Each participant can choose the task they wish to carry out during the cleaning sessions.

4 / COMMUNITY

For Buddhist monks, cleaning the temple together in the morning is an essential part of monastic life.

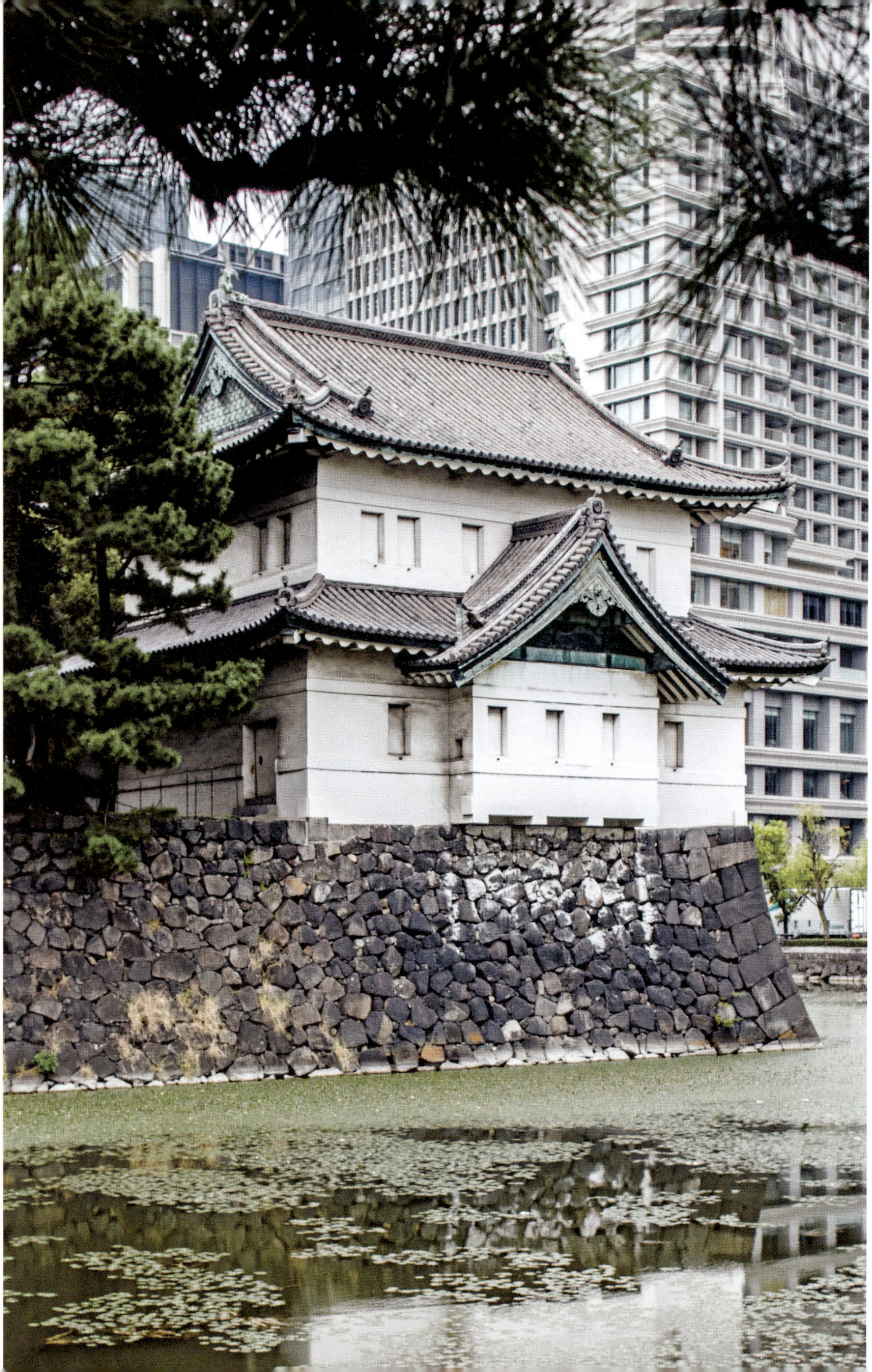

ABOVE

Security is particularly important in this part of the city, with its concentration of government offices and ministries.

OPPOSITE

Tōkyō's Imperial Palace was built on the former site of Edo castle and is surrounded by a moat and thick walls.

*Work gives way to fun in the hustle and bustle of Akihabara, just to the north of Chiyoda,
a favorite destination for* otaku *(fans) of computers, video games, and anime.*

ATION
PRIZE OUT
PRIZE OUT
両替機
COIN CHANGER
両替
りょうがえ
COIN CHANGER
GET!!
GAME

FREE
愛客旺
ラムタラ
メディアワールド
アキバ
在庫量No1
Blu-ray
DVD
PC-GAME
フィギュア
圧倒的な品ぞろえ。新しい何かを見つけよう
SEGA
SEGA
SEGA
SEGA
SEGA
SEGA
SEGA 2号
万世橋
中央通り
Chuo-dori Ave.
フレスカ
B1

ABOVE

Collectors will find figurines and other items depicting their favorite characters in Akihabara's stores.

OPPOSITE

Garish signs are appearing on more and more buildings as amusement arcades join the sex-toy stores and duty-free outlets.

DEEP DIVE

CLIMATE

AND NATURAL CATASTROPHE

Surrounded by the Sea of Japan to the west and the Pacific Ocean to the east, the archipelago of Japan is volcanic and very mountainous. It has always had a close relationship with a natural world that can be both beautiful and deadly.

The Japanese climate varies widely between Hokkaidō and Okinawa. The archipelago is so stretched out that its northernmost reaches are in the same latitudes as Canada while the south is level with Cuba. The north island of Hokkaidō and northern Honshū enjoy hot summers with long, cold, snowy winters, while the Ryūkyū islands to the south have a tropical climate. with temperatures that never drop below 50 degrees Fahrenheit (10 degrees Celsius). Tōkyō has a damp, subtropical climate, benefiting from relatively mild winters with little or no snow but experiencing hot summers (77–86 degrees Fahrenheit/25–30 degrees Celsius), with heatwaves approaching 104 degrees Fahrenheit (40 degrees Celsius) and great humidity. Inhospitable terrain and the harshness of the climate in certain regions have prompted the population to group in other areas where conditions are more clement.

Japan lies at the junction of several overlapping tectonic plates on the Pacific Ring of Fire and is exposed to a number of natural hazards (volcanic eruptions, landslides, earthquakes, and tsunamis). The Japanese population has long since learned to live with these phenomena and alert exercises are organized regularly.

One thing the entire country has in common is the rain, of which there is no shortage, and Japan is one of the wettest countries in the temperate zone. Typhoons form in the South Pacific throughout the year, moving across the ocean before hitting the archipelago, and some thirty or so make landfall every year.

There are numerous flood plains in Tōkyō and the heavy rains that fall in the city in June and September can sometimes spell disaster. To protect the area, the municipal authorities constructed the "G-Cans" between 1993 and 2006; known as *shutoken gaikaku hōsuiro* in Japanese ("metropolitan area outer underground discharge channel"), it is the largest flood-prevention system in the world, comprising five concrete containment silos 203 ft (62 m) deep and 105 ft (32 m) across, 4 miles (6.4 km) of tunnels more than 33 ft (10 m) in diameter, and an immense reservoir (the "underground temple"). This gigantic, subterranean basin excavated beside the Edo River is open to the public during the dry season. There are fifty-nine pillars, each weighing 550 tons (500 tonnes), and the whole structure is 580 ft (177m) long, 256 ft (78 m) wide, and 60 ft (18 m) deep. It has seen use more than a hundred times in the last decade.

THE GEOLOGY OF JAPAN

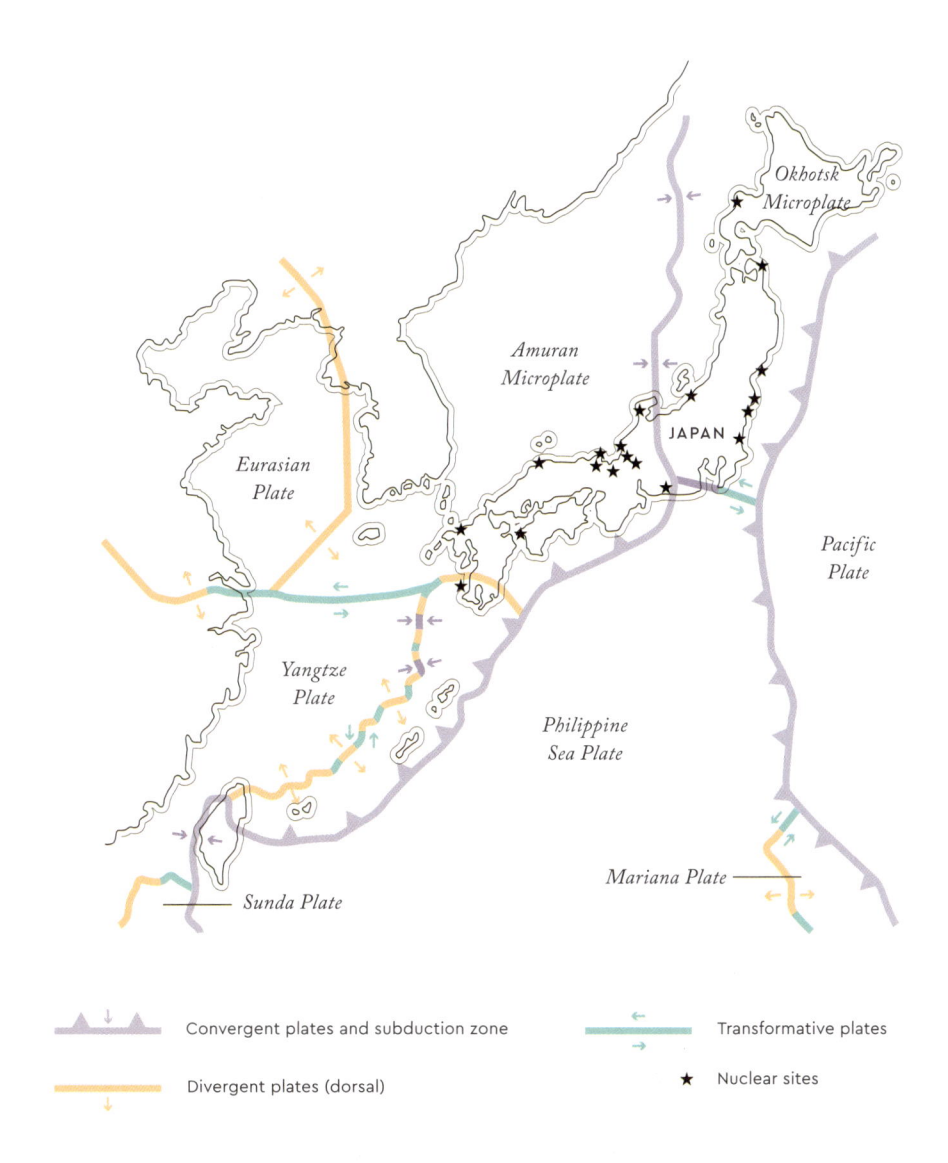

Okhotsk Microplate

Amuran Microplate

JAPAN

Eurasian Plate

Pacific Plate

Yangtze Plate

Philippine Sea Plate

Mariana Plate

Sunda Plate

— Convergent plates and subduction zone
— Divergent plates (dorsal)
— Transformative plates
★ Nuclear sites

A MAJOR INTERSECTION OF TECTONIC PLATES

Japan lies at the junction of several tectonic plates and there are earth tremors of differing magnitudes every day, ranging from an imperceptible shiver to devastating earthquakes, as was the case on March 11, 2011, when the force of the upheaval registered as 9.1 on the Richter scale! An average of 1,500 seismic events are recorded in the country every year.

ARCHITECTURE
THE BUSINESS DISTRICT

YURAKUCHŌ

The fourteen floors of the Tokyo International Forum house both a conference venue and an arts center, the largest in the city. The boat-shaped building was designed by architect Rafael Vinoly in 1996.

THE RHYTHM OF THE YAMANOTE

Yurakuchō Station has been in service since 1910 and the city is unimaginable without it.

HIBIYA KOEN

Hibiya's Park is surrounded by skyscrapers.

BUSINESS

Marunouchi-Otemachi and Yurakuchō are home to the headquarters of the eighty-three biggest companies in Japan.

LUNCH AL FRESCO

Hibiya Park is an ideal natural setting for a spot of lunch away from the office.

ALLEYWAYS

Individual buildings and terraces of houses are connected by very narrow alleyways known as *rōji* in Japanese.

SPICK AND SPAN

Tōkyō is a very clean, almost immaculate, city. Skyscraper windows are spruced up very regularly, as here on the Tokyo Skytree.

UNDER THE RAILS

Yurakuchō is famed for its *gadō-shita*, *yakitori* and *gyoza* restaurants located beneath the tracks.

CULTURE

The Tokyo International Forum hosts gigs, sporting fixtures, and artistic events throughout the year.

ABOVE

Jimbōchō boasts nearly 200 bookstores selling every possible genre from manga to novels, in editions that are limited and sometimes quite expensive.

OPPOSITE

There are several luxury hotels, including the Imperial Hotel and the Peninsula, in Hibiya district, next 0to Yurakuchō. Its narrow, busy streets are crammed with izakaya (Japanese pubs) where executives come to relax after work.

24時間
日本の祭典
一軒まるごと！
日比谷産直飲食街
都久志屋
九州
鶏
北海道
牛
牧場
嘉
小澤
牛酒場
牛〇本店
創業明治26年(1893)
魚〇本店
貝
消火栓
自転車を除く
一方通行
高圧ガス
SAPPORO
22-50

254 | *Tōkyō* | CHIYODA

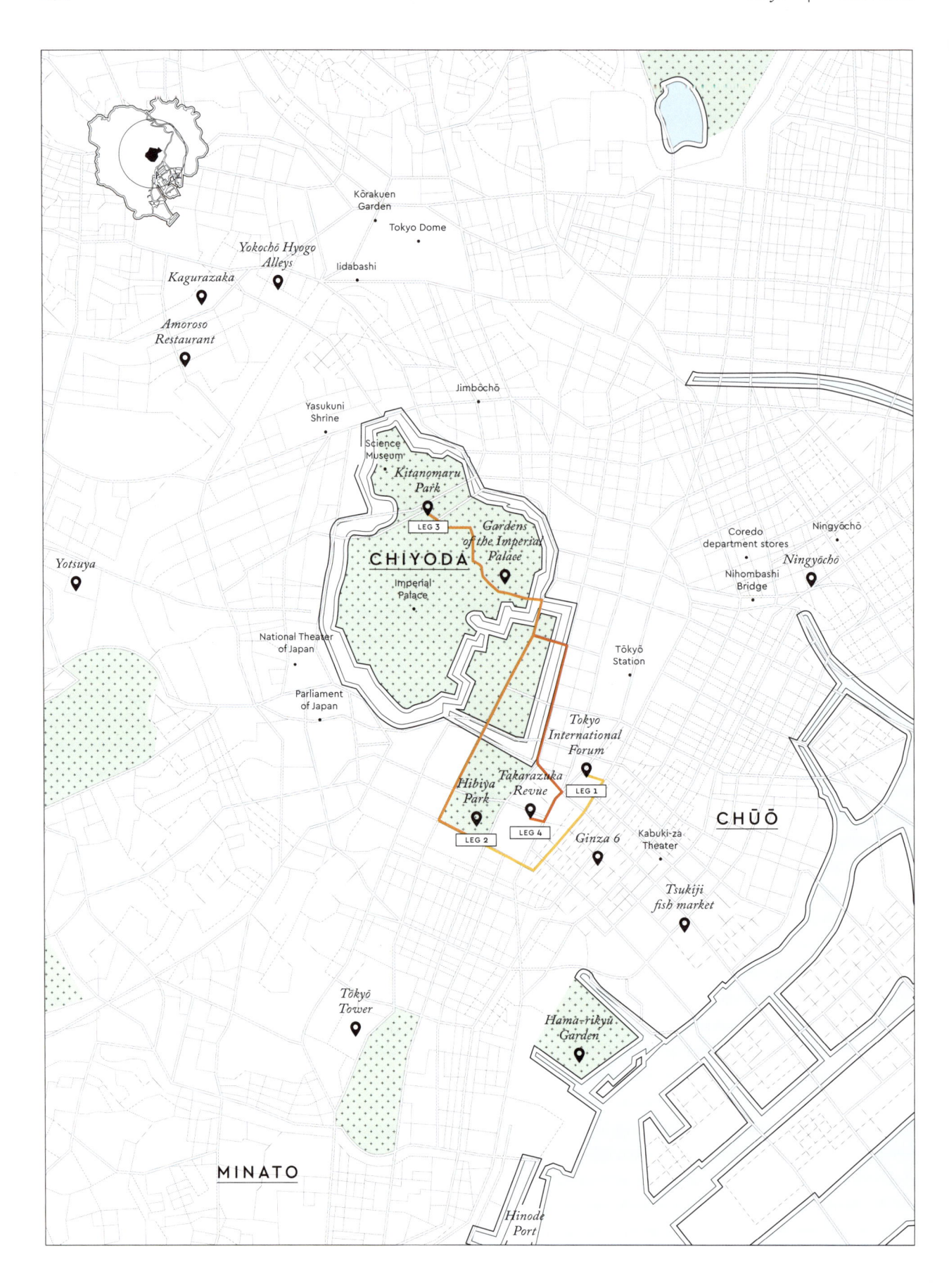

WALKING TOUR

IN THE FOOTSTEPS OF JAPANESE *SALARYMEN*

From Yurakuchō to the Imperial Palace, Chiyoda is mostly an area for government officials and executives in suits and ties, the famous *salarymen*. Following in their footsteps in Chiyoda will show you a new side of the capital.

LEG 1: A STROLL TO YURAKUCHŌ

The Yurakuchō business district to the east of the Imperial Palace gardens is essentially the preserve of office buildings and the world of *salarymen*. Exploring this part of the city offers an opportunity to experience the daily life of a Japanese executive first-hand. Why not join the throngs of employees picking up lunch from one of the food trucks serving salads, curries, and Thai or Vietnamese food on the terraces of the Tokyo International Forum complex, a venue for exhibitions and conferences.

LEG 2: A BENTŌ IN HIBIYA PARK

Hibiya Park is another popular option for a lunch break. It's a lovely place to spend a few moments, especially when the cherry trees are in blossom, but also in the fall, when the maple leaves turn extravagant shades of yellow, deep red, and orange. Hibiya Park was previously a private garden for the Mōri and Nabeshima clans during the Edo period but was opened to the public in 1903. It also became the scene of major unrest in 1905 as rioters reacted violently to the Treaty of Portsmouth that ended the Russo-Japanese war. Hibiya is now a leisure park, boasting an open-air stage for concerts, tennis courts, and festivals with different themes that are held throughout the year.

LEG 3: THE GARDENS OF THE IMPERIAL PALACE

While the Imperial Palace is closed to visitors, you can take a stroll in the surrounding gardens (there are three, all open all year round). There are even a couple of museums in Kitanomaru Park in the northwestern corner of the estate. If you are there at New Year, it is one of the rare moments when you can slip into one of the palace courtyards to hear the emperor address the public.

LEG 4: AN EVENING OF MUSICAL THEATER

Founded in 1914 with an exclusively female cast, the Takarazuka troupe has made a name for itself throughout the country. Depending on the show, the revue will strike up numbers from American musical comedies or enact scenes from the life of Napoleon Bonaparte. All the roles, including the male roles, are played by (single) women. A visit to the Takarazuka revue is a unique experience, although best planned in advance; performances are very often sold out.